Midnight Marquee Studio Series

HAMMER FILMS

Midnight Marquee Studio Series

HAMMER FILMS

Edited by Gary J. Svehla and Susan Svehla

Midnight Marquee Press, Inc.
Baltimore, MD USA

Copyright © 2011 by Gary J. Svehla and Susan Svehla
Interior layout and cover design by Susan Svehla
Copy Editing by Linda J. Walter

Without limiting the rights under copyright reserved above, no part of this publication may be reproduced, stored in or introduced into a retrieval system, or transmitted, in any form, or by any means (electronic, mechanical, photocopying, recording or otherwise), without the prior written permission of the copyright owner or the publishers of the book.

ISBN 13: 978-1-936168-24-8
Library of Congress Catalog Card Number 2011962451
Manufactured in the United States of America

First Printing by Midnight Marquee Press, Inc., December 2011

Dedication
To all our FANEX Hammer fans...

TABLE OF CONTENTS

8 Introduction

VAMPIRES
10 Hammer Films and the Resurrection of Dracula
22 Peter Cushing, Terence Fisher and Hammer's Vampire Mythology
32 Christopher Lee, Count Dracula and Hammer Films
46 Peter Cushing and Van Helsing
50 The Dracula Films with No Dracula!
54 Hammer's Hunt For A New Vein of Vampire Film: Three Semi-Classics from the 1970s
73 Why the 1970s Bite
86 Let Me In: The Return of Hammer and the Spirit of Val Lewton

FRANKENSTEIN
92 Evolving Worlds of Hammer's Baron Frankenstein

SCI-FI
129 X—The Unknown
141 Val Guest and Nigel Kneale: Hammer's Dynamic Duo

FANTASY
167 Surviving the Lost Worlds of Hammer
185 The Hammer Factory:
    Hammer Films, Corman Style
191 The Abominable Snowman
193 The Curse of the Werewolf
195 The Devil Rides Out

MUMMIES
197 Christopher Lee Is The Mummy;
    Peter Cushing Is Kharismatic
202 Hammer Films Unearth The Mummy

PSYCHOS

242 The Phantom of the Opera
245 Paranormic and Nightmare
249 To the Devil... a Daughter

WAR
252 Hammer Declares War
263 Night Creatures

266 Hammer Memories

Introduction

With the re-emergence of Hammer and their new releases including *Let Me In* (2010), which received critical praise, and their forthcoming 2012 release of *The Woman in Black* starring Daniel Radcliffe already garnering interest, we wanted to take a look back at our old faves and wallow in fond memories —even as we anxiously await their new films.

As is mentioned in many of the following chapters, the old Hammer horror films were not favorite films of most critics. But times have changed, as can be seen in this review by Peter Travers in *Rolling Stone* for *Let Me In*:

> I thought for sure that any Hollywood remake of Tomas Alfredson's artful Swedish vampire film, *Let the Right One In*, would be a crass desecration. Well, color me blushing. Director Matt Reeves (*Cloverfield*) proves expert at tracing Alfredson's footsteps, creating a mood of chilling terror even while moving the setting from Stockholm to 1980s New Mexico with Reagan raising fears about the Evil Empire. Better yet, Reeves plugs in a live wire to play Abby, the girl vampire who's been 12 for, well, a very long time. That would

be Chloë Grace Moretz, an acting dynamo (see *Kick Ass*) whose mesmerizing performance goes deep. Abby fascinates her new neighbor, Owen (Kodi Smit-McPhee of *The Road*), a boy victimized at school by bullies. He wants to be fearless like Abby, whose only parental figure is a guardian, played by the great Richard Jenkins. For the sake of newbies to this story, I'll say no more, except there will be blood and surprising tenderness. Moretz and Smit-McPhee will stay with you, especially in a delicate scene where he asks her to be his girl. "I'm not a girl — I'm nothing," she says. Prepare to be wowed. It's a spellbinder.

So, for all those fans, who were vampire and Frankenstein and werewolf fans before it was cool, we offer a series of chapters on our favorite Hammer films. This book is not a complete listing of Hammer films—that's been done. Nor is it a chronological listing of their cinematic output. Rather it comprises articles from *Midnight Marquee* as well as several new entries that we think Hammer fans will enjoy.

VAMPIRES

Hammer Films and the Resurrection of Dracula

by Gary J. Svehla

When Hammer Film Productions introduced *Horror of Dracula* (*Dracula*, in England) to American film audiences during the summer of 1958, a new era of Dracula and vampire cinema was upon us.

Or was it?

Both general movie aficionados and horror film fanatics are quick to jump into two camps concerning the supremacy of individual screen Draculas, most selecting either Bela Lugosi, who single-handedly created the popular conception of a "horror movie star," and Christopher Lee, who frequently essayed the Dracula role for Hammer Films.

The Lugosi supporters cite his European elegance and aristocratic demeanor, his deliberately delivered dialogue, his suave veneer and his subtle animal magnetism. Actor Lugosi still remains the popular conception of the Count in the American consciousness, starring in what Universal Pictures called "the strangest passion the world has ever known." And although steeped in wonderfully Gothic surroundings (the "broken battlements" of his Transylvanian castle are a masterpiece of set design), Lugosi's vampire remained sexy: More than 90 percent of the actor's fan mail came from women. His Dracula was proof that vampires were frightening *and* attractive. "They wanted to know if I only wanted maiden's blood," the actor later recalled. And while tastes in what is and isn't attractive have changed, Lugosi's peculiar charm introduced the element of sensuality missing from Stoker's hoary creation.

Christopher Lee's Count primed his sexual pump with gushes of sensual magnetism and animal savagery. In his brief scenes at the beginning of *Horror of Dracula*, he quickly turns from bland aristocrat to demonic fiend. While Universal Studio's ad campaign suggested that "he [Dracula] kisses with crimson lips," Hammer showed us those blood-smeared chops in glorious Technicolor, close-up and bestial. As Lugosi slowly lunged for his victim's throat with a furtive sexuality, Lee's approach was more seductive and erotic, at first tenderly nuzzling his female victim's face and neck before baring his fangs and digging in for the kill.

To be honest, both interpretations of Dracula are surprisingly much more similar than has been suggested in the annals of film criticism. Neither actor closely adheres to Stoker's original concept of the vampire, and neither actor has starred in a film that can legitimately be called a definitive adaptation of the novel. However, both actors are elegantly European, cultured and dangerous, albeit in their own individual ways.

When Lugosi's Count pays a visit to his eventual victims in the privacy of their opera box seats, or when he greets the overwhelmed Renfield (Dwight Frye) at Castle Dracula, Lugosi always exudes a disquieting old world charm.

Lee plays a similar scene when greeting Jonathan Harker (John Van Eyssen) at his castle, and though he has less dialogue than Lugosi, he is an equally attentive host. And while Lee's barbaric, hissing attack upon Jonathan Harker in the library is more visceral than anything in Lugosi's *Dracula*, Lugosi does indeed display his predatory nature when Renfield cuts his finger on a paper clip. His creepy slow crawl forward, arm outstretched, maniacal smile on his face, reveals the blood-loving beast underneath the veneer of the composed Count.

But even more revealing is Dracula's quick anger upon looking into Van

Above: Bela Lugosi as Dracula
Below: Christopher Lee as Dracula from *Dracula Has Risen From the Grave*

Bela Lugosi in a portrait for *Abbott and Costello Meet Frankenstein*

Helsing's (Edward Van Sloan) mirrored cigarette box. When the vampire's nemesis tricks the Count into revealing his vampirism (by lack of reflection), Lugosi responds with a hateful, feral look of fury.

The most apparent differences between the interpretations of Lugosi and Lee are found in their body language and movement. Since Lugosi's Count is a creature of stately deliberation, it would be impossible for Lugosi to create the frenetic energy that Lee displays at the climax of *Horror of Dracula*. In that film's well-remembered climax, Dracula and Van Helsing (Peter Cushing) settle their dispute in a ferocious bout of hand-to-hand combat. Such exertions seem beyond Lugosi's Dracula, who creeps and floats as though he were starring in an opera whose musical rhythms dictate his movement. Christopher Lee's Count is more the cornered wolf whose guttural wails and biting, clawing brutality echo his need to survive at any cost.

Yet in spite of these and other differences, both interpretations of Count Dracula are ultimately similar in the following ways: Both are romantic figures whose interests primarily lie with the female of the species, both are of patently aristocratic stock, both can generate a false charm to disarm victims, and both are unrepentant monsters hiding under a surface of cultured European breeding.

For far too long Dracula buffs have been trying to separate Christopher Lee and Bela Lugosi into opposite points of the compass, stressing the differences in their interpretations in an effort to paint one actor as being superior in the role to the other. I disagree with many film historians and favor Christopher Lee's visceral performance over Lugosi's theatrical interpretation of the Count. While Lugosi's performance is *different,* it's every bit as good, and I have no fault over those critics who favor Lugosi's performance.

It is the frequency of Lee's Dracula performances on film that has also helped him put his individual stamp upon the role. Lugosi played Dracula in 1931 and did not repeat the role again onscreen until 1948 when he appeared in the comic spoof, *Abbott and Costello Meet Frankenstein,* despite more than two decades of stage appearances in the role too numerous to chronicle in these pages.

But Christopher Lee created Hammer's Dracula franchise, which allowed him to essay the role in seven films: *Horror of Dracula, Dracula—Prince of Darkness, Dracula Has Risen from the Grave, Taste the Blood of Dracula, Scars of Dracula, Dracula A.D. 1972*, and *Satanic Rites of Dracula* (*Count Dracula and his Vampire Bride* in the U.S.). Whether or not one views Christopher Lee's performance as superior or inferior to Bela Lugosi's, the fact remains that no actor in movie history has portrayed the evil Count as many times on the screen. (Lee did his own riffs on *Abbott and Costello Meet Frankenstein* when he parodied his Dracula portrayal in *Uncle Was A Vampire* and *Dracula Father and Son*. He also worked outside Hammer to appear in director Jess Franco's abysmal *Count Dracula*.)

This is the first major accomplishment that Hammer Film Productions added to the evolution of *Dracula* cinema: the concept that the infamous anti-hero could headline a cinematic franchise and carry the audience simply on the basis of Christopher Lee's image, name, and box office appeal. To a new generation of horror movie fans, Christopher Lee *was* Count Dracula, and Hammer the new home of Gothic cinema. Even though the early Hammer *Dracula* films most successfully stand the test of time, especially the first, *Horror of Dracula* (considered by many to be Hammer's masterpiece), *Brides of Dracula* and *Dracula—Prince of Darkness* are superior productions as well. The subsequent sequels grow less and less ambitious: *Taste the Blood of Dracula* is the last entry worthy of serious critical attention, while *Scars of Dracula, Dracula A.D. 1972*, and *Satanic Rites of Dracula* not only tarnish the reputation of Hammer Films, but drag Stoker's creation to new lows.

Despite the eventual degeneration of the series, Hammer's *Horror of Dracula* is pivotal to the history of *Dracula* films for bringing the subtext of Tod Browning's film into stark relief: the perversity of vampirism and the all-consuming seduction of evil.

Christopher Lee in a portrait for *Dracula—Prince of Darkness*

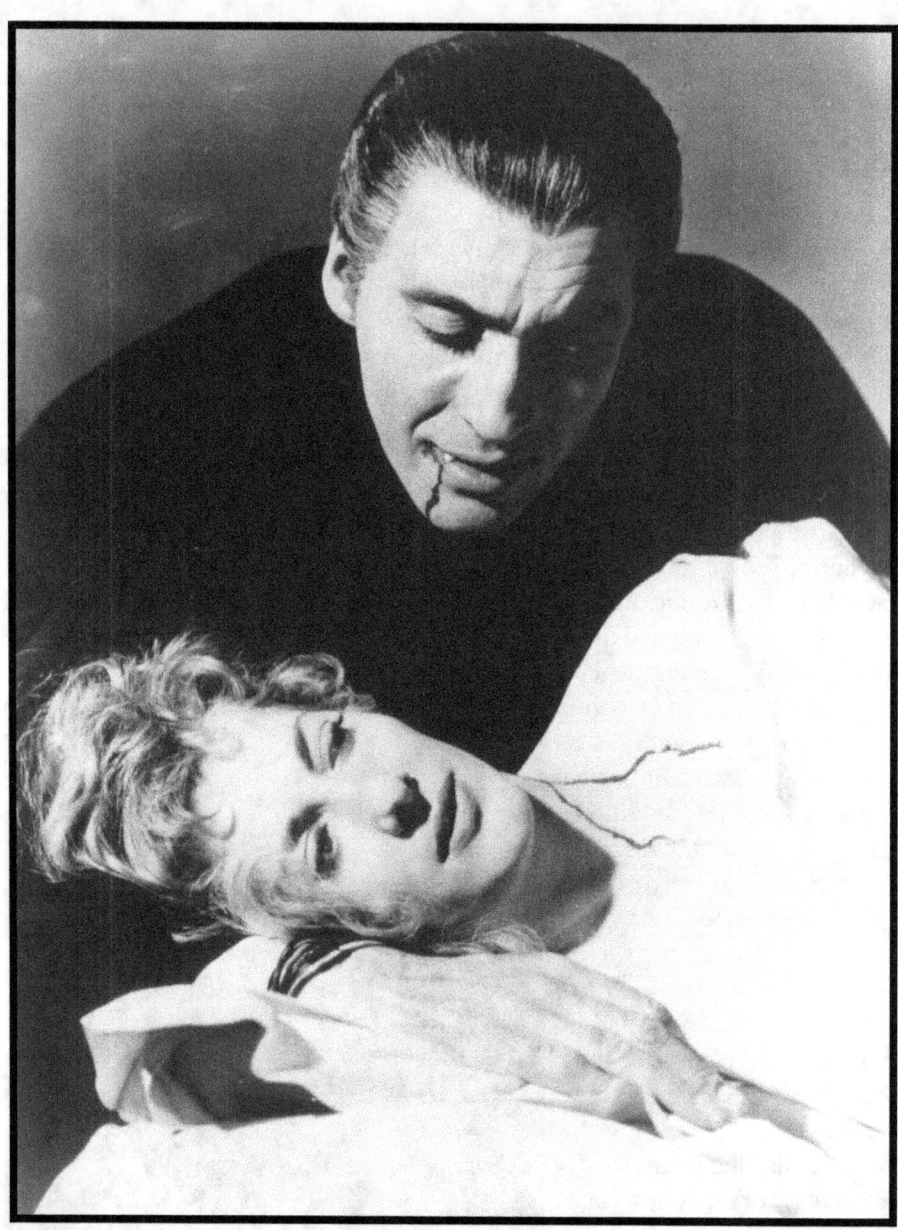

Bela Lugosi's Dracula looked and acted evil, and while he appears dominantly handsome outside of Carfax Abbey, the persistence of his evil both repels and attracts. However, Christopher Lee's unconventional good looks go beyond the similar virtues, which Lugosi brought to the cinematic table. Lee's Count is openly sensual and erotic, and his two female victims are eager to be savaged by their dark and bloody seducer. First the youthful and virginal Lucy (Carol Marsh) is slowly sapped of her energy as she longingly looks beyond the bay windows as the autumn leaves rustle and blow past. Her breathing becomes forced and rhythmic, her bosom heaves up and down, as her blatant sexual urges await satisfaction at the mouth of Dracula. Her naked passion leads to a nocturnal visit from the dreaded Count. Soon the undead Lucy's sexual abandon reaches greater perversity as she stalks children, becoming a vampiric child molester. The vampire's all-consuming sexuality even extends to incest: Lucy attempts a nightgown-clad seduction of Holmwood (Michael Gough), her own brother, who initially resists. Fortunately the hidden Van Helsing rescues him as she attempts to "kiss" her brother's vulnerable throat.

Interestingly enough, Hammer's latter-day entries in the erotic vampire sweepstakes—*The Vampire Lovers, Lust for a Vampire*, and *Twins of Evil*—which are much more blatant and soft-core in their sexuality, fail to generate the erotic perverse intensity inherent in these earlier, more subtle Hammer entries. These 1970s Hammer films are much more titillating upon a surface viewing, but their cheap eroticism lacks the intensity and artistic expression displayed in these earlier Gothic films.

Later in *Horror of Dracula*, Holmwood's wife Mina (Melissa Stribling) becomes the latest "bride" of Dracula, hiding the Count's coffin in the cellar of her own home. Wearing high collars or scarves to hide the mark of Dracula's "kiss," Mina's smirks and smiles cannot deny the hidden satisfactions, which she has encountered as willing victim of Dracula. Her cold, aloof and dogmatic husband Arthur seems passionless and pallid compared to her nocturnal lover, a sexual outlet that Mina obviously needs. In such an interesting romantic triangle, Mina seems so much more alive during her necrophilic "affair" with Dracula than with her cold-fish husband. In this Victorian worldview, Dracula's romantic power is the root-cause of his menace. If sex is anti-social and evil, then the sexless Van Helsing's zeal to eradicate such a blatant sexual monster makes him a worthy opponent of the sexually active vampire king. Here *Horror of Dracula* anticipates the spate of "slasher" films in the 1970s and 1980s, where sexual release is often met with physical punishment and violent death. In this mythic vision created by Hammer, vampirism is akin to sexual experimentation... and to be stopped at any cost! By repeatedly making vampirism both sexual and dangerous—as seen first in Stoker's text and later in Universal's *Dracula's Daughter*—Hammer has underlined an important part of Dracula cinema.

Even though Stoker created much of the accepted lore concerning vampires—that a vampire must sleep in consecrated soil, that a vampire casts no reflection in a mirror, and that a wooden stake through the heart may destroy a vampire—Hammer dramatically recast those rules by portraying vampirism as a cult or a perverted religious sect. In the capable hands of Hammer's scenarists (mainly Jimmy Sangster and Anthony Hinds/John Elder), the "new rules" of vampirism resulted in a Religion of the Undead.

This is another major contribution that Hammer made to *Dracula* cinema: a radically new way to perceive vampirism. The concept was best explored in

Hammer's *The Kiss of the Vampire*, whereby the vampires, under leader Dr. Ravna (Noel Willman), were actually a cult whose members, during their ceremonial meetings, wore white robes and initiated new members into vampirism. Such an undead cult was merely hinted at in Hammer's *Horror of Dracula,* and its successful sequel, *The Brides of Dracula*, as Peter Cushing's Van Helsing speaks frequently about "the cult of the undead." Later, the vampire cult idea could be found in both *Vampire Circus* and *Captain Kronos: Vampire Hunter*.

In these and other vampire films, Hammer, like Universal, focused upon the anemic, strength-sapping illnesses of the otherwise healthy and young female victims of vampirism. Their energies and spirits are sapped by some unseen malady; eventually, the victims die a slow, tragic death, their energies only returning when they rise from their graves. It is in these sequences especially that Hammer infused "new blood" into the genre. These reanimated corpses, now seductively dressed and burning with renewed energy and sensual power, roam the woods and graveyards by night, searching out new victims for blasphemous sexual crimes.

Hammer also liked to paint religious paraphernalia in bold, symbolic colors. In the classic Universal films a vampire would snarl and flee from the appearance of the small crucifix on a chain; in Hammer's world, a larger, silver cross would be held outstretched like the Holy Grail, forcing the condemned vampire to squirm and slowly back away in agony. Sometimes, the vampire would vanquish its tormentor, and stare down the cross-wielding crusader. Harking back to Stoker's novel, Hammer had religious symbols burn impressions into the flesh of vampires touched by them. Such fear and loathing would be registered by orgasmic breathing, a heaving of breasts, and ultimately screams of pain as the flesh was burned by this symbol of good. In the hands of Hammer's directors and writers, vampire hunters wielded huge crucifixes and large stakes, perhaps too blatantly phallic, all the more visually symbolic of their goodness in fighting the disease of vampirism.

The reanimated seductress would then be lured back into her unholy resting place, back into her crypt, back into her coffin, where only the knowledgeable vampire slayer could bring peace to the tormented victim of the undead. The horror of vampirism for Hammer, like Stoker before them, is best manifested as a voluptuous, wanton lust in the female of the species. Thus, when Van Helsing drives a wooden stake through the shrieking vampire's heart, vivid crimson spurting as the wooden shaft is buried deep in the vampire's chest, the sexual subtexts that drive both novel and film adaptations are consummated. Finally, after turning away from all this bloodletting, the camera would inevitably return to the face of the vampire, now in peaceful repose, having been freed from the vampire's sexual hunger through a "cleansing" act of brutal sexual healing.

Such horrific stakings, blood spurtings, and peaceful redemptions would be repeated in such Hammer films as *Brides of Dracula, Kiss of the Vampire,*

Van Helsing (Peter Cushing) uses a crucifix to threaten the vampire Lucy (Carol Marsh) in *Horror of Dracula*.

and *Dracula—Prince of Darkness*. These sequences powerfully demonstrate the mythic, ritualistic and religious dogma, which Hammer created around its interpretation of vampirism. And to reinforce the concept of vampirism as a perverted cult or unholy religion, Van Helsing was soon replaced in the Hammer series by actual men of the cloth, including such clerics as Father Sandor (Andrew Keir) in the monastery-set *Dracula—Prince of Darkness* and the Monsignor (Rupert Davies) from *Dracula Has Risen from the Grave*.

Hammer chose to illustrate the battle of good against evil with imagery more overtly religious than anything found in the Universal films. The vampire myth was revised in *Dracula Has Risen from the Grave* to include the proviso that a vampire can only be killed by a wooden stake if its attacker is a true believer in God and manages to say a prayer before Dracula pulls out the bloody toothpick.

Finally, the early Hammer films offered the lush Technicolor photography of cinematographer Jack Asher and others, aided in large part by the budget-minded yet inspired production design by Bernard Robinson. With the use of color, Hammer established that lush hues and Gothic horror could go hand-in-hand. In the 1950s to early 1960s, Technicolor photography was at its artistic peak, and *Horror of Dracula* and *Brides of Dracula* remain as examples of Hammer's most inspired use of color photography, perhaps the most creative in the history of horror cinema.

Horror of Dracula

Universal was fortunate in having the genius of German-born Karl Freund to create the look of *Dracula* in all its monochromatic splendor, and the set design for Lugosi's Transylvania castle remains the most dazzling ever recorded in a horror film. Hammer, however, dared to add color and period detail to its horror Gothics, employing a veneer of Victorianism more consistently than Universal.

Horror of Dracula—though it is difficult to convince people who never saw the film theatrically—is a totally different film when viewed in its original Technicolor. Its later reissues (both on video cassette and laser disc), in more muted Eastmancolor, rob the film of much of its splendor. In its original form, the deep saturated hues and tones of Castle Dracula's interiors are awe-inspiring.

Hammer changed the look of horror films when it lensed *Horror of Dracula* in rich primary colors. Even the drops of blood that fall upon the crypt inscription of "Dracula" during the opening credits are redder than red. Universal successfully proved that Gothic films do not have to depict reality, but rather suggest an alternate world of light and shadow. The Gothics of Hammer were no more natural than Universal's, but Hammer used a more colorful palette to illustrate Dracula's unnatural world.

Reality isn't the goal of Christopher Lee's horrific entrance during the library sequence in *Horror of Dracula*—his fangs bared in depraved intensity, blood smeared all over his mouth and face—just stark terror. Director Terence Fisher and cinematographer Jack Asher ably accomplish their goal—to bring scares back to the horror film and the Baby Boomers that wanted them.

Even in the more subtle sequences of *Horror of Dracula*, with the daylight fading and autumn leaves blowing wildly just outside of large French windows, a somber mood is generated through inspired color photography.

For the climactic struggle between Dracula and Van Helsing, Hammer set designers decorated Dracula's study with antique curios, book-lined shelves and period furniture, creating an ambiance of ancient evil. Against this backdrop, the color photography makes Dracula all the more frightening in his funeral clothes and black cape, appearing like the Devil incarnate. Cushing's Van Helsing dives for the curtains to reveal the first rays of sunlight, again abetted by superb color lensing, creating such an impact as the image of sunlight—so white, so pure—contrasts the dark evil that the black-caped Dracula represents. Dracula's graying, decomposing flesh slowly turns to ash, eventually blowing away with a cleansing breeze, leaving only his ring within the colorful astrological circle painted onto the floor. Again, such a contrast would not be nearly as effective if filmed in black and white. The key sequences in Hammer's films were created and designed to take advantage of color photography.

Finally, while Hammer continued the already hallowed tradition of turning away from Stoker's novel, they also avoided the stagy elements of the Hamilton Deane–John L. Balderston play. *Horror of Dracula* is not the definitive interpretation of Stoker's novel, nor does it try to be. But by parting from the text of the play, the Hammer film avoids the talky, stage-bound quality that hobbles the Lugosi film. Jimmy Sangster's tight screenplay manages to keep the action moving at a brisk clip while never losing an opportunity to maintain a high level of scares. Characters are sketched quickly, but never caricatured, and events speed forward with an internal logic sometimes missing from Stoker's novel. For speed, economy of narrative, and story momentum, *Horror of Dracula* remains the best of the Dracula movies.

As Sangster states in his autobiography *Do You Want It Good or Tuesday?* (Midnight Marquee Press, 1997): "In the novel, Dracula came to England by sea. There was no way that Hammer was going to go for that... so we settled for a journey on a horse-drawn carriage, crossing a border manned by one customs-immigration official. That they could shoot in the grounds of Bray Studios." And just as he did with *The Curse of Frankenstein* a year earlier, Sangster fashioned his screenplay around Hammer's resources, providing a showcase for their abilities. Sangster did manage to use some of the novel's many characters—Jonathan Harker, Mina Murray, Lucy Westenra, Arthur Holmwood—but pared away many of their relationships and personal histories. Sangster's 82-minute movie script instead concentrated on the Gothic implications of bringing to life a monstrous, undead Vampire King who thirsts and lusts for human blood.

"The terrifying lover who died yet lived... the blood in his veins once flowed through hers!" declared the ads for the American release.

It is amazing to think that Jimmy Sangster only made £750 (or $1,200 at today's current rate of exchange) for writing *Horror of Dracula*, the unofficial Hammer masterpiece. In his autobiography, Jimmy Sangster writes: "Okay, so it was a pretty good movie... But masterpiece! Come on!"

Mr. Sangster's legions of fans beg to differ.

Like Stoker's novel, Sangster's Dracula is the focal point of attention even though he is mostly offstage. Actor Christopher Lee only appears onscreen for a total of some seven minutes, yet he remains the catalyst for the film's action. He also completely reshaped and recast the Lugosi persona to create his own interpretation. By appearing in six additional Hammer productions, he became the omnipresent Dracula of the Baby Boomer generation. Freely acknowledging Lee's many limitations as an actor, it cannot be disputed that his performance in *Horror of Dracula* is a classic in its own right. More so than Lugosi, Lee's Count Dracula is a terribly flawed anti-hero. However, just as soon as the audience comes to sense the loneliness inherent in the state of vampirism, his feral demonism breaks through; Dracula becomes the cornered beast that will gladly kill rather than be killed. And thus emerge both the sad Byronic hero and the insidious, seductive fiend, all housed within the character of Count Dracula, onscreen for less than 10 minutes in this 82-minute film.

Jimmy Sangster's script reserves its main focus for the athletic, monomaniacal vampire hunter Dr. Van Helsing, for once not portrayed as an elderly savant. Sangster casts Van Helsing as Dracula's sole nemesis, rather than the leader of a band of vampire hunters found in Stoker's novel, and the tension between these two adversaries creates the dramatic core of the movie. Sangster's pulse-pounding ending provides a truly dramatic confrontation between Van Helsing and Count Dracula, something missing from *every* earlier movie version. And this climax, even today, remains a treasure.

Hammer Film Productions of England never had the resources available at Universal Pictures, lacking the American studio's money, top-drawer performers and Hollywood's masterful technicians. However, with *Horror of Dracula* Hammer had a vision. Limited by a low budget, hampered by a restrictive censor board, and hoping to repeat the lucky financial success of their earlier *The Curse of Frankenstein*, Hammer happened to combine a screenwriter of immense creativity, a director who understood the dramatic tension inherent in horror films, a cinematographer who was a master of Technicolor photography, a production designer who could perform miracles on a limited budget, and two acting talents who each found his niche in modern genre films. Against all odds, *Horror of Dracula* became a landmark film, one that became much more than just a remake, but a film that redefined the expectations of cinematic Gothic horror to become the trendsetter for all subsequent Dracula films to be produced for the next two decades.

Horror of Dracula is a classic horror film, and Christopher Lee's performance as Dracula is a revitalization of the character. The question is not whether his performance is better than Lugosi's, for Bela Lugosi's identification with the role is too complete and encompassing for any actor to do more than offer variations upon its theme. But Hammer and *Horror of Dracula* redefined the vampire-Dracula cinema for Baby Boomers, cutting new creative trails through unknown terrain, a terrain that is waiting yet to be further explored by a new generation of horror film and Dracula aficionados.

Peter Cushing, Terence Fisher and Hammer's Vampire Mythology

by Gary J. Svehla

It took director Terence Fisher only two movies—*Horror of Dracula* (1958) and *Brides of Dracula* (1960)—to create horror film's most sophisticated vampire mythology, a mythos based in part upon vampire literature and also Universal's monster classics from a generation before. Hammer's vampire mythos is primarily visual and not just a verbalized series of rules. Director Terence Fisher, cinematographer Jack Asher, screenwriter Jimmy Sangster, and most especially actor Peter Cushing made Fisher's world of vampirism immediately recognizable: sexy, dark-haired, negligee-wearing vampire brides; frail female victims with swollen neck bites who seem attracted to this newfound erotic evil; claustrophobic castles meticulously decorated; burial vaults filled with vampires bloated with blood; aristocratic barons or counts who are so polite at first but so animalistic later.

Even though Christopher Lee as Count Dracula and David Peel as Baron Meinster are classic embodiments of human corruption and evil—cinematic vampires of the most resonating sort—it is vampire slayer Dr. Van Helsing who becomes the focal point of Fisher's world of vampirism. Cushing's performance as Van Helsing is perhaps his best. At the very least, it's an iconic performance equaling his Sherlock Holmes and Baron Frankenstein: Every strength and idiosyncrasy that Cushing brings to the screen can be found in his first two performances as Van Helsing. For me, Cushing was never better.

Peter Cushing's performance as Van Helsing is very British: He wears a hat and sports a dress overcoat on top of a jacket and tie, his medical bag always at his side. Just as Dracula and Meinster are devoted to evil, Van Helsing is devoted to good—though perhaps *obsessed* is the better word, for Van Helsing is always intense, focused, almost humorless, and seems the cold-blooded scientist dedicating his life to the eradication of the world's oldest malady, vampirism. Cushing's typical expression is one of piercing superiority; his thin, almost nonexistent lips form a sliver above his determined chin; his aquiline nose serves as the regal focal point of his face; and his cold, penetrating eyes burn like coals punctuating the curt orders he delivers to everyone. Peter Cushing's Van Helsing is not generally warm and fuzzy, at least not in *Horror of Dracula*, although, like many doctors, he can turn on the charm if necessary.

To find a demonstration of his cool intensity, one need only look as far as the 23-minute mark of *Horror of Dracula* when Van Helsing enters both the local tavern and the film, looking for his colleague, Jonathan Harker, who has

disappeared. Van Helsing asks for a brandy and some food, and the innkeeper responds that he serves only simple meals and that strangers are urged to hurry along. The pretty young barmaid seems to remember Harker from a week ago, but the disapproving gaze of the overpowering innkeeper silences her tongue immediately. "What are you afraid of?" Van Helsing asks in tones as sharp as that gaze. Noticing the garlic flowers, he notes, "Not for decoration, are they?" Van Helsing, hoping to force information out of the innkeeper, adds that such garlic flowers are not merely artifacts of superstition, that the danger is real. But the innkeeper remains silent, although the barmaid secretly slips Van Helsing Jonathan Harker's bright red journal, stating she was told to burn it.

Maintaining his deadpan intensity, Van Helsing drives a stake through his friend's chest at Castle Dracula, then journeys to visit the Holmwoods in his capacity as Harker's "friend and colleague," to pass on the bad news of Harker's death and cremation. The always brusque and pompous Arthur Holmwood (Michael Gough), brother of Harker's fiancée, Lucy (Carol Marsh), is upset that Van Helsing won't reveal where or how Harker died. Since Arthur won't allow Van Helsing to see the young woman, Van Helsing asks Holmwood to "please express my sympathy to Miss Lucy."

In one of Cushing's most didactic sequences, Van Helsing is alone, listening to his Dictaphone, on which he records important pieces of vampire lore. We hear the formal voice of Van Helsing rattling off vampire mythology in a point-by-point manner: "Light... vampire allergic, fatal. Garlic... vampires repelled by the odor of garlic. Crucifix... power of good over evil. The power of the crucifix is two-fold. It protects the normal human being, but it also reveals the vampire or victim in advanced stages... Victims detest being dominated by vampirism but are unable to relinquish the practice—like addiction to drugs." While listening to such dramatic audio recordings, "Props" Cushing demonstrates his talent for small details. Sitting in a red pinstriped chair, Van Helsing crosses his legs and holds the red journal in his hands. He scrunches up his face to read fine details and uses a pen to both make notes and underline key points. As he listens, he gets brand-new ideas, which he tries to incorporate into his note making. After being briefly interrupted by a servant, he begins to record new information into his dictating machine. Peter Cushing's attention to detail and his inspired use of props is always a delight to behold.

Van Helsing, when necessary, can rely on his bedside manner and be most charming: His smile illuminates his entire face, a warm hand on the shoulder offers needed emotional comfort and support. Perhaps the duality of the characterization can best be seen in one of *Horror of Dracula*'s finest moments, the sequence where the vampiric Lucy, rising from her tomb for the first time, attempts to lure the servant's daughter, Tania, to her tomb to feast on the child's blood. Arthur, who is hiding and watching in the misty shadows, calls out to his sister, who barely covers her newly sprouted fangs, smiles and approaches her terrified brother, enthusiastically proclaiming, "Come, let me kiss you," her welcoming arms upraised to hug him. Suddenly, a gloved hand from the right of the screen abruptly thrusts a silver crucifix outward toward Lucy, causing the terrified vampire to grimace and back away. Approaching with unfaltering courage, Van Helsing touches the cross against Lucy's forehead, sizzling its impression into her newly dead flesh. She then runs off into her crypt, with Arthur in pursuit. Instead of joining Arthur, Van Helsing removes his coat and wraps it around the confused Tania. In a fatherly manner, he tells Tania to "put this on... we will all go home together." Then he hangs the crucifix-rosary around Tania's neck, asking, "Will you wear this pretty thing?"

Van Helsing (Cushing) gives Tania (Janine Faye) a cross to protect her before he deals with Lucy in *Horror of Dracula*.

Continuing to calm the startled child with his warm smile and comforting words, he tells Tania to watch the horizon... "You'll see the sun come up." Then he bundles her securely in the coat, smiles broadly, and joins Arthur in the crypt, trying desperately to persuade the equally confused adult that he must allow his sister to lead them to Count Dracula. But all Arthur can think about is freeing Lucy's soul from this possession of evil. Van Helsing calmly explains that this is Dracula's revenge—Lucy is to replace the vampire mistress whom Harker destroyed at Dracula's castle.

In this one pivotal sequence, we see how the steely, scientific Van Helsing melds into the sympathetic and compassionate human being. Just like the soldier during wartime, Van Helsing is not allowed to let his guard down, not even for an instant. When Arthur seems disgusted by the thought of driving a wooden stake into Lucy's heart to release her soul, Van Helsing speaks convincingly. "It's only a shell, possessed and corrupted by the evil of Dracula. Liberate her soul... we must destroy that shell for all time. Believe me, there is no other way."

In the movie's climax, Arthur and Van Helsing stand guard outside the house, but when they go back in, they discover Mina has been ravished by Count Dracula, finding the almost dead woman sprawled across her bed with blood dripping down her neck. The momentarily outsmarted doctor gives Mina a life-

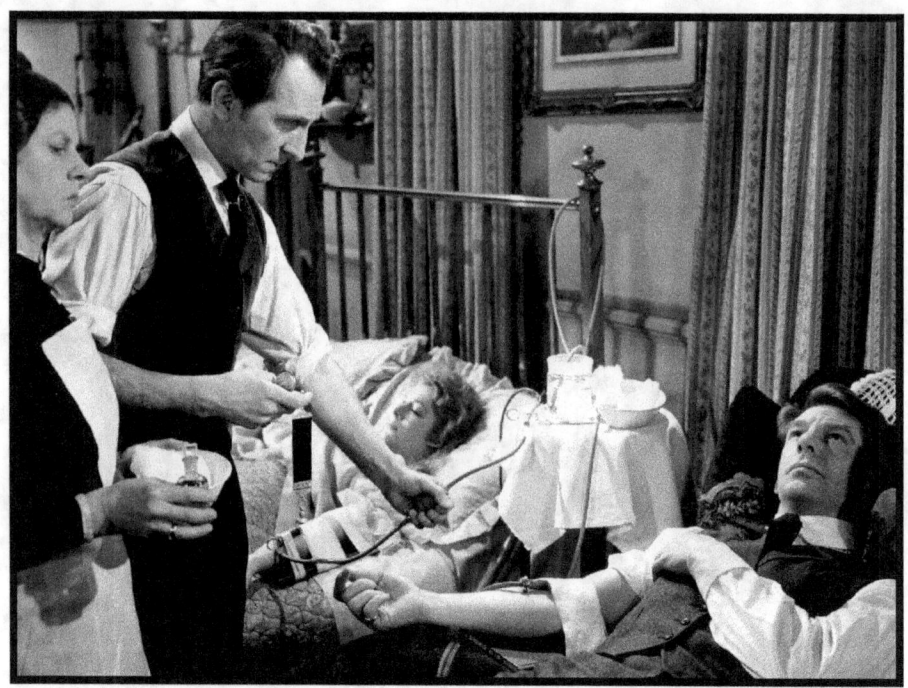

Gerda (Olga Dickie) helps Van Helsing save Mina (Melissa Stribling) with her husband Arthur's blood (Michael Gough) in *Horror of Dracula*.

saving transfusion using Arthur's blood, Van Helsing once again turning on the bedside manner. "Just sit still for a minute," the good doctor smiles. Suggesting that Arthur drink some wine to replenish the missing blood, he jocularly urges, "Go and have some now... there's a good fellow." And, once again, during the blood transfusion sequence, "Props" Cushing is in his glory, tilting a bottle of alcohol to wet a cotton swab to bathe Arthur's arm as he pulls the needle out, curling the arm up, and methodically undoing the transfusion apparatus. Cushing's attention to detail never fails to hold an audience spellbound.

The final aspect of Van Helsing's character, as created by Peter Cushing, is his physical prowess and energy: He runs into danger at the drop of a hat. After Arthur and Van Helsing are seated, wondering how Dracula could have gotten into the house, maid Gerda enters and nonchalantly mentions that Mina made her promise never to go down to the cellar. Almost immediately, Van Helsing's eyes pop open; he sprints out of the sitting room, rushes down to the cellar (his energy aided in large part by James Bernard's thunderous musical score), sees the empty white coffin containing Dracula's native soil, and plops his ever-present crucifix into the coffin, to prevent Dracula's return—just as Count Dracula, momentarily appearing at the cellar door, closes it and locks Van Helsing inside. Once Arthur frees the energetic door-banging doctor, Gerda tells them that Dracula ("he looked like the devil") scooped up Mina and carried her away in the carriage. Van Helsing knows that, since Dracula cannot return to his coffin in the cellar, he must make for his home. And, in *Horror of Dracula*'s final four-and-a-half minutes, the climactic chase begins! Dracula futilely attempts to quickly dig a grave outside his castle as Van Helsing's carriage arrives. While Arthur runs to comfort his wife, Cushing runs full throttle in pursuit of Dracula.

Van Helsing darts up the castle stairway, two steps at a time, and soon finds himself dodging a metal candlestick thrown by the Count. In hand-to-hand combat, Dracula strangles the life out of Van Helsing, who reacts in classic Cushing style (his eyes bulge dramatically, and he goes limp; Cushing plays this same trademark slipping-into-unconsciousness sequence in *Horror*, *Brides of Dracula*, and *The Mummy*). Count Dracula, gloating and pausing before bending down for the kill, is stunned by the immediate reanimation of Van Helsing, who forcefully throws the Count backwards. As Van Helsing retreats, his eyes quickly dart across the room to see a stream of light peeping through the heavy drapery. With a single thought in mind, Van Helsing climbs atop the huge wooden table and leaps toward the curtains, tearing them from their mountings, flooding the room with the fresh rays of the sun. Dracula writhes in pain and begins to decay. Van Helsing uses two candlesticks to form a crucifix, keeping the vampire pinned down as the burning sunlight fries the vampire to ash and dust. Briefly resting by sticking his head outside the windows for fresh air, Van Helsing pushes his hair back with his hands (another Cushing bit of business), staring down at the ashes of what was once Count Dracula. And so ends *Horror of Dracula*!

Two years later, Dracula is dead (Christopher Lee was off doing other projects); Peter Cushing's name appears above the title (the blood-red credits read "Peter Cushing in *Brides of Dracula*"); and the movie belongs to him—even though the supporting performances of David Peel as vampire Baron Meinster, Martita Hunt as the Baron's mother, and Yvonne Monlaur as the French student teacher are particularly strong. Surprisingly, the characterization of Dr. Van Helsing has changed significantly, as his scientifically detached persona presented in *Horror of Dracula* has finally succumbed to the kindly bedside manner persona, which appeared only sporadically two years earlier. With seemingly more of the focus on the character of Van Helsing, the team of screenwriters, including Jimmy Sangster, smoothed the vampire slayer's harsher edges, casting Van Helsing as the film's true hero and passing the hard-shelled, obsessive nature of his former characterization on to Fred Johnson, who plays the village priest. The priest thanks God for the arrival of the world's foremost authority on evil, but Van Helsing's smiles and arm-tugging reassurances contrast with the priest's steadfast, unwavering commitment to the eradication of vampires in his village. Johnson plays one-dimensional determination to Cushing's multi-dimensional anti-vampire zealot, comforter and friend.

Christopher Lee worked solo in *Horror of Dracula*—a vampire king who, without the hint of a Renfield-esque slave, managed to move his coffin from his Transylvanian castle to J. Marx's Undertaker establishment and finally to Arthur Holmwood's home. In *Brides of Dracula* all the vampire references allude to a wicked community of evil. Even the film's opening narration calls vampirism a cult corrupting the world. When speaking to the just-rescued Marianne (Yvonne Monlaur), who escaped from Chateau Meinster, Van Helsing declares: "I've been asked to make a study of a strange sickness—partially physical, partly spiritual... have you heard of the cult of the undead? It must be stamped out. That's why I am here!" Later, when speaking to the priest, Van Helsing reveals, "The vampire by its kiss—taking of blood—makes that victim another vampire, so the cult grows." Also speaking to the priest, Van Helsing warns: "These colonies must be wiped out... only then will this bondage of hell be removed from the world."

Brides presents David Peel initially as the brooding, Byronic hero who is soon revealed to be an insidious vampire, chained to his chambers in his own home by a mother who supplies him with female victims. However, Marianne, conned by the Baron's charm, steals the key to release him from his captivity. His first victim: his own mother, the Baroness. Soon Greta (Freda Jackson), Meinster's childhood nurse, becomes his human disciple and protector. In a wonderful sequence of pure horror, Van Helsing visits the chateau and retracts the curtains that hide the Baron's coffin. From the back of the scene, now wearing the drab gray favored by her son, the Baroness appears, slowly slinking closer to Van Helsing. Revealing herself, she covers the bottom of her face, embarrassed by her vampiric fangs, telltale signs of her undead affliction. Suddenly, in full-spread glory, Baron Meinster appears, triumphant, wide-eyed, with his glorious fangs barred in a stance of defiant power. In sequences such as these, Cushing's acting talent triumphs. In rapid-fire succession, Van Helsing thrusts forward his crucifix, causing the Baron to grimace and recoil, but the Baron flings a candlestick holder at Van Helsing (those Hammer vampires—always tossing candlesticks!) and overturns a huge dining-room table to make a hasty escape to his carriage outside. While cinematography and direction are succinct and inspired, Cushing's physical performance—whether it be the deliberate rhythms of slowly turning and thrusting his crucifix or the jerk-action fancy foot-work to evade flying chunks of metal or overturned tables—makes these actions appear choreographed (as the scene-blocking surely was), and his nimble physical reactions make all of this real.

At the climax of *Brides of Dracula*, when Van Helsing journeys alone to the vampire's lair in the abandoned windmill (populated by a veritable cult of the undead: Greta, Meinster, and two iconic dark-haired vampire babes, Marie Devereux and Andrée Melly), the physical power of Cushing's performance comes into full light (and he was pushing 50 at the time). Van Helsing has

Van Helsing (Cushing) swoops down on the Baron (David Peel) in *Brides of Dracula*.

hardly begun his quiet investigation of the spooky windmill's interior when Greta sends her vampire maidens after him, but he uses the power of the crucifix against them. However, Greta, still human, grabs the crucifix and falls to the bottom level and her death below, the crucifix firmly clutched in her hand. Next the Baron enters, swinging a chain. Van Helsing swoops down on a rope and, with the full weight of his body, kicks the Baron backwards (Errol Flynn could not have done it better). The victory is short-lived, however, for soon the Baron has Van Helsing against a post and uses his chain to strangle the good doctor into unconsciousness. Then Meinster spreads his cape and goes down for the kill, gleefully rising up with blood smeared on his lips and teeth, and smugly exits the mill. Van Helsing awakens, shakes his head to regain his senses, rubs his head with his hand and finally feels the vampire bite marks. In a marvelous reaction, Van Helsing momentarily panics but quickly regains his composure, his mind abruptly shifting to a state of deep thought. Suddenly he jumps up, starts a fire and places a branding iron in the blaze. Once the fire is at its absolute hottest, he anchors himself with a rope and burns the "seal of Dracula" from his neck, extinguishing the crispy flesh with Holy Water. He then falls into unconsciousness; time-lapse photography shows the vampire

Van Helsing is told, "You must humor local customs," in *Brides of Dracula*.

wounds vanishing. The sequence, as enacted by Cushing, is simply incredible. Cushing's rapidly changing facial expressions, his groggy reawakening segueing into physical intensity, and his quick, calculated movements are the craft of acting worth savoring.

Amazingly, Peter Cushing first appears in *Brides of Dracula* at the 31-minute mark, entering even later in this film than he did in *Horror of Dracula*, but from that point, Cushing dominates the movie, and (in an expansion of his beside-manner charm from the first film) exudes kindness, starting with his initial sequence, in which he has his carriage driver stop to help the unconscious, alone-in-the-woods Marianne. In his best "Props" Cushing exhibition, he rapidly produces a bottle of smelling salts, cracks it open and uses it to revive the French beauty. Taking her to the inn, he orders cognac and coffee for Marianne and a room for himself, and learns that adjacent to the bar a wake is occurring: A young girl lies in an open coffin wearing a garland of garlic, the obvious victim of vampirism. Her father tells Van Helsing, "You must humor local customs." Van Helsing responds quite seriously: "There's usually a good reason for all those old customs!" Returning to Marianne, Van Helsing asks her to tell him everything, in detail, not leaving anything out. Then his intensity melds into fatherly kindness, and, smiling, he states, "Then forget it, forget it completely and never mention it to anyone." Leaving the obsessiveness and rigidity to the village priest allows Cushing to play Van Helsing with more heart and soul.

Van Helsing escorts Marianne to her new job as student teacher at a ladies' academy, where Frau Lang, the wife of the director, informs them that her husband does not tolerate tardiness. When the starchy Herr Lang raises his voice to reprimand the scared young teacher, Van Helsing intervenes, facing up to the unwavering authority figure: "I assure you, sir, this was unavoidable, I'm a doctor..." passing his card to Lang, who eyeballs Van Helsing's accomplishments with wide-eyed wonder. When Lang notes Van Helsing is a graduate of Lyndon University, he bubbles, "Almost a colleague." And, as he rattles off Van Helsing's degrees—doctor of philosophy, doctor of theology, doctor of metaphysics—he immediately bends the academy's rules and allows Cushing visiting privileges at any time. "The rule is already rescinded, in your favor," the formerly rigid Lang smiles. Before leaving, Van Helsing tells Marianne, "Don't let that ogre in there frighten you!"

Sometimes Peter Cushing's face says it all. In a pivotal sequence where servant Greta hugs the freshly dug grave of the village girl who just died, Van Helsing waits in the shadows, watching Baron Meinster's nurse help reanimate this victim of the undead. "Wake up... no, I can't help you. You have to be strong, push!" A human arm emerges from the fresh earth as the coffin lid is slowly opened, and Greta removes the garlic flowers from around the vampire's neck. During this entire sequence, the editor cuts back and forth, recording Van Helsing's wonderment, revulsion, shock and even sadness. Only the ill-timed sudden arrival of the priest—"Stop in the name of the Almighty!"—breaks the spell, as Van Helsing jumps out of the shadows to demand the priest step back, and a vampire bat (whose ridiculous presence is the only black mark in an otherwise superior movie) attacks Cushing, who fights by swinging his medical bag.

Peter Cushing's trend-setting performances as Van Helsing are helped immeasurably by the fact that these Terence Fisher movies are outright horror-movie classics. *Horror of Dracula* is superior by nature of its originality and freshness and its overpowering performance by Christopher Lee. *Brides of Dracula* presents a much more sanitized vision of vampirism; The stakings and bloodletting are not nearly as gruesome. And, while the windmill climax is exciting and horrific, Meinster's non-climactic death (burned with Holy Water and finished off by the shadow of the windmill blades forming a cross) cannot hold a candle to *Horror of Dracula*'s frantic final five minutes. But each of these classic Hammer films is creatively kicked into overdrive by the well-rounded performance of Peter Cushing, a performance that is by turns sensitive, obsessive, warm, and frenzied, sometimes all within the same sequence. When it comes to naming the best horror-film performances of all time, many would say look no further than Peter Cushing's Van Helsing as demonstrated in these two movie classics. Such an argument would be difficult to dispute!

Christopher Lee, Count Dracula and Hammer Films

by Gary J. Svehla

Horror of Dracula, along with *Bride of Frankenstein*, remains for me the best horror film classic ever produced. And the success of *Horror of Dracula*, more so than Hammer's earlier *The Curse of Frankenstein* (a very good trial run for the superior *Horror of Dracula*) and the black-and-white science fiction *Quatermass* classics, was chiefly responsible for Hammer Film Productions becoming iconic and the major producers of horror cinema since Universal set the bar during the 1930s. And at the time unknown British actors Christopher Lee and Peter Cushing quickly became the horror genre stars for a new generation of fans.

Christopher Lee, never better, captivates *Horror of Dracula*, although appearing only 18 minutes or so onscreen. His performance—combining the mysterious (his caped entrance greeting Harker), aristocratic (his conversation with Harker commenting upon his fiancée's beautiful portrait), monstrous (his blood-soaked teeth and visceral entrance into the library, after Valerie Gaunt attacks Harker) and totally undead (his animal-like predatory advance upon defenseless Harker in the underground vault after Harker stakes the vampire woman)—is iconic. Lee's Dracula is not necessarily the incarnation of Bram Stoker's vision from the novel, but contrary to Lee's decades-long rants, this is not really a bad thing. As translated by the Hammer production team of Anthony Hinds, Michael Carreras, director Terence Fisher and screenwriter Jimmy Sangster, this truncated re-visioning of the Stoker novel is played more for its Gothic horror quotient. The role of Dracula, as written for the film, casts Lee as a centuries-old predator, an Undead with an aristocratic history, who believes he is unconquerable. Dracula, as seen in *Horror of Dracula*, can be romantic, debonair, revengeful, commanding and slightly aloof. When he welcomes Jonathan Harker to his home, his words have a formality and haughty tone that more than implies he is the boss and Harker is the hired hand. So when Dracula leaves Harker alone in his room, it is no surprise that we hear the clicking of the key that locks him in, perhaps for his own protection. We understand that Dracula is more than attracted to Lucy, but his interest is fueled by his sense of revenge, since Harker destroyed his vampire mate. Count Dracula feels he must take Harker's woman away from him. Dracula's manipulation of power essentially drives him (not necessarily his lust for blood).

In fact, when he invades and declares all-out war upon the Holmwood household, he of course visits the beautiful, vulnerable Lucy (Carol Marsh)

Dracula (Christopher Lee) enters the bedroom of Lucy (Carol Marsh) in *Horror of Dracula*.

nocturnally, appearing through open French windows that are wind swept by the autumn breeze and leaves that swirl outside. Director Terence Fisher lingers on the open window, the leaves whipping past, as the majestic musical score by James Bernard amps up the tension, with a cut-away before Dracula appears (although the viewer is anticipating his immediate appearance). When we finally cut back to Lucy's bedroom, we are greeted musically by the iconic James Bernard bombast and a tight full-frame shot of the leering vampire. Dracula commands the very will of Lucy and can have her in any way imaginable. Dracula still can influence Lucy, even after vampire hunter Dr. Van Helsing appears on the scene to give his second opinion of her condition. Van Helsing sees the puncture wounds on Lucy's neck and commands Arthur to close all windows and surround the room with garlic flowers. However, kind-hearted maid Gerda gives in to Lucy's pathetic moans that she cannot breathe and needs some air. After the garlic is removed and the window opened, Count Dracula enters and drains Lucy of her blood—she is found dead the next morning. Once again Count Dracula's commanding power makes this human chess tournament exciting for a Count who has lingered for centuries and by now must find life and humankind very dull indeed. When he meets a worthy adversary such as Van Helsing (Peter Cushing's performance is classic and drives the movie as much as Lee's does), Count Dracula's "the game's afoot" spirit rises to the surface.

After Lucy rises from her coffin as a white-gowned predatory vampire, she tries to entice little Tania, the young daughter of maid Gerda, into approaching her. Van Helsing's stakeout at her tomb for several nights allows him to be present when she attempts to dine on Tania. His firm hand and crucifix jut into the frame from the lower right and Lucy, gasping in orgasmic rhythms, backs away from the conquering cross. Van Helsing touches the metal to her forehead, immediately burning an impression as the totally frightened vampire woman flees to her tomb. It is Arthur Holmwood's fear and weak will (symbolically representing the human frailties that allow the vampire to remain supreme) that force Van Helsing to drive in the stake himself and bring peace to Lucy rather than use her (as Van Helsing implores) as a lure to find Count Dracula.

Dracula, continuing his clever cat-and-mouse games, moves his casket to the Holmwood cellar so he can operate his reign of terror from within the Holmwood house—a brilliant and rather gutsy ploy. In one of the movie's best sequences, Count Dracula appears to seduce Arthur's wife Mina in their own bedroom, forcing her down onto her own marriage bed, nuzzling her face as she surrenders willingly to the Count's physical, sexual charms. Most interesting, although a devious predatory beast, Count Dracula delights in the fact that his victims are sexual conquests and totally abandon themselves to his lusts and passions—and that they enjoy this deadly initiation into the world of the Undead. During these Victorian times, the socially restricted females are frisky in their nocturnal sexual appetites and seem to want to play the anti-social bad girls—with pleasure (at least in the world of Hammer)! Count Dracula, from the outside looking in, understands human nature. He was once a member of the human race, but his centuries as one of the undead living among flesh-and-blood mortals allows him to use his experience and knowledge to dominate and control people. This expertise, as well as his all-consuming evil, enables him to appear indestructible. It is rather an act of ego that allows Count Dracula to continually drain Mina of her blood and to draw the formerly polite, prim and proper wife into Dracula's free-spirited sexual abandon of vampirism (although she is never totally transformed). Imagine, Count Dracula, Mina's Undead lover, lives in the very cellar of the Holmwood residence and Dracula has his way with Mina whenever he desires under her husband's very nose. Such arrogance is one of Dracula's defining characteristics.

Only after Van Helsing figures out what has been occurring and finds the Count's white coffin in the basement (placing a crucifix inside, preventing Dracula's return) is the vampire king forced to flee. In the film's classic climactic sequence, as Count Dracula hurries by carriage back to his home chateau, with the goal of burying Mina alive in a freshly dug grave and making her a vampire at last, we have a tense chase through the countryside and soon through the nooks and crannies of Count Dracula's home, as the vampire emerges from trap doors hidden in his home that help to protect him. In a gut-wrenching battle to

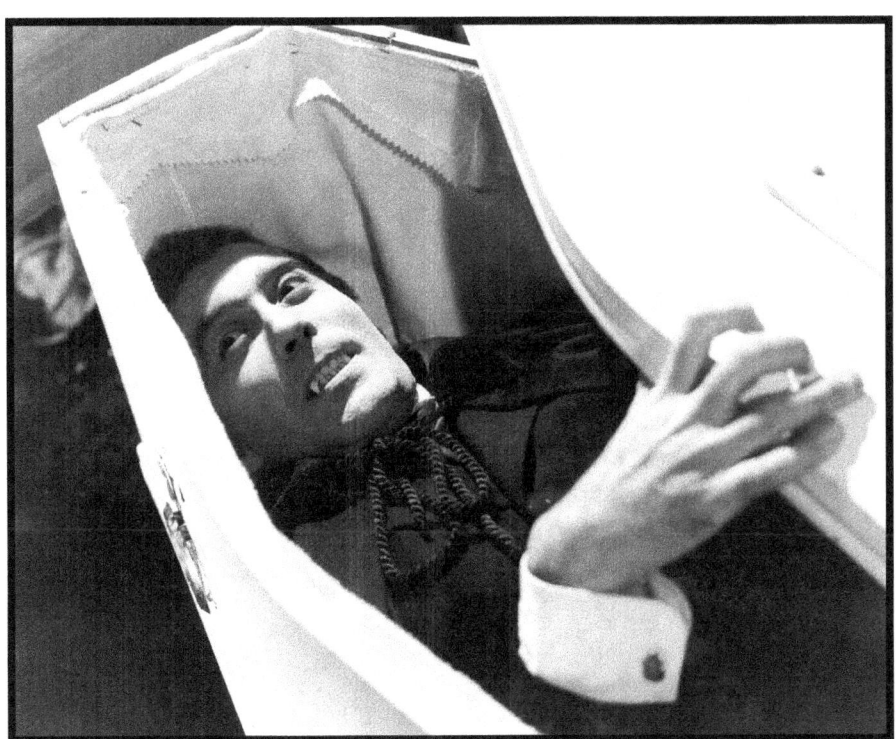

The Count hides in the very cellar of his victim and right under the eyes of his arch-nemesis Van Helsing in *Horror of Dracula*.

the death, Dracula and Van Helsing meet in hand-to-hand combat, with Dracula gaining the upper hand, strangling the life out of the vampire hunter. But the wily Van Helsing, seeing the deadly rays of the morning sun peep from behind the huge curtains, makes his final play by diving across a huge table and leaping to tear the curtains from the large windows, thus bathing Count Dracula in the rays of light that will destroy his evil forever, or at least until the next film. In this ultimate battle between good and evil, evil is not destroyed but momentarily defeated, with the suggestion that evil is an ever-present entity that must be constantly defeated for the short term.

Count Dracula is a character of few words in *Horror of Dracula*. His physical presence, contained beneath a black cloak that makes the vampire appear rigid and tall, commands more authority than his words alone ever can. Coming from such a demonic presence, Christopher Lee's line delivery is succinct and authoritative. His few words, delivered by that towering figure, speak volumes. He can smile and chat politely when communicating with Harker, but it is his eyes and teeth that flare with violence in the library sequence, where Dracula throws Harker around like a rag doll, revealing the extent of his demon spirit, cruelty and self-preservation. As stated, in a supporting role in the movie with his name in the title, Count Dracula permeates every sequence with his

A seemingly helpless beauty (Valerie Gaunt) begs for help from Harker (John Van Eyssen) in *Horror of Dracula*.

power, whether he is physically present in that scene or not. Christopher Lee's performance as Count Dracula in *Horror of Dracula* is classic, rivaling if not surpassing Bela Lugosi's totally different take on Count Dracula. Whether Lee will ever admit it or not, his Count Dracula in this production is the 20-minute performance that fueled his decades-long ascent as international star.

Just as essential to Lee's performance as Count Dracula is director Terence Fisher's visual creation of the world of vampirism. Yes, Fisher acquiesced to the stereotype of vampires having long, pointed fangs and wearing a flowing cape, but his vision of the Undead is totally unique and remains for me the ultimate vision of such an evil cult and the loneliness of vampirism. Fisher emphasizes the sexual dominance and manipulation of the human victim. Just as much as humans fear the kiss of the vampire, they long for their seduction into naughtiness and evil. In the Victorian age, pent-up passions (mostly female) scream for playful release. Even if it means their lives are forfeited, the appeal of life everlasting with wild sexual abandonment might very well be worth the sacrifice. But it is the look of the Hammer vampire that Fisher created and made iconic. Think of these three major sequences and you get the point. First, Valerie Gaunt's sexual come-on to Harker in the library, pleading that Count Dracula abuses her and that she wishes to escape with him, seemingly offering herself sexually if he helps her. The raven-haired woman, adorned in a white nightgown, seems frightened to death and vulnerable. But at the same time she is alluring, beautiful and pushing herself on Harker. As the foolish male gives in to this vampire's trickery, we watch as he hugs her and she lunges for his neck, Count Dracula angrily interrupting her defiance. Just observing her facial transformation as she morphs from vulnerable female victim to predator with animalistic fangs bared is exactly what I mean by Fisher's portrayal of vampirism. Cut to the second sequence, immediately following. Christopher Lee as Dracula, formerly stiff, aristocratic and proper, suddenly appears with red eyes, elongated face and blood-smeared teeth. He hisses, more like an animal than a human being as he prances over tables. He grabs his vampire mate, shakes her around and easily handles the weaker Harker. who is forced to the ground (where he stays put). Again, the transformation from seemingly human Count Dracula to Undead vampire king is horrifying and shocking. Finally, let us cut to the sequence in Count Dracula's underground burial vault, where Jonathan Harker foolishly decides to kill Dracula's vampire mate before dispatching the Count himself, leading to the triumphant entrance of Count Dracula, who mysteriously has moved from his stone coffin (where Harker stares at his corpse, forgetting that the sun is rapidly fading) to the doorway, now powerful and confident that he can easily destroy his enemy. With a smirk and smile, Count Dracula, liberated by the death of the day and return of darkness, slowly approaches Harker, who cowers in fear, to be found by friend Van Helsing weeks later, now gaunt, lifeless, physically violated, sporting fangs and occupying the former resting place of Dracula's mate. Never has a vampire seemed so overwhelmingly powerful and evil. Christopher Lee and Terence Fisher create this new violent and sexual image of the Undead, an image that would rule vampire cinema around the world for decades.

For Christopher Lee, the two immediate Hammer sequels, *Dracula—Prince of Darkness* and *Dracula Has Risen from the Grave*—are the only two artistically worthy of Lee and the only two that embellish his characterization of the immortal Count. But nothing that followed comes close to 1958's *Horror of Dracula*, the movie that symbolizes and becomes the microcosm for everything that is meant by the phrase "Hammer horror." While *Horror of Dracula* is the classic symphony, all the sequels are basically variations on a theme.

Dracula—Prince of Darkness (1966) should have impressed by having Jimmy Sangster (screenplay, but hiding beneath the pen name John Sansam) and Terence Fisher (director) repeat their roles, but it is Christopher Lee who stretches himself creatively while the efforts of Fisher and Sangster disappoint. In almost every sequence of merit in *Prince of Darkness*, there is a direct counterpart in the far superior *Horror of Dracula* that shows just how inferior the sequel was. But this criticism does not extend to Christopher Lee and Barbara Shelley. In this production the character of Dracula is mute and does not speak, and much as Lee demonstrated while playing Kharis the mummy in *The Mummy* and the Creature in *Curse of Frankenstein*, his ability to communicate emotion and character with his rigid posture, facial expressions and piercing eyes is undeniable. Helping to again maintain the horrific tone of dread is the bombastic score by James Bernard, repeating many themes from the earlier production, as well as adding new musical brushstrokes. Of course Lee complained about doing the character of Dracula in 1958 without incorporating Stoker's dialogue directly from the novel. But of course the actor was further enraged that he had absolutely no dialogue in this 1965 widescreen sequel. However, happy camper or not, Lee performs remarkably as the mute vampire king, who still commands an aristocratic, otherworldly presence. The film's major flaw is the fact that almost half the movie involves the resurrection of the vampire king, slitting one poor bastard's throat (Charles Tingwell) and spilling his blood over Dracula's ashes, ashes poured into his burial resting place by manservant Klove (Philip Latham). Klove's mysterious entrance in silhouette, dramatically announced by a Bernard musical stinger, suggests that Philip Latham might well be Dracula, this tease becoming one of the movie's best sequences. But too much of the film is wasted on something that in 1940s monster-rally Universals would have taken mere moments to present. And too much time is spent on the mundane—traveling here, traveling there, entering a room, sitting at a table, etc. Terence Fisher does not do much generating of mood in Dracula's castle; this time out Dracula's abode lacks the air of malevolence that it maintained in the earlier production.

But once Christopher Lee reappears with (this time) his black redlined cape and equally blood-red eyes flaring, the movie takes off. Embellishing the Undead mythos, Sangster and Fisher focus upon Barbara Shelley's character of Helen Kent, a typically repressed and rather stuffy wife to the equally boorish husband Alan. However, after bitten by Lee, she starts to breathe in sensual rhythms and wears sexy, form-fitting nightclothes that focus upon her heaving bosom. For Helen vampirism becomes something playful, exhilarating and personally liberating. And Dracula's more blatant sexuality continues as he appears both frightening and dashing in dark sitting rooms, using his own sharpened fingernail to draw blood down his slightly exposed chest, intending for the transfixed nubile blonde Diana (Suzan Farmer) to drink his blood as an act of evil initiation. This ritual introducing innocents to the world of the Undead becomes more an act of seduction than rape, and Dracula's blood lust is only equaled by his physical lust for his beautiful and innocent victim (Father Sandor states that since Dracula touched her, he now feels he owns her).

Yet in sequences of direct confrontation by so-called human aggressors, Dracula and his mate Helen either appear demonic and powerful or recoil and hiss when confronted by the holy cross, their eyes defiant and enraged, ready to strike, fight back, even break a sword in half and overpower puny humans

Dracula seduces the innocent Diana Kent (Suzan Farmer) in *Dracula—Prince of Darkness.*

by any means necessary. Their arrogant facial expressions and piercing stares demonstrate their air of superiority. No matter how iconic and effective Christopher Lee was portraying Dracula in *Horror of Dracula*, he is able to play Dracula in mime and somehow bring an added dimension to his performance. He is here less human and more an incarnated spirit, but his body language, expressions and movement establish Count Dracula's ungodly character and convey his aristocratic dominance. Some consider the climax of *Prince of Darkness* rushed and silly, Dracula's demise resulting from his coffin sliding off a carriage onto the frozen lake surrounding his own castle. As Charles vol-

Dracula tumbles into the freezing water to his death in *Dracula—Prince of Darkness.*

unteers to crunch across the ice to stake Count Dracula, Father Sandor (Andrew Keir) yells for him to run away, as the sun's rays are dying and Dracula darts out of his coffin, grabbing hold of Charles (Francis Matthews). Sandor fires a series of rifle blasts, creating a broken ring of ice around the Count, who less than aristocratically teeters on the loose block of ice that tips and sways in the water. In a quite silly balancing performance, Count Dracula tumbles into the chilling waters underneath, seemingly to his death. The sequence is visually interesting and is the first time (crossing running water will drown a vampire) this important vampire mythos has been shown on film. Performance wise, Christopher Lee is able to transform from arrogant and superior to fearful and defeated within a matter of seconds, much to his credit. Perhaps slightly silly, it is nonetheless audacious to show Count Dracula maneuver atop a frozen sheet of ice. Of course this climax lacks the dramatic build and extended surprises offered by the end of *Horror of Dracula* (that climax is repeated at the beginning of *Prince of Darkness* and many consider that reprise the best part of this first sequel), one of the best climaxes of any horror classic.

But *Dracula—Prince of Darkness* reveals an even more confident Christopher Lee extending the definition of vampirism through a bravura physical performance that demonstrates that a mute Count Dracula can be even more supernaturally threatening and commanding of his Undead domain. Many critics bemoan the fact that Lee is rendered speechless in this first sequel, but such limitations perhaps motivated this under-rated actor to dig deeper into his acting bag of tricks to produce a performance that both parallels and broadens the exemplary one that Lee delivered back in 1958. Lee's performance, whether gloating, leering, exuding dominance, seducing or angrily flaring his nostrils, brings a new dimension to Count Dracula. Instead of simply repeating his earlier performance, Christopher Lee approaches his interpretation freshly.

Christopher Lee's last significant Dracula sequel, *Dracula Has Risen From the Grave* (1968), offers many creative changes, including the replacement of director Terence Fisher by Freddie Francis, a gifted cinematographer. "John Elder" (producer Anthony Hinds' *nom de plume* when he wrote Hammer screenplays) replaced Jimmy Sangster. Thankfully James Bernard returned to compose another archetypal Dracula musical score.

By the time of *Dracula Has Risen From the Grave*, Hammer Dracula movies were becoming boilerplate and all the archetypes were becoming predictable paint-by-numbers by their lack of creativity. Peter Cushing's career-defining performance as Dr. Van Helsing from the original morphed into a series of generic vampire-hunting clergymen, all of whom paled in comparison. Andrew Keir's performance from *Prince of Darkness* was quite effective as Father Sandor, but he was still no Peter Cushing. In the latest sequel Rupert Davies, playing the Monsignor, is even less effective, although he does a serviceable job. We now have the female in jeopardy performance (the beautiful blonde Suzan Farmer in *Prince of Darkness* and the even lovelier Veronica Carlson in a similar performance here in *Dracula Has Risen From the Grave*), where an innocent and sexy young woman is threatened by Dracula and must be rescued before she is doomed to vampirism. While Farmer and Carlson submit memorable performances, their roles as written lack the complexity of better productions where the Barbara Shelley fem lead transforms from sexually repressed to sexually liberated. Also, remember that Lucy from the original *Horror of Dracula*, innocent and sickly when we first meet her, becomes tainted and ultimately destroyed by the evil of Dracula, but Carol Marsh and Barbara Shelley each created memorable female leads that were unique and deftly written. In the resulting sequels, the leading ladies in these Hammer Dracula movies became little more than just another pretty face (and body). As written, their roles did not allow the creative complexity that we witnessed in the first two Hammer Dracula movies.

Dracula Has Risen From the Grave relies too heavily on the conflict between religion and atheism and the dramatic climax involves Christopher Lee, physically majestic as always, being staked in his coffin and writhing, struggling and finally pulling the stake out of his chest because the staker, an atheist, cannot manage to say a prayer that would allow the Count to die. In John Elder's screenplay, we have a weak-willed priest unceremoniously resurrect Count Dracula by tripping, falling and bleeding onto the ice that houses the corpse of Count Dracula. Another boilerplate moment is the sometimes silly returning to life of the formerly dispatched vampire king. So perhaps the film's major theme this time out is the lack of spiritual commitment, where even clergymen can be seduced into the cult of the Undead, or at least become the mindless servant of Dracula.

Into this world comes the privileged blonde beauty Maria (Veronica Carlson), who lives with her mother and the Monsignor and is madly in love with Paul (Barry Andrews), the already referenced atheist who becomes the flawed hero. Maria loves to sneak out across village rooftops (a magnificent set design that is used effectively to provide a creepy nighttime setting of doom) to visit Paul, and her love and innocence becomes the opposite extreme to Dracula's evil. As contrast to Maria we have lusty and not-so-innocent barmaid Zena (Barbara Ewing), with whom Paul flirts and whom Maria sees as an unfair rival (unfair because the loose Zena is more than willing to put out but Maria, living with the Monsignor, must always be the good little girl). It is apparent that Count Dracula will experience difficulty in attempting to seduce Maria to his side, but Zena is ripe for the throat ripping. And when Zena submits to Dracula's charms after being lured to his den, she becomes his servant and slave while human, but once Dracula grows tired of her and drains her of all her blood, killing her, she remains bloody and dead and does not resurrect as a vampire. Maria, soon hypnotized and possessed spell-like in a dreamy haze, walks dazed and barefoot across a wooded field to fall into the awaiting arms of Count Dracula, who caresses her before the bite. Perhaps the pivotal sequence occurs when Count Dracula attacks Maria, entering her bedroom and demonstrating his masculine seductive powers, ultimately having Maria eagerly submit to his vampire kiss, biting the young innocent in the neck as she clutches rhythmically and then drops her teddy bear, simulating orgasm as the vampire king's fangs penetrate her neck. Christopher Lee's "courtship" continues to be romantic and seductive until the final moment when his blazing red eyes and bared fangs reveal the extent of his animalistic bloodlust.

Not much new occurs with Lee's performance here. Once again he retains Svengali-like powers over the possessed priest (Ewan Hooper), the slutty barmaid Zena and the innocent Maria. In an interesting display of jealousy, Zena becomes enraged that Count Dracula now desires the sweet blonde over her ("Take me!" she implores), and her tantrum leads to her destruction at Dracula's hands (and for once we cannot blame Count Dracula). Count Dracula's sexual prowess instigates women to fight over who will be his bride tonight. Obviously, a guy wrote such a script.

Paul is finally able to resolve his religious faith dilemma and say a prayer at the movie's end, destroying Count Dracula one more time. Christopher Lee unfortunately crosses the line that separates the demonic from the ridiculous

In *Dracula Has Risen From the Grave*, the Count (Christopher Lee) has Svengali-like power over Maria (Veronica Carlson) and Zena (Barbara Ewing).

and, while still effective with bloody tears falling from his eyes, looks more than silly attempting to pull a huge metallic crucifix from his torso. In the hands of director Terence Fisher the integrity of Christopher Lee's performance would be preserved. But in the gifted hands of new director Freddie Francis, Count Dracula's aura of the Undead and his fearsome persona is compromised and diminished. At this point Christopher Lee has morphed from being the most innovative interpreter of Count Dracula to a gifted actor submitting to B movie silliness, and the creative slide would continue in the sequels to come.

Still to follow were Hammer's *Taste the Blood of Dracula* (1970), *Scars of Dracula* (1970), *Dracula A.D. 1972* (1972) and *The Satanic Rites of Dracula* (1973), all these films worthy but often worthy in spite of the presence of Christopher Lee as Dracula. Director Peter Sasdy's *Taste the Blood of Dracula* wasn't even supposed to feature Christopher Lee as the Count, but Lee was finally coaxed to return to his role (at conventions and in print Lee often stated that his guilt over putting production crews out of work forced him to return to a role that was becoming more and more a parody) and the script was rewritten. Three upper-class Brits, bored with their humdrum life, restore Dracula's ashes to life but kill Dracula's servant, and the revived vampire vows revenge, cleverly orchestrating their deaths at the hands of their own children. Sasdy's direction is very effective and visually interesting for the time, and the simplistic story works well as a revenge tale. With Dracula's meager presence, often included as a quick insert, pointing and stating "the next" to emphasize the latest victim

At least Count Dracula (Christopher Lee) has a larger screen presence in *Scars of Dracula*.

to be dispatched, the vampire king is reduced to almost meaningless status. Count Dracula is almost an after-thought in his own movie.

In the low-budget-looking *Scars of Dracula* (the opulence and succinct claustrophobia of Bray Studios and their Gothic set pieces are long gone), at least the character Count Dracula has a much larger screen presence and many more lines of dialogue to deliver, but the pasty-faced Lee (even the makeup appears subpar) is becoming a sadist and blood-thirsty in a cruel, not romantic, way. The complexity and internal performances of the best Hammer Dracula productions have been replaced by poorly scripted interpretations by writers who fail to build upon the iconic performances of the first two or three productions. Instead, these stand-alone productions feel tossed out, and even Christopher Lee's performance seems professional but not inspired. He never embarrasses himself and manages to elevate the production, but he realizes the subtlety and brilliance of classics such as *Horror of Dracula* are long gone. At least this production, directed by the generally excellent Roy Ward Baker (with a script by producer Anthony Hinds that is not mindful of the earlier productions, some of which he wrote), has some Hammer Gothic mood and puts the vampire king pretty much front and center again. But besides the film's reliance on more cruelty and blood shed (perhaps a compromise for modern horror audiences?), the character of Count Dracula is played rather one dimensionally. At least *Scars of Dracula* includes one dynamic sequence that Lee applauded— Count Dracula, in a sequence directly from the Stoker novel, crawling lizard-like up the outside wall of his castle.

The final two silly sequels (both directed by new hire Alan Gibson in a nondescript manner) attempt to update Count Dracula for modern British society. *Dracula A.D. 1972* includes the clash between a vampire cult, lead by a young hippie type called John Alucard, and British rock 'n' roll youth who are fascinated by Satanism and devil cult worship. Lee's role as Dracula is limited and undistinguished. Not even the return of Peter Cushing as Van Helsing or the bouncy delights of Caroline Munro can save this production. The film's opening sequence, featuring Van Helsing and Dracula fighting to the death atop a coach, is the best sequence in the movie. And when Count Dracula takes a broken wheel spoke through the heart, well, visually, this film shines. But Count Dracula as envisioned by Christopher Lee is much more than a demonic vampire who fights in action sequences that feature clever special effects. Any stunt man could do that.

Even worse, Count Dracula goes corporate in the generally subpar *The Satanic Rites of Dracula*, recasting Dracula as a reclusive businessman. Peter Cushing is back as Van Helsing (a descendent of the original) but does not have much to do, nor does Christopher Lee as Count Dracula. Besides waging war with the Van Helsing clan, Count Dracula tries to hatch a diabolical plot to unleash bubonic plague (quite fitting for a person as old as Count Dracula) upon an unsuspecting world. But such a plot would seem better suited to one of Lee's Fu Manchu movies. Once again, not even the presence of the always-reliable Freddie Jones or beautiful Joanna Lumley can salvage this dreary, listless movie. *The Satanic Rites of Dracula* does not need a stake to destroy the now pathetic Count. Here, Count Dracula is dead on arrival.

Christopher Lee, in many ways, was correct in protesting the lack of quality and the failure to recreate Bram Stoker's vision of Count Dracula in these Hammer productions. However, his performances in *Horror of Dracula* and *Dracula—Prince of Darkness* are faithful to Stoker's vision and remain enthusiastic, inspired, complex and sophisticated portrayals of cinematic evil over 50 years later. For me, seeing that quick cut of Dracula's vampiric face, elongated, blood-soaked in extreme close-up (hissing/breathing on the soundtrack), his face and teeth smeared with human blood, transcends the artifice of acting. In that quick cut and the sequence that follows, Christopher Lee becomes otherworldly and ethereal—transforming himself into the king of the Undead. He does not appear to be acting. Instead, every fiber of his body has been transformed into Count Dracula. Never again in his screen-acting career has Christopher Lee ever appeared so out-of-body transformed by any one performance. Christopher Lee's Count Dracula in 1958's *Horror of Dracula* remains among the classic performances in horror film cinema. It is a career-defining performance, and it demonstrates why *Horror of Dracula* is among the top-10 horror movies ever produced.

Peter Cushing and Van Helsing

by Tom Johnson

Peter Cushing, the screen's most prolific (five films) Van Helsing, was born in Surrey, England on May 26, 1913. After the usual false starts common to most actors' careers, Cushing took the bold step of going to Hollywood to break into movies with little experience other than community theater productions. After lucking (and, he admitted, lying) his way into the cast of director James Whale's *The Man in the Iron Mask* (1939), Cushing made six more movies before returning to the U.K. due to World War II.

Cushing became associated with future Van Helsing, Sir Laurence Olivier, and appeared with him as Osric in the Academy Award–winning *Hamlet* (1947). By the mid-1950s, Cushing had become England's most honored television actor and had scored in several movies (notably *The End of the Affair,* 1954). Sought and caught by Hammer Films to play the Baron in *The Curse of Frankenstein* (1957), Cushing became typed in horror roles and never looked back, appearing in over 75 more pictures. Effectively cast as heroes (Sherlock Holmes in *The Hound of the Baskervilles,* 1959) and villains (Grand Moff Tarkin in *Star Wars,* 1977) and everyday people (Mr. Fordyce in *Cash on Demand,* 1961), Cushing was the most versatile actor to be associated with horror movies. He brought all of his considerable skills to the Van Helsing role in Hammer's *Dracula* (1958).

On the trail of his friend Jonathan Harker (John Van Eyssen), who has failed in his attempt to destroy Dracula (Christopher Lee), Van Helsing enters an inn and confronts its frightened, surly owner (George Woodbridge). "What are you afraid of?" Van Helsing asks. "Why all these garlic flowers over the window? They're not for decoration, are they?"

"I don't know what you're talking about."

"I think you do... and I think you know something about my friend. He came here with a purpose... to help you."

"We haven't asked for any help."

"You need it all the same."

"You're a stranger here in Clausenberg," the innkeeper sniffs. "Some things are better left alone... such as interfering in things which are beyond our powers."

But Van Helsing will have none of this. "Please don't misunderstand me. This is more than a superstition... I know! The danger is very real."

And so is Van Helsing, played by Cushing not as a cliché but as a fully developed character, a recognizable human being.

"Can Dracula really be as old as it says here?" asks the skeptical Arthur Holmwood (Michael Gough), whose wife Mina (Melissa Stribling) is the Count's next target.

"We believe it's possible," Van Helsing asserts. "Vampires have been known to have gone on from century to century."

"Another thing... I've always understood that *if* there were such things," Holmwood continues, "I thought they could change themselves into bats or wolves."

"That's a common fallacy," says Van Helsing, grounding the picture in reality and saving Hammer hundreds of pounds in special effects.

Cushing's Van Helsing, a combination of sensitivity and sternness, dominates the movie and is one step ahead of Dracula's fleeting, shadowy appearances. Despite Dracula's awesome powers, we are not at all surprised when Van

Van Helsing (Cushing) is ready to meet Baron Meinster in *The Brides of Dracula*.

Helsing puts him away. In the picture's famous climax, Van Helsing uses both his mental and physical prowess; trapped in a beam of sunlight by Van Helsing's makeshift cross, Dracula whips and thrashes in a well-deserved destruction.

Van Helsing was back two years later in *The Brides of Dracula*, and not a second too soon. Baron Meinster (David Peel), a vicious Dracula wannabe, has been terrifying a Transylvanian village. An ineffectual priest (Fred Johnson) fails to comfort the father of a recently vampirized girl. "Poor man," he mutters. "And I am powerless, powerless..."

"Perhaps I can help," says a confident Van Helsing.

"Who are you?"

"You sent for me... Dr. Van Helsing."

"Oh!" gushes the priest. "Thank God you've come! Thank God!"

With God's help, plus some holy water, the cross-like vanes of a windmill, and plenty of guts, Van Helsing makes short work of the upstart Baron.

Peter Cushing got it a *bit* wrong in an interview with *Little Shoppe of Horrors,* a magazine devoted to analyzing Hammer's horror films: "Stoker had described [Van Helsing] as a *little* old Dutchman with a *bald head* and sporting a small beard. Therefore, all the production team got together and decided that it would be better to inject more vigor into the character. So I played the part more or less as myself."

This meant a civilized charm that could turn a bit chilly when called for, or a wild athleticism: a perfect—and necessary—match for Christopher Lee's energetic Dracula. Cushing's greatest strength in horror pictures (other than his impeccably 19th-century look and mannerisms) was his ability to make the most absurd line or situation believable.

Unlike past and future Van Helsings, Cushing's character was a lone wolf. Combining both intellectualization and physical prowess, his Van Helsing needed no one at all to help subdue the Count or his disciple Baron Meinster. This gave Cushing's interpretation an additional boost, even though it's at odds with Stoker's gang leader. Due to Hammer's focus on action, Cushing was as perfectly cast against Lee as Van Sloan was against Lugosi.

Van Helsing made a comeback in *Dracula A.D. 1972*.

Van Helsing did not appear in Hammer's next four "period" Draculas, but made a comeback (of sorts) in *Dracula A.D. 1972* and *Satanic Rites of Dracula* (1973). As Lorrimer Van Helsing, a descendent of the original, Peter Cushing was unable to lift both films out of the ordinary (which is testimony to their mediocrity). In these latter day versions, Van Helsing has, due to Cushing's advancing years, joined forces with the police (Michael Coles), to considerably less result.

Cushing gave his final performance as Van Helsing in *Legend of the Seven Golden Vampires* (1974). This Dracula/Kung fu combo filmed in Hong Kong isn't as bad as it sounds (how could it be?), but is almost as far from Stoker's original as it's possible to get.

After leaving the Van Helsing role, Peter Cushing appeared in 20 movies, ranging from the excellent (*Star Wars*) to the execrable (*Tendre Dracula*, 1974). He died of cancer in August 1994, leaving a legacy of fine film performances and devoted fans, both outside and inside the film industry.

The Dracula Films with No Dracula!

by Gary J. Svehla

The Brides of Dracula is a film worthy of being in my top-10 horror classics of all time, but a film nevertheless inferior to the greatest Hammer production of all time, *Horror of Dracula*. Revisionist theory now holds with *Brides of Dracula* being a superior film, and while it is a better movie in itself, it is too derivative of *Horror of Dracula* to be called the better film. David Peel is one of the finest movie vampires, with his gray cape, flaming red hair—so brilliant in Technicolor—and deliberate line readings, but he is just not Christopher Lee. Let me support my claim. David Peel's performance includes two extreme variations in his character of Baron Meinster. First he is the brooding, romantic Byronic hero (the shackled man who stands on his castle ledge, apparently ready to jump; the handsome young man who comes to visit Marianne at her teaching academy). Second, he is the bestial vampire (with his well-kempt hair becoming more frizzy, his eyes bulging, his evil sneer radiating and a mouthful of fangs flashing). However, when he confronts Gina (Andrée Melly) to vampirize her, he appears in the animalistic stage with little attempt made to romance the almost willing victim. After courting and romancing Marianne (Yvonne Monlaur), he storms into her room and takes her by force. Here is Peel's major flaw—he can play both extremes effectively but lacks the subtlety to effortlessly meld one into the other. Christopher Lee could be the animalistic vampire (during the brutal library entrance) and the dashing romantic (his early sequences with Harker), but when he seduces both Mina and Lucy, we see layers of both extremes in his performance. Peel's performance lacks this depth.

Brides of Dracula has perhaps the faster-paced and more effective rhythm throughout, but *Horror of Dracula* contains more outstanding sequences. In *Brides of Dracula* we have Van Helsing (Peter Cushing's performance in both films is perhaps the most outstanding in his career and he is equally impressive in both) returning to the chateau to confront the Baron in a shorter rehash of the climax to *Horror of Dracula*. This is followed by the wonderful sequence with Martita Hunt where she reveals his incestuous relationship to her own son the Baron. And we have the superb windmill sequence with the two vampires protected by their nurse Greta (Freda Jackson in a wondrous over-the-top performance) before the Baron appears. These are *Brides of Dracula*'s money sequences (along with perhaps the eerie resurrection sequence of Marie Devereux coaxed by the vampiric mid-wife Greta). *Horror of Dracula* features the nightmarish sequence where Harker goes alone into Dracula's crypt and kills Dracula's bride Valerie Gaunt, failing to kill the Count before sunset. Then we have the landmark sequence in the library where Harker is infected. Finally

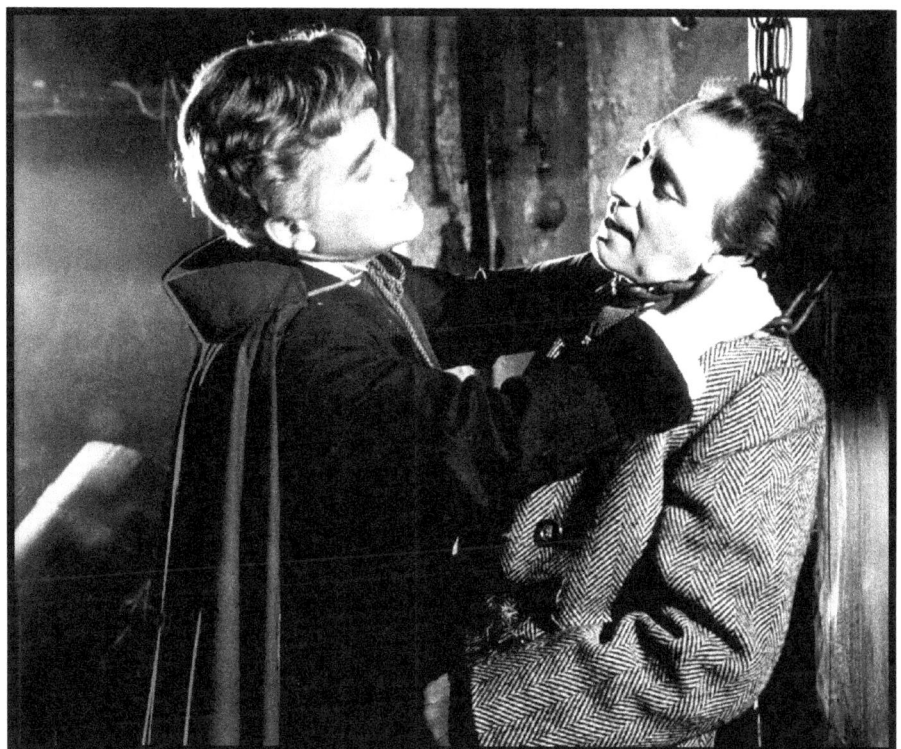

Baron Meinster (David Peel) tries to throttle Van Helsing (Cushing) in *Brides of Dracula.*

we have the outstanding climax where Van Helsing chases Count Dracula throughout his castle and ultimately destroys him in the blinding sunlight. And did I almost forget the subtlety and dread in the sequence where vampiric Lucy attempts to seduce the young Tania but is dramatically foiled by the sudden intervention of Van Helsing? *Horror of Dracula* has endless sequences that are simply superior to those outstanding sequences in *Brides of Dracula*. And so many of the best scenes from *Brides of Dracula* are obviously modeled after the similar sequences from the originator. Simply compare the pulse-pounding climax from *Horror of Dracula* to the disappointing one from *Brides of Dracula* — a short fight with the Baron, holy water, which acts as acid on the face, and finally the shadow of the windmill in the image of a cross. Second rate all the way when compared to its predecessor.

But while this revisionist theory of the superiority of *Brides of Dracula* has obviously colored this review, I must state that both films are in my top-10 and both reflect the absolute best work created by director Terence Fisher, whose world of vampires is unholy, other-human and the finest realization of the world of the undead yet captured on film. While other vampire films go for the gusto, the dramatic, the special effects and the over-acted, Terence Fisher's

Noel Willman as Dr. Ravna is no Christopher Lee as he entrances Jennifer Daniel in *Kiss of the Vampire*.

vampires are subtle, multi-layered, sensual and pathetic (and horrifying), all at the same time. The use of garish Technicolor photography to embellish this world of fairy-tale depravity only helps to capture this cinematic world of the undead to perfection. And *Brides of Dracula*, with its photography, Technicolor, direction and performances, becomes a classic for all time.

Kiss of the Vampire, directed (unfortunately) by Don Sharp, is a film inferior to *Brides of Dracula* (but the gap in quality is greater between *Brides* and *Kiss* than was the gap between *Horror* and *Brides*), mostly because Don Sharp's vision of vampirism is at times too imitative of Terence Fisher's and at other times too flat and literal without all the wonderful visual layers of Fisher's vampiric world. Let me state that *Kiss of the Vampire* is a solidly entertaining Hammer vampire movie filled with a few marvelous performances—especially Edward de Sousa as Gerald, one of the finest Hammer heroes, with a performance that requires him to play drunk, romantic bliss, fear of insanity and the horror of confronting vampirism. *Kiss of the Vampire* features a musical score by James Bernard, and his piano sonata is one of his finest contributions to horror cinema, as the overall score also excels. Perhaps the set direction by Bernard Robinson (featuring both the interior of the castle and the hotel interior) is among his finest work. And the script, penned not by Hammer regular Jimmy Sangster, but by John Elder (Anthony Hinds), is mysterious and haunting. But where is the wonderful pacing of a Terence Fisher film? Too much time is spent with the newlyweds' motorcar breaking down and the couple entering and meeting the proprietors of the hotel. Where are the outstanding horror sequences? Where is the sense of the vampires as undead? The brother and sister, who travel by coach and hide beneath parasols, rushing back to their protective carriage, hurriedly pulling down the purple shades, comes closest to capturing this sense of the undead. Noel Willman as Dr. Ravna is very subtle and quite effective as the leader of the vampire cult (although one's

Sadly, *Kiss of the Vampire* lacks a Van Helsing, instead offering Clifford Evans as Professor Zimmer, here tempted by Isobel Black.

eyes constantly go to his hair extensions that embellish his widow's peak), but he is definitely a vampire cast in the "actors who resemble Christopher Lee" mold. And while Willman's underplaying works very nicely, he is definitely *not* Christopher Lee.

Most disappointing is the lack of a Van Helsing or powerful vampire hunter in the vein that Peter Cushing made a Hammer staple. Instead Clifford Evans (the father from *The Curse of the Werewolf*) portrays Professor Zimmer, a drunken shell of a burned-out man, who lives in solitude, mysteriously but conveniently appearing to sniff out the undead. If we had a back story or some evidence of a characterization that would make the audience care about this broken man, his performance might have resonated and been more profound. But here he is just the gruff man, who appears out of nowhere to provide the necessary help. Even his pivotal sequence confronting the evil vampire Tania (Isobel Black), who is attempting a vampiric resurrection sequence similar to the one performed by Freda Jackson in *The Brides of Dracula,* is truncated and cheaply shot, substituting mountains of fog for a carefully rendered set. When Zimmer confronts the sensual vampire girl, he is bitten on the hand and forced to stick his hand in fire, repeating the similar branding sequence from *Brides of Dracula*, but to far less effect.

Hammer's Hunt For A New Vein of Vampire Film: Three Semi-Classics From the 1970s

by Dennis Fischer

As Hammer entered the 1970s, they saw indeed that times they were a-changin', and tried to think up new approaches to horror which would attract the new horror audience. This led to such projects as *Hands of the Ripper* (1971), *Dr. Jekyll and Sister Hyde* (1971), *Demons of the Mind* (1972), *To the Devil a Daughter* (1976) and the Karnstein trilogy (1971), as well as Jimmy Sangster's misfired remake of *Curse of Frankenstein—Horror of Frankenstein* (1970). In the past Hammer had had hits with non-Dracula vampire films *Brides of Dracula* (1960) and *Kiss of the Vampire* (1963).

The results of these attempts were a mixed bag, which contained both a hint of freshness and plodding doses of the same-old same-old. Perhaps the best were the three nontraditional vampire films that the studio attempted. The first, and unfortunately least, of these was *Countess Dracula* (1970), which featured a female vampire, who according to Raymond McNally and Radu Florescu, authors of *In Search of Dracula*, was a female descendant of Stephen Bathory, the general who had helped Vlad Tepes to reconquer Wallachia.

Instead of following the path of *Dracula's Daughter* (1936) by introducing some fictitious relation of the vampire count, Hammer and Hungarian director Peter Sasdy decided to base their story on Elizabeth Bathory. Much of the information printed on Bathory has proven to be inaccurate, but there was enough to suggest a sensational (in both senses of the term) new approach to vampirism.

Elizabeth Bathory was born in 1560 in Hungary and was related to Sigismund Bathory, Prince of Transylvania. Her family was distinguished in both the noble and the perverted sense and included a brother recorded as being sexually insatiable, a devil-worshiping uncle, and an aunt who was a lesbian witch.

At the age of 15, she was married to Count Ferencz Nadasdy and resided in Castle Csejthe in the Nyitra County in northern Hungary. The Count was known as "The Black Hero of Hungary," and was frequently involved in military campaigns against not only the Turks, but also Spanish and Italian mercenaries hired by the Hapsburgs. Consequently, his young bride was frequently left alone and probably sexually frustrated.

History books claim she hated her mother-in-law and surrounded herself with astrologers and magicians. She learned occultism from a manservant named Thorko, though her childhood nurse, Ilona Joo, also apparently had some

knowledge of witchcraft. She supposedly cavorted with witches, and had an affair with a young nobleman who was reputed to be a vampire.

After 10 barren years, she gave birth to three boys and a girl. Her husband died in 1600, leaving her alone once more. Now mistress of the castle, she sent her mother-in-law away and practiced lesbianism with her two beautiful maids.

According to authors NcNally and Florescu, Bathory lost her temper one day as her maid was combing her hair. She struck the maid, causing a nosebleed, and became convinced that the droplets of blood rejuvenated her skin. Thorko and János Ujvary murdered the maid, and then Elizabeth stripped and bathed in her blood.

She became a distaff Gilles de Rais [French serial killer of children in the 1400s], and the corpses of 50 girls were found buried in the castle grounds. Rumors of the murders of children and teenaged girls, as well as stories of girls being kept in dungeons and fattened like cattle because Elizabeth believed that the fatter they were, the more blood was in their veins reached King Mátyás, who failed to take action until one of her victims escaped and went to the authorities.

On December 30, 1610, Elizabeth's cousin György Thurzo led a band of soldiers into the castle and discovered a girl whose body had been drained of blood and another who was covered with small punctures made by a sharp instrument, and in the dungeons were more girls in the same gruesome condition. The Countess had been "milking" her victims of their blood until they died.

Countess Bathory was put on trial, but never appeared and refused to plead innocent or guilty. Ujvary, the major domo, testified that he knew of about 37 girls who had been killed, six of whom he brought into the castle with promises of jobs as maids. The judge ordered the beheading of Thorko, Ujvary and all her accomplices. Her nurse Ilona Joo had her fingers torn out one by one, then was burned alive. Because she was a noble, it was against the law to execute the Countess.

The King demanded Elizabeth's death, but she was not sentenced. Instead, her sentence was delayed indefinitely, per Count Thurzo's request, and she was walled up within her own chamber with only a small aperture through which she might receive food. Three years later she died at the age of 54. Discovered among her documents was an invocation to the Devil, written apparently on the eve of her arrest, to send 99 demon cats to tear out the hearts of Mátyás, Count Thurzo and other officials.

In addition to *Countess Dracula*, Bathory is also directly referenced in the films *Daughters of Darkness* (1971, directed by Harry Kumel), *La Noche de Walpurgis* (1971, *The Werewolf Versus the Vampire Women*) and its sequel *El Returno de Walpurgis* (1974, *Curse of the Devil*), as well as influencing numerous other films.

The film does make the mistake of assuming that the Countess took her husband's name, so the main character played by Ingrid Pitt is called Countess Elisabeth Nadasdy when in fact the Count assumed his wife's name because of her family's importance.

The hero of the film is Imre Toth (Sandor Eles), a young officer whose father, General Toth, had served the Count. Imre has been summoned because he has been mentioned in the Count's will. The hero's name not only conjures up memories of the Scroll of Thoth for horror fans, but also means "death," an interesting surname for a heroic soldier. Early in the film his youthful virility is displayed by his admiration of a serving wench.

In a brief scene Sasdy initiates the theme of the aristocracy as figurative vampires who live off the blood of the peasantry when a peasant pleads to an unheeding and uncaring Countess that his family will starve unless he gets a job that the late Count promised him. The Countess' carriage runs him over. This prompts curses of "Devil woman! Devil! Devil!"

At the reading of the will, faithful family steward Captain Dobi (Nigel Green) receives only some armor, the library goes to Master Fabio (Maurice Denham), the stables to Toth, and the rest of the estate divided between Elisabeth and her daughter Ilona. Elisabeth is visibly disturbed at this news, but indicates she will follow her husband's wishes.

Sasdy introduces his inverse Jekyll-and-Hyde theme in a playful manner (inverse because it is the normal "Elisabeth" that ages rather than her transformed self). The Countess is just about to take a bath when Terry, a serving maid, is

Countess Dracula (Ingrid Pitt) and Captain Dobi (Nigel Green) have more than a working relationship.

scolded for having made the water too hot. Terry pours in a pitcher of cold water and pronounces it cooler, but Elisabeth scalds Terry's hand in the water, and then orders the maid to peel a peach, a D.H. Lawrence bit of female sexual symbolism. Terry accidentally cuts her hand and the Countess strikes her. The girl's blood splashes onto the Countess' face, which magically appears younger. Sasdy juxtaposes the key elements—bath, blood, sexuality and sadism—which make up the Countess' mania, but although more blood will be spilled, this is the last time we really see it on camera.

When servants inform Dobi that Terry has disappeared, he suggests they look in the whorehouses, but Terry's mother insists that she is pure, establishing the importance of virginity to the blood sacrifice. Dobi is shocked to see Elisabeth looking 20 years younger. It is quickly make clear that they are lovers and he looks to her to reward his years of faithful "service."

The Countess' daughter Ilona (Lesley-Anne Down) is in a carriage traveling home when highwaymen, under instructions from Dobi, waylay her. The villains kill her driver and carry her off. Meanwhile, the now youthful Elisabeth makes a play for Toth by arranging for him and Fabio to come to dinner while she passes herself off as Ilona.

Sasdy helmed *Taste the Blood of Dracula* (1970) as well, which also included a theme of vampirism destroying the foundations of family life, and here he adds the popular late '60s theme of the older generation preying on the young. As part of flirting with Imre, Elisabeth reveals that Dobi has been the Countess' secret lover for many years. Imre is willing to take her up on her enticing offer but Elisabeth glances at a mirror and sees she is once again her true age and hastily gets rid of her would-be lover.

The character of Fabio represents science and knowledge; he is a scholar who loves his books but is beholden to the patronage of social superiors. He remarks to Nurse Julia (Patience Collier) that when Ilona left, she favored her father in looks but now that she is back (actually Elisabeth), she is image of her mother. Through careful detective work, Fabio figures out what is going on, but rather than share the truth, he becomes an accomplice in the Countess' homicidal doings, allowing him continued access to the family's library. Dobi later murders Fabio, although his death is pronounced a suicide. Dobi manages to plant evidence pointing to Fabio as the murderer of Elisabeth's next victim, a Gypsy fortune-teller.

Director Sasdy's macabre humor is evident in the Gypsy's death scene when the young lass telling the Countess' fortune predicts that a "young lover will lift away the veil of widowhood" and that she "will be young in her heart again." The Countess pretends to be pleased with her fortune, and the girl has no idea she is the next blood donor.

Elisabeth's willingness to sacrifice the lives of others for youth helps underscore the film's theme of the folly of worshiping transient youth. Her character is calculating and manipulative; however, her desperation is believable—so that while she is never sympathetic, she often seems more pathetic than evil. Her main flaw is that she never questions her presumed "right" to do with others as she wishes. She inspires loyalty in Julia and devotion in Dobi, but never love in Imre, who is only transfixed by her illusionary beauty. Her most dangerous quality is her ability to convince others to do anything to help her achieve happiness. Dobi realizes that she prefers Imre and tries to make him look bad by bribing a local whore to seduce Imre. When Dobi then leads her to the rendezvous, the whore complains that Imre can't do it and Elisabeth has Dobi offer the woman twice her expected price for visiting the Countess.

Elisabeth discovers that the woman was no virgin and her blood is tainted, and does not make her younger. However, she uses it to threaten Imre with murder if he doesn't marry her. The wedding must be soon, for the Countess is rapidly aging. Toth himself had earlier admitted to physical inexperience—"I have much to learn," he says, to which Elisabeth responds, "Then let me teach you," before kissing him.

When Dobi gets Imre drunk at the local pub, the befuddled lad suggests a double wedding, he to daughter Ilona (really the Countess masquerading as her daughter) and Dobi to the Countess, little realizing that they are the same woman. He toasts their good fortune in having found a virtuous woman, who is everything in one—mistress, friend and mother. But the limitations of this view are apparent when one considers that by turns, Elisabeth is all these things and yet by no means virtuous.

In fact, her undoing is her willingness, nay, her desire to supplant her daughter. She usurps her daughter's inheritance, imprisons her, steals her destined lover—in their brief meeting it is indicated that the real Ilona and Imre had a major attraction to each other. Elisabeth is prepared to sacrifice her only daughter to retain her youth and beauty, even for a short time. But during wedding ceremony she begins to age. Nurse Julia, who was willing to do anything for the Countess until she discovers that Ilona is to be the next victim of the Countess and Dobi, sets the real Ilona free.

The Countess discovers that only the blood of a virgin will bring back her beauty in *Countess Dracula* after she murders Ziza (Andrea Lawrence).

All is revealed when Elisabeth attempts to kill Ilona. Imre leaps to protect Ilona, and Elisabeth stabs her erstwhile lover instead. The film ends with Elisabeth, called "Devil woman" and "Countess Dracula," in a jail cell. That is the only time she is referred to as Countess Dracula apart from the title over Ingrid Pitt's face in the opening credits

The film's most positive attribute is that it provides the lovely Ms. Pitt a chance to prove her acting mettle. The Polish-born actress has an appropriately exotic accent for the role and her body movements establish her predatory nature. Ingrid alters her performing style nicely between the younger and older versions of herself; we never lose interest in either of her characters. Unfortunately, the talented and lovely Ms. Pitt never received many parts she could really sink her teeth into, though her subsequent appearances in such fare as *The Wicker Man* and *Smiley's People* were most welcome. Her favorite performance was as Heidi in *Where Eagles Dared* (1968) with Richard Burton and Clint Eastwood. [Ingrid passed away Nov. 23, 2010. She loved her fans and the many friends she made on the horror film convention circuit will sadly miss her devilish laugh and the twinkle in her eyes.]

Her co-star, Nigel Green, passed away in 1972. Green appeared in films such as *Jason and the Argonauts* (1963, as Hercules), *Zulu* (1964), *The Masque of the Red Death* (1964) and *The Skull* (1965). Green shines as Captain Dobi, the older man who realizes that his mistress prefers another but can't deny her wishes, however depraved. Green unfortunately died of an accidental overdose of sleeping pills a short time after the release of the film.

Hammer's next vampire epic, *Vampire Circus*, was number three on the list of Donald C. Willis' Twelve Best Genre Films from 1971-1981. Willis admired the film for the way it "imaginably plays on, sharpens our double sense of horror films as narrative/spectacle, the sense that 'it's only/it's not only' a movie" (*Horror and Science Fiction Films II*).

Director Robert Young and editor Peter Musgrave do a superb job of adding style and keeping *Vampire Circus* lively, even upon occasion wondrous. Debuting director Young tries his wings not with flashy camera angles but as a master of montage and evocative imagery.

As the film opens schoolmaster Professor Mueller (Laurence Payne) is reading a book while Jenny Schilt (Jane Darby) is frolicking in the forest. Suddenly, Anna Mueller (Domini Blythe), dressed in black, leads Jenny to the castle of Count Mitterhaus (Robert Tayman), who appears just below his portrait.

We soon learn that the Count is a vampire and Anna, his willing love slave, has brought Jenny to him as a victim. "One lust feeds off the other," says Count Mitterhaus, oozing sexuality as he caresses Anna, who reacts rapturously. The scene equates vampirism and sexual desire—they get off on offing people.

Mueller has summoned the local villagers for help. They storm the castle and find Jenny dead. Mitterhaus confronts Mueller, knocking the ineffectual schoolmaster aside. When the vampire is stabbed, he slits his would-be attacker's throat. The Burgermeister (Thorley Walters) impales Mitterhaus on a huge stake, but he simply breaks it in two. (A line of dialogue makes plain that the stake must pierce his heart.) The Count places a curse on the town before being energetically dispatched in a continuous action sequence that could easily have been the climax of another movie.

As the villagers burn the castle down, the Burgermeister pronounces, "The Count is dead. We've rid our village of evil." Rather than being the thesis of the film, this proves to be its antithesis.

The film's story was written by Judson Kinberg (screenwriter of the excellent thriller *The Collector*, 1965), and was based on John Fowles' novel, from a story by George Baxt (the screenwriter for *City of the Dead* [1960, aka *Horror Hotel*] and *Circus of Horrors*, 1960) and Wilbur Stark. The plot is designed to demonstrate that evil can never be fully eradicated.

Vampire Circus opens with the death of Jenny (Jane Darby), whose body was found by Professor Mueller (Laurence Payne).

The mood Young creates here is downbeat rather than upbeat, which is underscored in a scene where he cuts from a shot of Jenny's corpse being borne through the streets of Stetl, to her parents grieving. Schilt (John Brown) demands Anna's death and tries to stab her. Instead, the town forms a gantlet as each man takes a turn whipping her, but in the confusion Anna makes her getaway.

Anna finds the body of her lover, and he temporarily revives after some of her blood drips on him. Mitterhaus tells her to seek out his cousin Emil. As she leaves, the villagers dynamite the castle, and in a pat bit of imagery, a bat emerges from a skull's eye-socket and flies away

Working with a restricted budget, Young makes the most of his images, abetted by Moray Grant's cinematography and Jill Carpenter's makeup. Even the images behind the long-delayed opening credits aren't wasted—they show a series of tableaux of the changing seasons around the destroyed castle while Mitterhaus' face is subtly but never fully superimposed, implying his continued influence over the region.

After the opening credits, the story resumes 15 years later during the midst of a medieval plague—with priests numbered among the victims, indicating that the Lord can't even save His own. Roadblocks have quarantined the infected village. The town council debates whether this is the result of a plague or a curse—Dr. Kersh (Richard Owen) insists that there is no such thing as a vampire and that what they killed was a man and not the living embodiment of some superstition.

It is a surprise when a Gypsy circus comes into town despite the roadblocks. A deceptive and heinous dwarf (Skip Martin) promises, "A hundred delights—the Circus of Nights!" (I can't help but feel that the "Circus of Nights" conception owes a debt to Ray Bradbury's 1962 novel *Something Wicked This Way Comes*, which is also about a sinister circus containing a life-altering Hall of Mirrors.) For a split second a bystander notices that the caged black panther is actually a man, Emil (Anthony Corlan). When asked why they have come, the dwarf answers, "To steal the money from dead men's eyes," followed by a shot of a plague victim being given his tokens for Charon (who ferries the dead across the River Styx).

The good doctor needs more information to fight the plague, and so must abandon the sick and evade the roadblock with the help of his son Anton (John Moulder-Brown), who draws the fire of the border guards and ends up thrown from his horse.

That night, the circus gives its first performance, one of the film's highlights, as dancers Serena and Milovan choreograph and perform an elaborate routine where a tiger is transformed into a striped, naked feral woman who tears the shirt off her trainer. The sequence is erotic and highly suggestive of animal passions, of a male-female, master-slave relationship that ends with the feral feline seemingly choked to death by her master's whip in her pursuit of gratification.

Anton appears at the circus, introduced by the dwarf with the lines, "Our hero returns. How goes the battle?" Clearly the battle is subtly ongoing. The Vampire Circus is fascinatingly deceptive by using the willing suspension of disbelief to trick the audience. We know that what the audience is seeing is "real," but the audience in the film believes it to be merely a trick. (An idea beautifully encapsulated visually in a gag where the dwarf pulls off a mask to reveal the same face underneath.) Hence, when the black panther transforms, via cutting, into Emil in mid-jump, the circus' audience applauds in the belief that it has seen a harmless conjuring trick rather than a vampire's animal-to-man transformation.

Neither are the cursed villagers all saints. When a boy is momentarily missing, age-old racism against Gypsies rears its unlovely head until Emil returns with the boy. The villagers are right to mistrust the Gypsies, but they do so for the wrong reasons, demonstrating their complicity in an ongoing evil.

Emil starts to put the moves on young Rosa (Christina Paul), the daughter of the Burgermeister, whose budding sexuality makes her easy to seduce, but Emil's partner and the Circus of Night's titular head, a matronly Gypsy woman (Adrienne Corri), warns him that the time is not yet ripe, so he withdraws his fangs.

A striped woman will tear the shirt off her trainer (Serena and Milovan) in an erotic sequence in *Vampire Circus*.

The next day Rosa refuses to stay at home although her mother is worried over her involvement with a circus performer (understandable, but yet another example of prejudice). However, as a parent she proves too permissive, allowing her daughter to have her way.

Meanwhile, the circus' silent strongman (David Prowse) uncovers the crypt of Mitterhaus. As in *Taste the Blood of Dracula* (1970), the "sins" of the fathers shall be visited upon the children, per Mitterhaus' curse. All the children of the village leaders will become victims of the vampires.

The second performance of the circus offers another of the film's most accomplished moments. In a visual pun, a pair of acrobats, Helga and Heinrich (Lalla Ward and Robin Sachs) transform into real bats. Shots of Bradforts-Amaros, real acrobats doubling for Helga and Heinrich, are cunningly intercut with slow-motion shots of bats in flight, playing up the similarity of movement and form.

At the end of the show, the Burgermeister is taken inside and introduced to the Mirror of Life. He is amused by a series of funhouse mirrors, and when asked what he sees, replies, "It's not life, its just distortions." However, in the last mirror, he sees himself being attacked by Count Mitterhaus, which causes him to collapse. In this film, the vampires, whose reflections cannot be seen in mirrors, travel by mirrors, often seen as symbols of truth and duplicity as well as gateways to other worlds. Mitterhaus is exacting his revenge on the Burgermeister even though he cannot be seen in the real world.

The devious dwarf offers to escort a small group of villagers (the unfortunate Schilt family) out of the infectious village and across the border, but he abandons them. A rapid series of cuts and animal noises make it plain that wild animals have attacked them— Emil as a panther. The only border crossed was between life and death ."That will keep the others from trying to leave," observes the dwarf malevolently, "tonight the children!"

Red crosses on the villagers' doors echo the plague of the firstborn in the Bible, commemorated by Passover, in which God killed the firstborn of the Egyptians, but spared the children of Israel, who sacrificed a lamb and applied blood to the top and sides of their doorways. This is a reminder that the anti-Christian vampires have declared their own plague on the children of the village. The villagers are fighting a losing battle against two plagues—disease and vampires.

Dora Mueller (Lynne Frederick), daughter of Professor Mueller and the runaway Anna, whom Anton believes is safe in the city, makes her way through the forest back to Stetl where she encounters the remains of Emil's victims. The next scene finds her lying on the ground and seeing what appear to be two menacing eyes, but in a clever switch they are revealed to be buckles atop the thigh-high boots of one of the border guards she is hiding from. He and his compatriots don't check long before they turn around lest they contract the dreaded plague.

In the village, Mueller argues that "fear will drive out fear, death will drive out death," an apt summation as the circus proves to be the source of the village's fears. Their fear of the strange circus will lead them to eventually dispose of their adversaries—who will then cease killing. In this atmosphere of fear Dora arrives.

Meanwhile, Anton argues against prejudice against the Gypsies and promises to take Dora to the circus that night. It is felt, and not inaccurately, that the circus is the one thing that keeps the people of the village from brooding about death (ironically by either diverting them or killing them). Mueller is right when he asserts, "They play no games; they are death."

The innocent Dora is frightened by the caged animals, symbols as we've seen of unbridled lust and animal passions. In an homage to *The Corsican Brothers*, Helga (Lalla Ward, better known for playing Romana on *Dr. Who*, 1979-1981) thrusts her arm into the tiger's mouth while her compatriot Heinrich reacts in pain, then she removes her arm unscathed to show Dora that the animals are really harmless, a good set-up for the acrobats' eventual demise.

The Gypsy Woman ringleader utters an ominous double entendre when she says, "Circus is for the young," to Jon and Gustav Hauser (Frederick and Barnaby Shaw), indicating underneath the cliché that this circus was created to entice the young for its own sinister purpose. She allows them into the Mir-

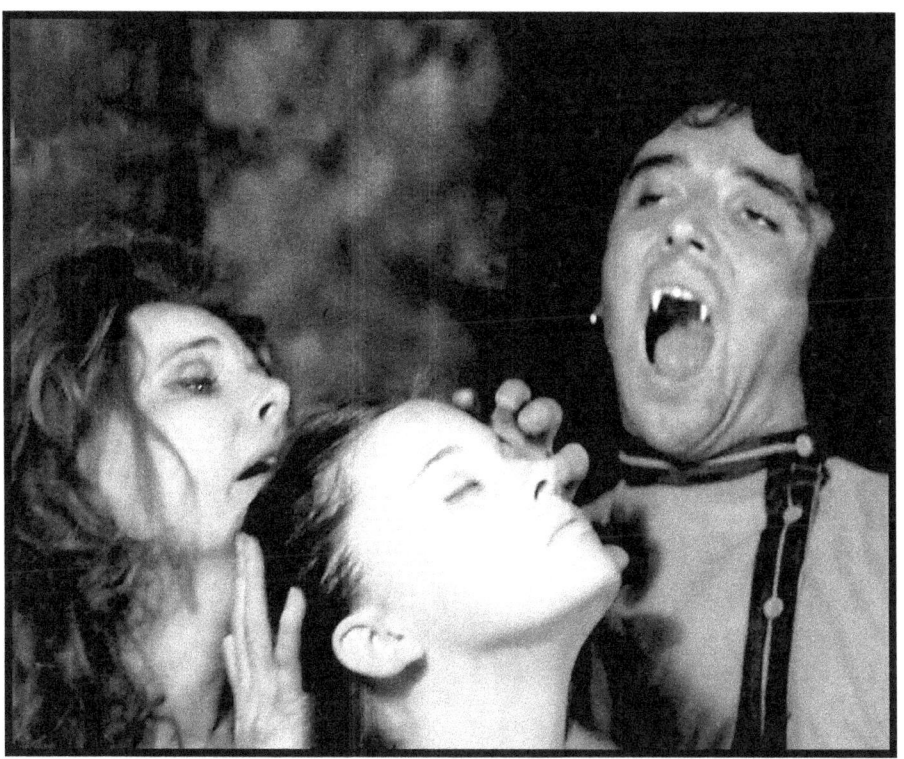

Anna (Adrienne Corri) and Emil (Anthony Corlan) have Dora (Lynne Frederick) in their clutches in *Vampire Circus*.

ror of Life tent for no money. There they see Helga and Heinrich in the mirror. Mitterhaus appears behind them, but is not reflected in the mirror. Rather he draws the children into the mirror where they are bitten, providing more blood for his eventual resurrection (the vampire as perverse parody of Christ, shedding the blood of others so that he might live eternally, rising from the dead to bring doom rather than salvation).

A group of villagers begin to persecute the members of the circus, beating up on the dwarf, who is rescued by the strongman. The Hausers are discovered dead with holes in their throats. The ever-fatuous Burgermeister advises destroying all the circus' wild animals, which some villagers resolve to do, beginning with a wholly innocent chimpanzee, then the transforming tiger. Emil escapes even after the Burgermeister has shot him. A flash cut reveals that the Gypsy Woman is an older version of Anna, who has aged considerably during the elapsed 15 years. Despite all the horrors in the village, Rosa remains anxious to be initiated into the pleasures of the flesh and places Emil's hands on her breasts, but he has other plans for her. He turns away and she follows him to the Count's crypt.

Dora is enticed by whispering voices to go to the mirror where Helga and Heinrich try to draw her inside, but she is protected by her cross and manages to

You can't keep a bad vampire down—Mitterhaus (Robert Tayman) is killed twice in *Vampire Circus*.

return to Anton on the other side of the mirror. She can't recall what happened, but remembers something about under the castle.

Finally Dr. Kersh reappears with two guardsmen. He has discovered that the plague is rabies carried by bats, that vampires really exist, and that the plague appears wherever the Circus of Nights appeared. The doctor begins to distribute medicine.

Anna and Emil now target the students at Mueller's school, causing Anton to rush upstairs to investigate. Anna, who is not a vampire, removes the cross from the neck of her abandoned daughter Dora, allowing the acrobats to chase her into the school's chapel. Anton, who is too late to save anyone upstairs, finds Dora on a perilous beam near the ceiling of the chapel. She knocks over the cross, impaling Helga and causing Heinrich to keel over in pain and expire as well. Anna screams, "my children," making them the possible progeny of Count Mitterhaus, to whom she planned to sacrifice her human daughter.

Anna and Emil flee, and Anton, Mueller and the doctor follow in hot pursuit, leaving Dora in the protection of Gerta (Elizabeth Seal). The strongman breaks into the chapel and Gerta tries to stop him by holding up a cross, but the strongman isn't one of the undead either, and takes Anna with him.

The frenzied climax leaves as many dead bodies in its wake as a Jacobean tragedy. One council member is seriously burned while burning down the Mirror of Life exhibit; the two dancers are discovered drained of blood; the strongman is killed; the dwarf pounces on Anton but gets his neck broken; Emil prepares to bite Dora, who slips away. Emil bites Anna instead, transforming her into her younger self; Emil causes a bat to knock a cross out of Anton's hand; several attackers in the Count's crypt are killed by the ferocious Emil until Mueller stabs him with the stake from Mitterhaus' body. He is bitten in the process and expires next to his ex-wife. Mitterhaus revives but Anton uses the cross on a crossbow to hold him at bay until he can place the crossbow mechanism around Mitterhaus' neck and decapitate him.

Dr. Kersh, Dora and Anton are the only survivors in the Count's crypt, and they wearily depart into the fog-shrouded air, but above them is the flying form of a bat—a reminder that evil will never fully be vanquished and danger is omnipresent.

Vampire Circus lacks complex characterizations, and its many characters have confused some viewers, but it is, nevertheless, a very lively film filled with thrills and indelible images. The sprawling narrative compacted into a relatively short running time makes the film a relief from some of Hammer's other vampire films of the same era where an overly simplistic revenge plot is duly stretched out to cover a similar, but seemingly much longer, running time.

***Vampire Circus* features a huge cast of characters, including Anna and Emil, who guard Count Mitterhaus.**

Though its making precedes the onslaught of the AIDS epidemic, it would be very easy to see the film as equating vampirism with AIDS. Vampirism, like AIDS, here is associated with sexuality; spreads like a plague and decimates families as well as causing fear in the uninformed.

The danger is right before the eyes of the audience, as it is for the villagers in the film. However, many villagers prefer not to believe in the evil, seeking escapism rather than having to deal with the suffering of others. Mankind has long been pacified by bread and circuses, but are we ultimately amusing ourselves to death? *Vampire Circus* may not have the answer, but while diverting, it does raise some interesting questions.

Captain Kronos is proficient with a samurai sword in *Captain Kronos: Vampire Hunter.*

Hammer hoped to start another horror franchise with *Captain Kronos—Vampire Hunter*, created by the most inventive talent on the famous *Avengers* series—Brian Clemens. Clemens also worked on *And Soon the Darkness* (1970), *Dr. Jekyll and Sister Hyde* and *The Golden Voyage of Sinbad*. Hammer was on its last legs, and subsequently only managed to pull off a few more features, none of which received major theatrical release in the U.S. The death knell sounded with the release of Don Sharp's lackluster remake of *The 39 Steps* in 1978. Soon after Kronos, the once most successful British studio was reduced to filming projects in Hong Kong such as *Legend of the 7 Golden Vampires* (1974) and *Shatter* (1975, U.S. title *Call Him Mr. Shatter*).

Still, *Captain Kronos* showed what could be done when talented people are given a creative hand. The idea behind the series was that Captain Kronos, late of the Imperial Guards, travels across the world with his faithful hunchbacked companion, Professor Grost, in search of various species of vampires to exterminate. While he was away at war, Kronos' mother and sister were vampirized. After having to kill the ones he loved, he declares war on all vampires.

Instead of your ordinary, everyday bloodsuckers, the films were to have featured interesting variations, asserting that there are as many species of vampires as there are of beasts of prey, and the methods, motives and means of destruction for these species vary extensively, meaning that our heroes cannot rely on lore but must learn each enemy's weakness.

The Paramount release didn't catch on with the public, and *Captain Kronos—Vampire Hunter* was the only film in the vampire swashbuckler series. Cheroot-smoking Horst Janson as Kronos might remind today's audiences of a Clint Eastwood wannabe, but his lack of charisma helped keep the character from catching on. Additionally, the character is presented as a withdrawn, taciturn man of action, rendering his companion (played by John Cater) as ultimately a far more sympathetic character.

One of the film's oddities was that the hero is adept with a samurai sword, though he can also fence with an epee or foil. Not many Western movies feature samurai swordplay—Terence Young's 1971 *Red Sun* being one of the exceptions—so this was quite an innovation for its time.

The film builds from the premise that vampires steal not only the life but also the youth of their victims. The vampires leave only a teardrop of blood behind, but their victims age almost immediately.

This film marked Clemens' directorial debut and shows a strong visual sense as well as an ability to build atmosphere and suspense. This is evident in the intriguing opening, where a vain blonde is combing her hair in a forest glen when she spies a black-robed figure in her mirror, upon which falls a drop of blood. The blonde's companion stares transfixed as a man approaches on horseback and discovers that the blonde is now an aged crone.

Composer Laurie Johnson provides a dynamic and rousing opening score emphasizing the hard-riding heroes who are on a quest—the martial overtones are much in evidence (both musically and narratively). Ian Wilson's cinematography is quite fine in the outdoor scenes, but unfortunately his lighting cannot disguise the barrenness of the castle set at MGM's Elstree Studios.

Fan favorite Caroline Munro plays Carla, a woman Kronos rescues from the stocks, whose part is little more than as a bedmate for Kronos and as an audience stand-in who asks Professor Grost the questions whose answers will forward the plot. She makes for a fetching bystander, but it would have been a far more interesting part if Clemens had given her the same dynamic characterization that he had given Diana Rigg's Mrs. Peel in *The Avengers*. However, women as mere props had been a long-standing Hammer tradition. Her lowly status is underscored in the plot; when the trio bed down for the night, Professor Grost informs her that they only have two beds—and the two men proceed to use them.

When Kronos goes to visit his old friend Dr. Marcus (John Carson), the audience is kept guessing as to whether Marcus is a friend or foe until Kronos smiles and calls him, "You old leech lover."

Kronos and Marcus, while discussing Professor Grost, provide my favorite line of the film: "What he doesn't know about vampirism wouldn't fill a flea's codpiece." For those unfamiliar with Renaissance accoutrements, a codpiece is a decorative bag placed in front of a man's breeches, which has the quality of emphasizing this portion of the anatomy. The Freudian among you will find *Captain Kronos—Vampire Hunter* rife with phallic symbols—swords, cigars, even Kronos' family crest, perhaps emphasizing his status as a force for life rather than death as the vampires prove to be.

As Grost lists the methods for dispatching a vampire—fire, decapitation, power of the cross for those who truly believe—Marcus maintains his scientific skepticism. "What could be more improbable than God? But I believe in Him," counters Grost, "if the miraculous can take a benign form, why not a malign form as well?

However, the film is not really interested in religious questions, only vampires. Clemens intersperses additional vampire attacks throughout the film. In one, a bracelet given to a small child is discovered on the arm of a withered old woman. In another, we see the shadow of a cross in a chapel. The arms of the cross start to bend and a cup of sacramental wine spills, representing the loss of another life.

To keep the audience guessing, the film sets up a pair of red herrings, Paul and Sara Durward (Shane Briant and Lois Daine). Their father, the world's greatest swordsmen, died seven years previously of the plague, and their mother Lady Durward (Wanda Ventham) blames Dr. Marcus for his death. The aristocratic Durwards are excellent candidates for vampires and a subtle tension underscores their scenes. Sara in particular is characterized as repulsed by her mother's aging, and Paul promises that they will never be like her. Once again, women are stereotyped as vain beings that worship at the altar of youth—and are ruthless in their pursuit of it.

In *Captain Kronos* Clemens manufactures a fanciful bit of folklore. Dead toads spring to life when vampires pass them. To discover who or where the vampires are, Grost buries several toads in boxes throughout the forest, marking the locations with red ribbons. Finding one alive would indicate that a vampire had passed that way.

Clemens does a Sergio Leone homage in a scene with Ian Hendry and two other toughs who torment Grost by addressing him, "Hey you, Crookback, how do you sleep?" Kronos comes in and makes short work of them with two too-fast-to-see swipes of his samurai sword leading to a delayed, I've-been-killed-and-collapse reaction.

Grost, agonizing over why his appearance should cause such a reaction, gives the film a small, but much needed, bit of heart. However, like most horror films, this one is more interested in trying to astound us than in exploring the inner conflicts of its characters.

After a visit to the Durwards,' Dr. Marcus hears his name whispered and sees a darkly cloaked figure. The frame freezes on running water and wind-blown leaves, indicating some aspect of reality has been altered. In fact, Marcus has been vampirized, and his realization of this and desire to be killed by his friends

Grost (John Carter) and Kronos (Horst Janson) have a difficult time destroying their vampirized friend Dr. Marcus (John Carson) in *Captain Kronos: Vampire Hunter*.

rather than live the life of the undead leads to one of the film's most outrageous sequences—Grost and Kronos unsuccessfully try one method after another to dispatch poor Marcus.

For these vampires, stakes through the heart aren't the answer. Marcus doesn't even bleed, because a vampire's heart only bleeds at the moment of death. They try hanging, but that fails. Finally they prepare to burn him when Kronos accidentally slams the doctor's cross into his chest (that's right, a cross-wearing vampire), which instantly turns Marcus' hair gray and he regains his soul before passing on, thus giving Kronos the necessary clue as to how to defeat the nosferatu.

Consequently, Kronos raids the local cemetery for a cross to melt down into a sword or cross blade, fighting off outraged locals who have heard from Marcus' servant that the captain was responsible for dispatching the good doctor. Here, Kronos fights Florentine style. However, the small number of attackers and a dull choreographed fight sequence rob this scene of its impact.

The vampire hunters decide to use Carla as bait, and send her off to the Durwards to spend the night. The vampires are capable of hypnotism, and soon have the curvaceous Carla under their spell. It is revealed that Lady Durward

has been wearing a mask to disguise her new vampire-acquired youthfulness, and that vampirism was used to bring Lord Durward back from the dead.

Kronos, having learned a trick from Perseus, has placed a mirror near the shaft of his blade and uses it to deflect Lady Durward's mesmerizing gaze back at her. This only leaves Kronos, the greatest swordsman who ever lived—or died—to be overcome. And he must be defeated using only the cross blade, as Kronos discovers when he tries a different sword. But good old Grost gets the cross blade back in time to dispatch both the lord and lady, who wither and turn into skeletons before the eyes of their astonished children.

As a swashbuckler, *Captain Kronos—Vampire Hunter* is somewhat tepid, but as an offbeat vampire thriller, it is fairly full blooded. Clemens demonstrates a command of style and finesse rather than flooding the screen with an orgy of bloodletting, as do so many modern horror films. Perhaps some of its appeal for me is simply its jaunty, "boys' own adventure" approach along the way. It delights in changing the rules and altering one's expectations. After so many repetitious, formula vampire movies, it is refreshing to come across one that tries to open a new vein.

Why the 1970s Bite

by Steven Vertlieb

As the 1960s drew to a close, Hammer was already in a major decline, its glory years sadly behind. There was still occasional brilliance, as witnessed by its final *Quatermass* outing, the breathtaking *Five Million Years to Earth* in 1967, but the fundamental essence of its creativity had ebbed. Its creative team largely dissipated, Hammer began to repeat itself in unflattering self-parody.

As a new decade was dawning, Hammer continued to release new excursions into the Dracula mythology, which usually proved little more than variations on an already exhausted theme. While the films themselves had dropped in quality, there were still moments of inspiration, which allowed the disparate parts to elevate the films on the whole. Hammer's Dracula films became much like sex: When they were good, they were terrific, and when they were bad, they were still pretty good.

Hammer Productions entered the new decade in the fall of 1970 with the release of its fifth Dracula film, *Taste the Blood of Dracula,* on September 16.

Alice Hargood (Linda Hayden) likes to be really close to Count Dracula (Christopher Lee) in *Taste the Blood of Dracula.*

Taste the Blood of Dracula failed to generate much excitement.

The film introduced the late Ralph Bates to the screen in the first of his horror film appearances at Hammer. It also starred Christopher Lee once again in the role he loved to hate, or, perhaps, hated to love. Increasingly dissatisfied with the growing mediocrity of his scripts, Lee voiced his displeasure at being typecast in a genre he had grown to loathe. Indeed, he threw open his arms to director Billy Wilder a year earlier and eagerly embraced the opportunity to portray Mycroft Holmes in Wilder's bittersweet romantic comedy, *The Private Life of Sherlock Holmes*. In the role that Lee later described as his personal favorite, the actor seemed to joyously poke fun at his own stiffness and pomposity while enacting Mycroft as a humorless civil servant.

One must eat, however, and so Lee reluctantly donned the regal cape of Transylvania's favorite son once more, inviting audiences to taste the now somewhat anemic blood of his romantic alter ego, Count Dracula.

Taste the Blood of Dracula was a pallid offering indeed. Audiences delighted in Lee's overbearing presence as Dracula, but his moments onscreen were simply that, mere moments. The rest of the picture seemed lacking in atmosphere or interest; indeed, everyone in the cast appeared to walk through a strictly by-the-numbers script. The sets, costumes and general atmosphere of the film were mostly first-class, as always, but Bram Stoker's demonic creation seemed mostly comatose at best. Peter Cushing, who elevated the status of any film with his presence, was sorely missed. *Taste the Blood of Dracula* simply failed to ignite sparks. Even in later years, when Hammer's Dracula series had degenerated still further, the presence of both Cushing and Lee assured audiences a degree of charm and romanticism. The absence of one or the other made the picture's shortcomings, like the Count's reflection (and, oft times, Lee's performances), all the more transparent. Dracula had risen again, but this was a grave endeavor for the Count, who played second fiddle to his misbegotten disciples. The teenaged daughter of one of his sworn enemies occupied more screen time than Lee, alluring and a lure for the downfall of her father and her friends. James Bernard, however, contributed one of his most exquisite scores to the picture, providing the few genuine moments of afterglow to an otherwise mediocre endeavor.

If its earlier effort featured little of the vampiric Count, Hammer's next foray into vampirism would obliterate him entirely.

The Vampire Lovers, released later that fall, was yet another retelling of Sheridan Le Fanu's *Carmilla*. Filmed originally in 1931 by Carl Dreyer in France as *Vampyr*, in 1960 by Roger Vadim as *Et Mourir De Plaisir* (*Blood and Roses*), and once more as *Terror in the Crypt* in 1963, Fanu's 1871 story has had nearly as many incarnations as his Carmilla has identities. *The Vampire Lovers*, it should be noted, did not imply affection for the undead on behalf of filmgoers; rather, it pointed to the previously understated sexual preferences of these naughty little suckers... in this case, lesbianism.

Ingrid Pitt played the cultured daughter of a countess, given shelter by General von Spielsdorf (Peter Cushing) and his family. Marcilla (Pitt) seduces and murders the general's niece and disappears into the night. Spielsdorf vows revenge, tracking Marcilla (now Carmilla) to her latest haunt, a sumptuous estate where she encounters a young girl with a sumptuous body. (Carmilla always liked quality.) Emma Morton (Madeline Smith) is lovely, innocent and virginal,

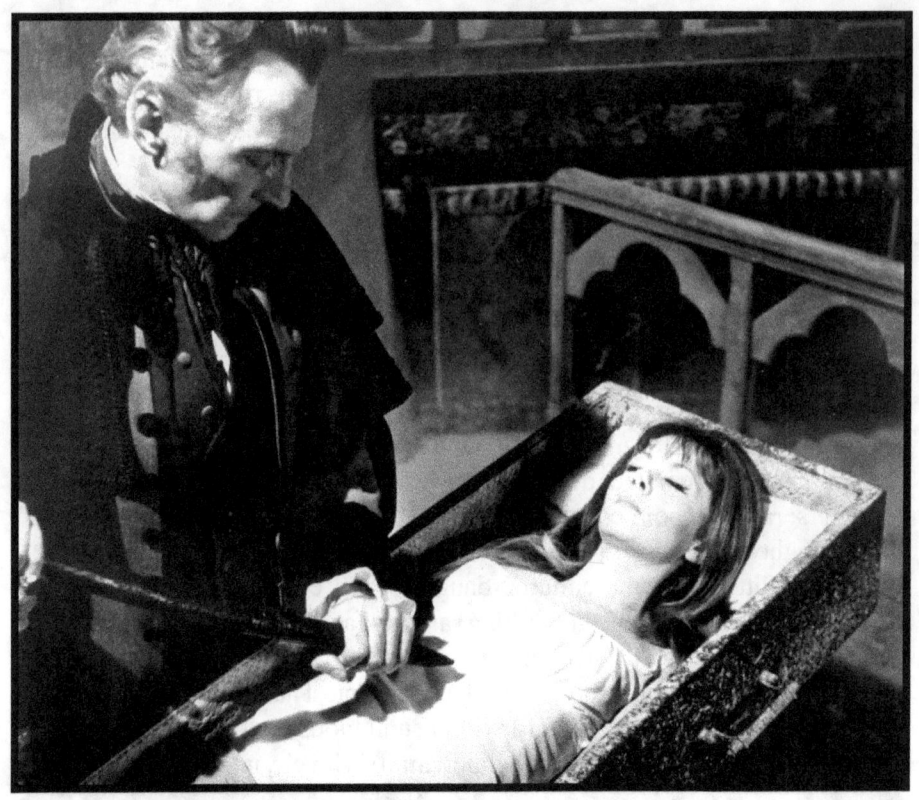

Peter Cushing and Ingrid Pitt in *Vampire Lovers*

succumbing to the tutelage of her calculating vampire friend who delights in biting her, not on the throat, but on the tips of her nipples. (Whenever Hammer could tap into an adolescent sex fantasy, it would.)

Carmilla, it seems, is actually a survivor of the infamous vampiric family Karnstein, and is bent on sharing her horrific legacy with partners both willing and unwilling. The General ultimately tracks down the bloody ingénue, rendering her harmless by means of decapitation. Hammer had found a way to give the General "head."

The Vampire Lovers was, in the final analysis, a success. Sincerely acted and rich with generous helpings of stylish eroticism, the film managed to overcome the absence of a definitive male vampiric influence, as well as cheesy color and a release in America by the even cheesier AIP. Peter Cushing managed to lend solid, if brief, support while a shadowy figure on horseback may or may not have been Dracula himself.

The first year of the decade will be remembered as a veritable blood feast at Hammer. Before the end of 1970 the studio released its second Dracula film of the year, and its third vampire feature. It's been said that not even plastic surgery could have saved *Scars of Dracula* from its fate, but despite its disas-

Scars of Dracula, **starring Christopher Lee, is a more interesting film that** *Taste the Blood of Dracula.*

trous reputation (and some scathing observations by its star), the film is actually more interesting than the earlier *Taste the Blood of Dracula.*

Directed by Roy Ward Baker (*Five Million Years to Earth*), and with a lovely score by James Bernard, *Scars of Dracula* returned the unholy Count to his castle in the Transylvanian mountains and provided the series with one of its most unforgettable images: the sight of Count Dracula climbing the outer wall of his castle. The stunning imagery, inspired by Bram Stoker's novel, was exciting to behold and an unnerving reminder of the vampire's rodent-like persona. This was, after all, not an aristocratic royal, but a vile, detestable creature of the night.

If the remainder of the screenplay was routine, the film distinguished itself in these inspired moments, including a wholly surprising finale in which the vampire prince is destroyed by a brilliant bolt of lightning. *Scars of Dracula* was, despite its unwarranted reputation of mediocrity, a welcome return to the quality of the earlier films of the series.

A worthwhile candidate for derision was the studio's next excursion to the crypt, *Lust for a Vampire*. The film was an unofficial remake of *The Vampire Lovers*, which had been released the prior year. *Lust* provided ample evidence that Hammer had simply run out of ideas.

LUST FOR A VAMPIRE

Evil, sinister, brooding, the ruins of Karnstein castle stand over the village of Styria, whose people whisper about macabre rites taking place there. Legend has it that every forty years the Karnsteins rise from their graves. They are the undead . . . the vampires.

A young Englishman comes to teach at a girls' school in the castle grounds. He falls in love with one of the pupils. Then several other girls are found dead — with fang wounds in their throats. The terrified villagers fire the castle, and there the ultimate horror is revealed . . .

Pressbook lobby card for *Lust for a Vampire*

The production was plagued by difficulties from the outset. Peter Cushing had been scheduled to star, but was forced to decline the assignment due to the illness of his beloved wife, Helen. Cushing was replaced by Ralph Bates, who took the role as a favor to the distraught actor. Director Jimmy Sangster became a last-minute replacement for Terence Fisher, who had broken his leg while drunk. (He must have read the script.)

Once again the terrible Karnstein family was wreaking havoc across the countryside in the person of their nubile daughter Carmilla (talk about juvenile delinquency!), cleverly changing her name this time to Mircalla. Perhaps Clark Kent's glasses might have made for a more effective disguise. The "lust" in the title told it all. Where *The Vampire Lovers* was erotic and suggestive, *Lust for a Vampire* was nearly pornographic. Star Yutte Stensgaard was selected for her twin abilities rather than for her sensibilities, and very attractive they were, too.

Sadly, however, she couldn't act. Nor could Mike Raven as Count Karnstein. Consequently, the film was an embarrassment for everyone concerned. For all of its notoriety and supposed titillation, the film is an incomparable bore.

Hammer fared better with its next film. *Countess Dracula*, released in October 1972 in the U.S., was actually more a historical drama than a horror film. Based on the life and crimes of true-life villainess Elizabeth Bathory, the picture recounts the bloody eccentricities of the infa-

Ingrid Pitt as *Countess Dracula* and her lover Dobi (Nigel Green).

mous "Blood Countess," who bathed in the blood of virgin women, and who was reputed to have murdered upwards of 650 people. Ingrid Pitt played the infamous Countess with customary relish as she discovered herself in a pickle over past and present indiscretions. While Bathory rivaled her male counterpart, Vlad the Impaler, for the sheer savagery of her brutality, this fictional Countess was somewhat more demure. Here, she embarks on her criminal career as an aged matriarch who discovers, quite by accident, that the blood of virgins, mixed with bath water and a little ginger ale on the side, is the magical elixir of youth.

Needless to say, the good Countess was never dirty again.

Distinguished British actor Nigel Green co-starred with Pitt as the loyal consort, Captain Dobi, in what, distressingly, proved to be his final performance. Critical reviews of the film were better than usual, but the public was indifferent to the Countess' charms. The picture premiered in England on the lower half of a double bill headlining *Hell's Belles*. Nigel Green took his own life on May 15, 1972, perhaps more from embarrassment than anything else.

Twins of Evil strolled down the Hammer aisle next in yet another variation of the already exhausted Carmilla theme. In this outing Peter Cushing appeared as a fanatical Puritan cult leader committed to eradicating the infestation of vampirism troubling his village. Count Karnstein has been borrowing from the village "library," a veritable treasure trove of nubile young virgins with whom he has his way. However, when the already unpleasant Count is drafted into service by the reincarnation of his undead, incestuous ancestor Mircalla, the Count's ugly demeanor becomes all the meaner. (If nothing else, *Twins of Evil* is a potent parable against extended family visits.)

Madeleine and Mary Collinson, real life twin sisters, appeared in both the film and a celebrated *Playboy* magazine pictorial designed to display their twin charms. The plot, in which one sister is infected with the vampire plague while her innocent sibling is unjustly mistaken for her, was a harbinger of the spate of "evil twin" television films in the 1980s. While Peter Cushing lent credibility to the well-traveled story, the film is remembered, somewhat unfairly, for its popular *Playboy* spread. Released in June 1972 in America, the film has much to recommend it apart from its sensationalistic umbilical connection to Hugh Hefner.

As Hammer continued its uphill struggle to retain control of the declining horror market, a quiet revolution was taking place across America, where a modest made-for-television movie, *The Night Stalker* (1972) and *In Search of Dracula*, a 1972 book on the historical Dracula were about to change the media face of vampirism forever. Dracula's friends and family members continued to proliferate throughout Europe and the British Isles. Hammer Films returned to the genre in 1972 with the release of *Vampire Circus*. Once again vampires set up shop in a middle European village, terrorizing women and children first, proving, of course, that chivalry is not dead... even if the women and children are. When the evil Count Mitterhaus (what is it with counts?) is finally cornered and impaled, he vows to return, a pale reflection of himself, and gain back his power by devouring the nourishing blood of others. Time passes while the accursed villagers suffer the slings and arrows of outrageous scripting. The village is soon consumed by some dread disease, and is ordered quarantined.

Astonishingly, a large and mysterious circus troupe manages to elude the city's protectors, arriving in town prepared,

Christopher Lee and Peter Cushing were reunited in *Dracula A.D. 1972*.

along with Mickey, Judy and a barn, to put on a show. It isn't long before a series of mishaps begin to befall the beleaguered townspeople. Virgins, of course, are the meal of choice, or the first course. Other family members soon follow. The dreaded circus performers change into panthers and assorted fanged beasts at will, recalling the plot (but not the style, grace, or subtlety) of Val Lewton's *Cat People*.

When the Count (Mitterhaus, not Dracula) finally returns to life, the future prosperity of the village of Schtettel is thrown seriously into doubt until a heroic young man manages to trap the Count's head in the bowstring of a crossbow, firing the fatal arrow that decapitates the unwelcome intruder.

They don't make movies like *Vampire Circus* anymore. We should be eternally grateful for small favors.

Dracula jointed the mod squad in late 1972, mixing sex, drugs and rockin' vampires. One of the silliest, if not the worst of Hammer's Dracula excursions, *Dracula A.D. 1972* was an embarrassing amalgam of traditional and juvenile narrative that pitted the once noble aristocrat against modern day teeny-boppers. The boppers win and Dracula is (or should be) covered in shame.

On the plus side was the joyous reuniting of Peter Cushing and Christopher Lee. As usual with their collaborations, it is the erstwhile Cushing who carries the proceedings. The highlight of the film remains the opening sequence, in

***Dracula A.D. 1972* was a miscalculated attempt to draw blood from a stoned generation.**

which the two old enemies battle atop a careening coach. While both actors had obviously aged in the years following their initial confrontation in 1958, their obvious joy in playing opposite one another once more was infectious. The film takes place 100 years after the last roughhouse between Dracula and Van Helsing (completely disregarding the Stoker timeline) in present-day London. There, Lorrimer Van Helsing seeks to protect his lovely granddaughter, Jessica (Stephanie Beacham), from the seduction of innocence. Dracula's descendent, Johnny Alucard (Christopher Neame), celebrates a black mass inside an abandoned church along with a group of terminally bored teenagers, including Jessica and the luscious Caroline Munro, as Laura.

Growing apprehensive at the sobriety of the ceremony, the callow congregation escapes a vaguely perceived impending danger, leaving behind the foolish Laura, who comes to regret her decision (like much of the film's paying audience). Dracula returns to life and wisely attacks the voluptuous Laura, unfortunately eliminating Ms. Munro from the remainder of the film.

Like his illustrious ancestor, Lorrimer Van Helsing specializes in researching and investigating occult practices and begins to suspect that his grandfather's evil nemesis has returned to exact a personal revenge. Not surprisingly, Dracula's method of revenge involves transfusing Jessica's blood with his own, taking her as his vampire bride. Or something. When Jessica's boyfriend becomes a vampire and summons her to the desecrated churchyard at the Count's command, Van Helsing lies in wait, blinding Dracula with holy water and sending the disoriented vampire plunging into an open grave lined with carefully placed stakes.

Other than a few memorable sequences reuniting Cushing and Lee, such as the opening moments between the Count and the original Van Helsing, *Dracula A.D. 1972* is a miscalculated attempt to draw blood from a stoned generation. Poorly directed by Alan Gibson, ineptly lit and photographed by Dick Bush, and with abysmal music by Michael Vickers, *A.D. 1972* is easily the weakest, most ineffectual entry in the series.

And that's saying something.

By comparison, Hammer Films' *Kronos*, released in America in June 1974 as *Captain Kronos: Vampire Hunter*, was a veritable breath of fresh air. Infused with boyish enthusiasm, *Kronos* was a swashbuckling adventure replete with swordplay, sorcery, sex and vampirism—not necessarily in that order. Hampered by an undistinguished performance by awkward newcomer Horst Janson, *Kronos* was, nevertheless, an innocent fantasy that attempted to reinvent the vampire legend with new rules and regulatory guidelines. The sparkling beauty of Caroline Munro was also very much in evidence, a far more tasty morsel to envision than the earlier depravity of Udo Keir. Directed by Brian Clemens (of television's *The Avengers*), and featuring the music of Laurie Johnson (*First Men in the Moon*), the film may have been a trifle too experimental for its own good. Ultimately, its box office failure was yet another nail in Hammer's coffin.

The Satanic Rites of Dracula **was the last reteaming of Lee and Cushing.**

Another failed experiment, Hammer's *The Satanic Rites of Dracula*, was released in England in January 1974. The film wouldn't see an American release until 1978, in an attempt to cash in on the success of Frank Langella's Broadway *Dracula*. *Satanic Rites* gained notoriety later as the film that transformed Dracula into Howard Hughes, as well as the long-overdue last appearance of Christopher Lee as the vampire prince.

In this telling, Count Dracula has at last tired of death on Earth and has decided to end the world, not only for himself, but, generously, for everyone else inhabiting the planet as well. He'll accomplish this task—no mean feat even for the Vampire King—by developing a deadly new strain of plague to eradicate the whole of humanity, thereby eliminating once and for all the annoying source of his needed blood supply. Disguised as business mogul D. D. Denham, Dracula has an unscrupulous scientist create a new strain of bubonic plague. As tycoon, Dracula has fully adapted to the lifestyles of the rich and infamous.

The film also generated some remarkably erotic and kinky imagery, including half-naked women shackled and chained in a hidden cellar. However, the most sexually arousing sequence involved a blatantly satanic ritual in which a willingly submissive young woman lies writhing naked upon an altar as drops of blood are spilt over her breasts, stomach and exposed vulva. (Poor Peter Cushing was obviously more interested, at this point, in retirement money than anything else.) Finally she is stabbed in the heart with a large, ritualistic dagger brandished by the cult leader, bringing her exquisite torment to a climax with a shuddering scream.

When Dracula's henchmen abduct Jessica, Van Helsing follows to prevent the girl from becoming the monster's bride. (It's interesting that, after all the heartache they have caused him, Dracula would want to marry into the Van Helsing family.) After the expected conflagration, Van Helsing entangles the vampire in the vines of a hawthorn bush, driving a stake through the monster's heart.

Satanic Rites of Dracula was Christopher Lee's final go-round as Count Dracula. Lee was particularly lucky in his vow to never don the vampire's cape again—for no one ever asked him. It was also, sadly, the final on-camera teaming of Cushing and Lee in a Hammer production. For both men, it was the end of an era.

Although a failure, Hammer obviously wanted to continue with a modern series of Van Helsing adventures. Cushing's Lorrimer Van Helsing was fast becoming the Sherlock Holmes of the monster set, aided by his equally heroic granddaughter Jessica and her Scotland Yard crony. Joanna Lumley replaces Stephanie Beacham in this film, and she's absolutely fabulous. The whole enterprise had a very Sax Rohmer feel to it, and, if not for the presence of Dracula, might have made a worthwhile thriller!

Easily the most bizarre addition to the Dracula legend by Hammer was *The Legend of the Seven Golden Vampires*, also known as *The Seven Brothers Meet Dracula*, and, *The Seven Brothers and Their One Sister Meet Dracula*. (I kid you not!)

It must have seemed an inspiration during the Kung Fu craze of the 1970s to combine the two genres, along with the great film studios of both England and Japan. Shaw Bros. eagerly accepted the offer to join with Hammer in producing the first martial arts Dracula film. Unfortunately for the two companies, it looked as though Matt Dillon was more adept at mastering martial arts than the seven brothers, who should have stayed home to sing, dance, and marry their seven brides.

Dracula was played by John Forbes-Robertson, who was, at best, an ineffectual Count. Of course, the little-known truth unearthed here was that Dracula, who had evidently tired of being a reclusive billionaire, had transformed himself into Kah, an Asian practitioner of occult rites. (Right.) Surely now the seven brothers would endure The Wrath of Kah.

Peter Cushing was enticed into portraying Van Helsing one last time, and if there is any joy to be found in this numbingly imbecilic enterprise, it is the enthusiasm this great actor brings to the part, combined with the wonderful music of Hammer's least appreciated genius, James Bernard.

Let Me In: The Return of Hammer and the Spirit of Val Lewton

by Gary J. Svehla

Wasn't it spine tingling to watch the beginning of *Let Me In* and see that gigantic Hammer logo with many of the classic images from its heyday drawn inside the letters? And then we observed the beginning title credit sequence, "A Hammer Films Production," and heaved a satisfied sigh that here is something us old farts remember.

The new reborn-from-the-ashes Hammer has nothing to do with the old company, except its sense of commitment to quality horror movie cinema. Matt Reeves' remake of the Swedish horror oddity *Let the Right One In* from a few years ago demonstrates that in rare instances the remake can equal or perhaps even surpass the original. At least for me the Hammer remake resonates more. I respected the original but was held at an emotional distance; here, I feel the angst and growing pains of the two young characters that hook me emotionally.

And when I watch *Let Me In,* I see the integrity of the better Hammer productions alongside the spirit of Val Lewton. I know, I know, Val Lewton is revered for his understatement and subtlety. Why show the gruesomeness of horror when shadows, loud sounds and psychological inner dread say it best.

I maintain the Lewton spirit is just as much about a malevolent tone, an ambiguity of morality where innocent victims do not actually understand the rightness or wrongness of the situation in which they find themselves. We have

Irena, from *Cat People*, who keeps herself chaste and abstinent as to not arouse the monster inside, so she can both protect and love her newlywed husband. Yet her inability to consummate her relationship only drives her husband into the arms of another woman. In *The Seventh Victim* we have heroine Jacqueline Gibson try to protect her younger sister Mary (Kim Hunter) from the urban horrors of Satanism. Mary, who comes from a sequestered private school, is a lamb in the lion's den

Jacqueline takes the only way out in Val Lewton's *The Seventh Victim.*

(or panther's cage?), no match for the obscenities to be found in the shadowy streets of Greenwich Village. So at the end of the story, the cult closing in, Jacqueline takes the only way out she can, suicide by hanging, which ends this bleak emotional roller coaster ride. In *Curse of the Cat People*, young child Amy Reed, daughter of Irena, must cope with the horrors of growing up. Her fantasy world protects her from the harsh realities of life, something her father Ollie fears, believing insanity and fantasy killed his former wife. Amy gravitates to the eccentric actress Julia Farren, her neighbor, whose daughter Barbara (the excellent Elizabeth Russell) is as alienated from her own mother (who seems lost in the clouds of dementia) as Amy is from her father. The heartbreak of waking up and discovering that none of her school chums are attending her birthday party is pretty devastating. Of course the fact that the invitations were never properly mailed explains the reality of the situation, but not its emotional reverberations as Amy's "friends" continue to taunt and ridicule the child. To me these themes constitute the Lewton aesthetic as much as subtlety of vision.

Yes, the Lewton films, existing 70 years ago, were tame and subtle and generally did not show monsters, fiends or the undead. *Let Me In* does that in spades. But the intense aura of dread and psychological horror that appeared in the Lewton oeuvre 70 years ago is channeled loud and clear in the Hammer remake. Kudos to young director Matt Reeves, the same director who made *Cloverfield* a few years back employing a shaky hand-held video camera to record the action. Here, doing a 180-degree turn, Reeves is the master of old school cinema, using a stationary camera and close-ups held long to compose his world of snowy vampirism in New Mexico.

Just like with *The Seventh Victim*, we experience a world of ambivalent morality where it is difficult to tell right from wrong. Author John Gardner reworked, in 1972, the classic Anglo-Saxon epic poem BEOWULF, rewriting the story from the monster Grendel's point of view, reminding us that Grendel, a child, ate human beings as food, much the same as humans lived off the "flesh" of fish. In *Let Me In* 12-year-old Abby (yes, she is much older but is trapped inside the body of a child victim) sadly confesses to her new friend Owen that she needs fresh blood to live. Yes, her feral transformations into an ultra-strong and fast demonic being are horrifying. When she attacks her victims, she is ferocious, ending up totally covered in the blood of her victims. Wise-in-years but young-in-appearance Abby seems more the victim of involuntary mortality. The appearance of the child walking barefoot in the snow only heightens her vulnerability. Abby kills to survive and, unfortunately, she feeds on humans. But just as Grendel elicited different points of view (monster or sad victim?), so does Abby.

Two telling sequences summarize what is outstanding about this coming-of-age vampire movie. Even though Irena and Ollie were adults in *Cat People*, I see the relationship between the two 12 year olds as very similar in *Let Me In*. We have Abby terrified to be aroused in front of the boy she befriends, just as Irena denied sex to her husband in *Cat People* because she feared harming him. The first sequence is when Owen and Abby go down to their cellar hiding place and he slices his thumb with a knife in front of Abby, undergoing the childhood ritual of becoming blood brothers/sisters with a close friend. When Abby sees the blood oozing from his thumb, flowing onto the floor, she looses control and reverts to her demonic self. However, even when aroused, she will not harm Owen. Running full throttle out of the cellar, she climbs a tree and sees an apartment resident and her cat walk past underneath. With silent determination she pounces below and devours both human and cat, satisfying her newly aroused blood lust. However, the telling moment is her ability to distinguish between her chosen victims, demonstrating her loyalty to Owen. She is indeed a blood-sucking monster, but she is also a human being with a heart. She is both predator and victim.

The second pivotal sequence involves the second time that Abby appears at Owen's apartment, where she again reminds him that he must ask her in so she can enter, according to vampire lore. For a moment he is horrified by what Abby has done and does not invite her in, but she enters the room anyway. Within seconds her body begins to quiver and blood begins to erupt from her scalp and cover her face. In shock, Owen grabs and hugs his friend and loudly announces that he invites her in. Within seconds Abby returns to normal and says that she knew Owen wouldn't allow her to be harmed. She trusted in his good heart. In an earlier similar test of friendship, Owen offers Abby candy that she first refuses. However, for friendship's sake she eats some, vomiting

Abby (Chloë Grace Moretz) bonds with outcast Owen (Kodi Smit-McPhee) in *Let Me In*.

as soon as the two of them go outside the store. Abby knew eating the candy would make her deadly sick, but for the sake of her friend she consumes some.

Just like little Amy from *Curse of the Cat People*, Owen is an outcast with his peers at school, but while the nasty actions of Amy's school mates was minor in the Lewton film, here in *Let Me In* Owen is tortured and tormented and almost killed by his bullies. He is bullied in the bathroom, given an almost castrating "wedgie," held underwater in the school pool by a tormentor, and carried almost naked by a gang of his peers and thrown into the pool. He is called a girl (he does have almost feminine features) and his tormentors want to see his penis as proof that he is indeed a male. And remember, Owen is only 12 years old. In the climactic sequence, Abby returns to slaughter a swimming pool full of his tormentors while Owen is held underwater, where he glances sideways to see the decapitated head of one of the bullies float past. In the Lewton style, the carnage and bloodshed occurs above the water with screams and splashing bodies dragged to and fro as seen from below, but other than the floating head, the carnage is more suggested than shown.

When was the last time you saw a modern horror movie that truly got under your skin and made you think and feel about the characters who occupied that world? Owen and Abby are similar outcasts who fight back in order to survive. Abby tells Owen you must fight back and hit them hard, and when Kenny, the chief tormentor, threatens Owen one time too many, Owen uses a metal pole to whack Kenny hard in the side of the head, taking part of his ear off. He too must

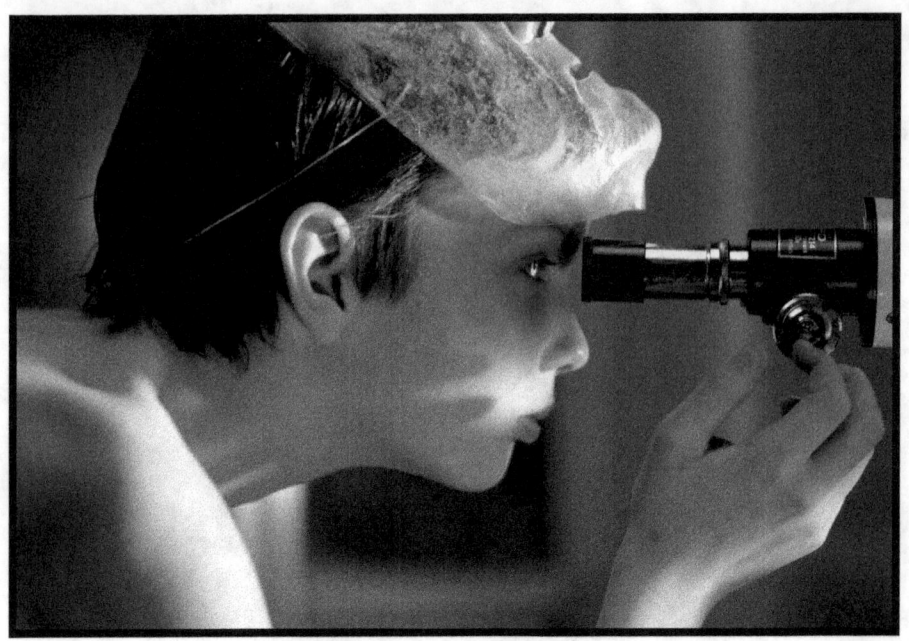

Owen spies on neighbors making love in *Let Me In*.

resort to violence in order to survive. But the evil that Kenny and the bullies evoke seems far more insidious than the survival killings of Abby. Ambivalent morality, deep questions about truly right and wrong acts seem watered down to simple blacks and whites in most horror movies (vampires are evil and vampire slayers are good, with no middle ground in between). *Let Me In* features a quietly intense musical score, almost classical in sections, composed by Michael Giacchino, that truly benefits the movie's atmosphere. Director Reeves allows long stretches of close-ups on faces and eyes. The camera studies the intensity of the eyes of Abby's adult companion, who pretends to be her father, and who stalks victims and drains their blood into plastic jars. During such killings he wears a trash bag over his head and the camera focuses on his eyes as he lies in wait. The movie features long stretches of conversation, accented by stark visual backgrounds of malaise and despondency. Even Owen's sexual awakening is illustrated as he sneaks a look, through a telescope, at other couples who live in his run-down apartment complex, one such couple preparing to make love, the woman's one breast fully exposed. When the puberty-bound Owen befriends Abby, he probably has more than friendship on his mind. And it is this intense childhood relationship that propels the Hammer remake above and beyond the Swedish original.

At the end of the movie, Owen has left home and is aboard a train, a trunk with Abby hiding inside by his feet. The two communicate by Morse code, Owen tapping on the trunk and Abby responding. Whether Owen is bound to

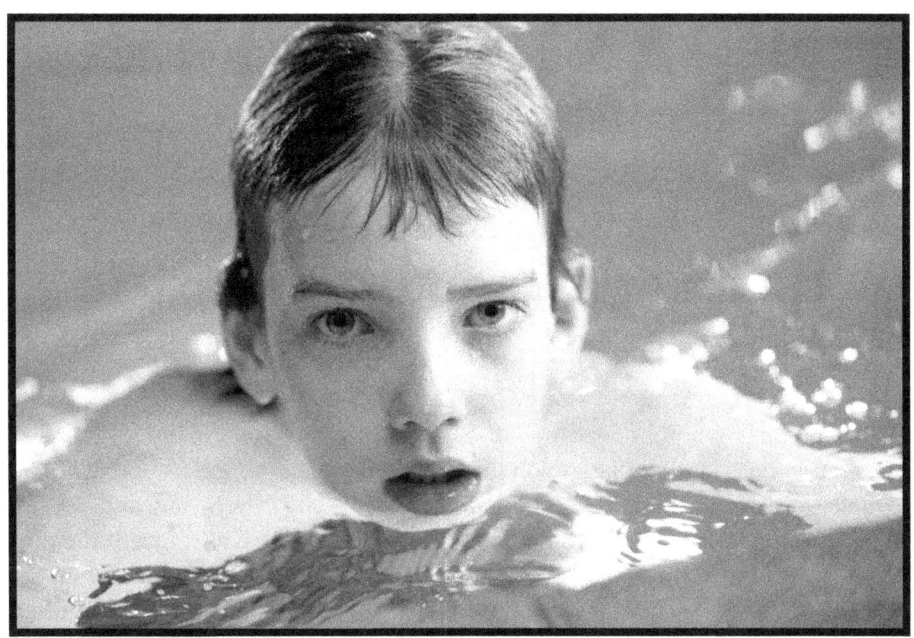

Matt Reeves pays homage to Val Lewton whether he know it or not—Above: Owen in a pool scene in *Let Me In*, and Alice takes a frightening swim in *Cat People*.

grow up and become the new "father" who acquires blood for Abby is never made clear. Right now we see two eccentric, lonely and alienated people bonding together to help one another survive. And at this point the morality meter is pointing toward the positive and not the negative, as the movie ends at the perfect moment.

While this reincarnation of Hammer horror forges new ground, it remembers its proud legacy. What an outstanding movie to inaugurate the rebirth of Hammer! And Matt Reeves pays homage, whether knowingly or not, to the best RKO Val Lewton productions of the 1940s. Stephen King calls *Let Me In* the best horror movie of the past 20 years, and compared to all the others, he very well might be right. After too many years of Hollywood-produced horror movie product, catering to date-night adolescents who only want a non-thinking roller coaster ride with plenty of horrific special effects, it is refreshing to experience an artistic horror movie geared to adults that wants us to think and feel. Isn't it about time!

FRANKENSTEIN

Evolving Worlds of Hammer's Baron Frankenstein

by Gary J. Svehla

After making their mark upon the world of science-fiction cinema with the Quatermass series *(The Creeping Unknown* and *Enemy from Space)* and *X—The Unknown*, Hammer Film Productions decided to now try to reinvent the cinematic world of Gothic horrors made so popular by Universal Studios during the 1930s—this time by adding deep saturated doses of color and English gentility.

When *The Curse of Frankenstein* was released upon American shores in 1957, Hammer had hit their financial and creative stride with a franchise series that would stretch well into the 1970s. *The Curse of Frankenstein* began the collaboration between Hammer superstars Peter Cushing and Christopher Lee, teaming the acting team with director Terence Fisher and screenwriter Jimmy Sangster for the first time.

Since the Hammer *Frankenstein* series has been analyzed to death in print, my focus here is *not* upon the merits or meaning of the series, it is *not* to contrast Freddie Francis' directorial style to Terence Fisher's. It is *not* to compare the relative creative opulence of the studio (utilizing minimal money for maximum results), its sets or its budgets during the Bray Studio period to its more expensive but more generic look in their later releases. It is not even to compare the Hammer series to the Universal series.

No, the focus of this chapter is to document the evolution of what I consider to be the quintessential Hammer character—Baron Victor Frankenstein—Peter Cushing's supreme cinematic triumph and obviously the characterization of his career, as portrayed in six films produced by the studio between 1956 and 1974. By focusing on Peter Cushing's performances in each of the series' entries, we see, not necessarily the betterment of the series over the years, but the metamorphosis of Peter Cushing's Baron Frankenstein into a classic movie role that stands the test of time. It is a persona so much a part of his humanity that Cushing often transcended the limitations of the scripts and budgets to produce a tour de force performance in each of the Hammer entries. Artistically, Peter Cushing's performance as the Baron is one of the principal reasons why the reputation of Hammer has transcended the "B" horror market. Let us examine why.

The Curse of Frankenstein

"I always had a brilliant intellect!"
1957, Screenplay by Jimmy Sangster, Directed by Terence Fisher

Jimmy Sangster's script immediately establishes the emphasis in the Hammer series upon the character of Monster-creator Baron Victor Frankenstein, instead of focusing upon the Monster, as Universal did 25 years earlier. However, the script of *The Curse of Frankenstein* spends too much time recasting the dominant elements from the Universal series (the obsessiveness of the doctor,

Frankenstein (Peter Cushing), guarded by the warder (Michael Mulchester), faces the gallows at the finale of *The Curse of Frankenstein*.

the conflict between Monster-creator and assistant, the blind hermit in the woods sequence, the damaged brain, the climax occurring on the eve of the Baron's weeding, the interference cause by the doctor's fiancé, etc.) that it seems afraid to break out of this set pattern (although Universal's copyright on the Karloff makeup caused Hammer makeup man Phil Leakey to concoct a new monstrous look for Christopher Lee's Creature). Indeed, as written, the script casts the role of Baron Frankenstein as an almost one-dimensional, obsessed scientist who dares to defy society's rules and the laws of nature. But Peter Cushing struggles to make the role so much more.

The film opens with a priest coming to visit the Baron in prison before his execution The script cleverly tells its story in flashbacks. Addressing the priest, Baron Frankenstein states he asked for him because, "I could think of nobody else...people trust you. Just listen. Tell me you'll stay!" The Baron's aristocracy begins to take over as his tone changes from gentle pleading to one of demands, even firmly planting his hand upon the priest's shoulder and soon both hands are clutching his neck. Threatening to leave the presence of this lunatic, the priest receives an apology from the Baron, "I won't forget myself again, I always had a brilliant intellect..." and tells of his childhood "where it all began."

As rewritten in the Hammer canon, Baron Victor Frankenstein lost his father and gained his title at the age of five. Ten years later, his mother dies and Victor inherits the family fortune. An aunt who is dependent upon the mother's monthly check to support herself and her daughter, Elizabeth, is concerned that the young Baron will discontinue their financial support. It is also understood that the young Elizabeth, the Baron's cousin, will someday wed the Baron. The Baron gladly agrees to continue the financial support. But what he needs now is a tutor to feed his ever-inquisitive mind. Thus enters Paul Krempe (Robert Urquhart), a man who is surprised that the teenaged Baron is conducting his own affairs with such sophistication. In voiceover, the Baron confides that Paul was "an admirable tutor" but that he learned all Paul had to teach in only two years. Cocky, self-assured, arrogant are phrases that categorize our earliest impressions of the Baron.

Paul and his student work intensely in the Frankenstein family laboratory bringing life to a dead dog. Here the Baron's obsessive one-dimensionality is made clear by Cushing's intense performance. While working, Cushing is always serious, he feverishly looks down at gauges, waves demandingly for Paul to cut off the machinery at a precise second, wipes his brow with his handkerchief. His blue eyes widen as he listens for the reanimated heartbeat of the now-revived dog. Smiling for the first time, he exclaims, "Paul, it's alive. We've done it!" Cushing's energetic eccentricity makes the Baron's inquisitive nature crystal clear. It is this linear obsession which dominates Cushing's performance throughout.

Soon the differences between pupil and tutor become clear. Paul, wishing to present their findings to a scientific meeting, is immediately shot down by the Baron: "We won't! We mustn't share it yet. We must move on to the next stage!" This attitude becomes an essential quirk in the Baron's character—as in a Shakespeare play, it becomes the Baron's tragic flaw. Once he has conquered knowledge at one level, instead of publishing his findings or sharing this newfound knowledge with his medical peers, the Baron simply wishes to immediately get back to work. In other words, instead of putting his scientific knowledge to practical use, he has an insatiable thirst to move onward, to discover knowledge for its own intrinsic sense, *not* to benefit humanity. Thus his quest for knowledge is more neurotic than self-satisfying—obviously he is unable to enjoy his accomplishments at any stage. He must constantly move forward. Simply stated, he is a driven man.

The Baron announces to Paul it is not enough to bring the dead back to life—"We must create a human being!" When Paul protests, calling such work a "revolt against nature," the Baron counters with the ironic, "Paul, you haven't shown scruples up 'til now!" The manner in which Cushing delivers this line, a slight all-knowing smile on his face, that evil glint in his eye, gives us new levels of insight into the up to now one-dimensional character. Throughout the movie, Cushing delivers similar lines with the same gusto. The Baron, looking at the huge hands on the rotting corpse he just snatched from the gallows, states, "Clod-hopping. No wonder he was a robber. He couldn't do anything

Frankenstein is obsessed with creating life, but Paul (Robert Urquhart) is not sure that this is a good idea in *The Curse of Frankenstein*.

else!" Eventually Paul can take no more and refuses to aid the Baron in his experiments, expressing his moral outrage. However, he does not leave the house because he has more than one interest there.

It seems the sudden, unexpected arrival of cousin Elizabeth (Hazel Court) complicates matters. Announcing her mother's recent death, she tells Paul (who she first mistakes for the Baron), "I've come to live with Victor." The Baron plans to proceed with his experiments despite the presence of a meddling female, and Paul's obvious attraction to Elizabeth establishes him as her great protector. Elizabeth, with no means of support, only too well understands the ramifications of her pre-arranged marriage to the Baron and his wealth.

Despite the presence of Elizabeth, the Baron is engaged in a torrid affair with the household maid Justine (Valerie Gaunt), who has set her sights on the Baron. She is more than a little threatened by the presence of Elizabeth and complains to the Baron that she is tired of meeting in dark corridors. The Baron knows what she wants. "What makes you think I'd marry you!" And with a double-entendre he cruelly orders her to "See to her [Elizabeth's] every need as thoroughly as you've seen to mine." Again, Cushing is embellishing these lines with nuance of a slyly sexual nature. Although saddled by the script that tries to keep Cushing's performance one-dimensional, he tries to bring something special to the role. Cushing utilizes every opportunity possible to imprint his character with underlying motives or nuance that deviate from the literal translation of the script.

The Baron begins toying with Paul's outrage, pretending he could continue with his unnatural work alone. "This will end in evil," Paul proclaims. Calmly the Baron responds, "Oh, I just rob a few bodies, but what doctor has not done that? How will we ever learn...My creature will be born with a lifetime of knowledge." Which leads to the question of a brain—and the Baron desires the brain of a great intellect.

Enter brilliant Professor Bernstein, the gracious dinner guest, who is soon sadistically pushed off the balcony to his death. Before his murder, the wise old professor warned Baron Frankenstein that scientists are "too concerned with discovery" and grow bored so easily that they too soon "go back into the darkness" of discovery instead of using that newfound knowledge to help mankind. Reinforcing Elizabeth's fear that the Baron spends entirely too much time in his laboratory, the Professor states that time slips away until "one is too old to enjoy life."

After the murder of Bernstein, Paul sees the Baron open the professor's coffin and remove his brain, stating, "I *can* stop you from using his brain." The Baron nonchalantly replies, "Why? He has no further use for it!" After a struggle, whereby the brain is injured, the Baron screams, showing his violent rage, "Get out of here, get out!" Thus Cushing's performance gravitates from aristocratic self-control, with an air of arrogance, to one of unhinged temper tantrums of uncontrolled anger and frustration.

Paul tries to warn Elizabeth one more time. She shows no inclination to leave, instead asking of Paul if he thinks Victor is "wicked or insane." Paul hits the nail on the head by saying, "Neither. He can't see the consequences, he's so wrapped up in his experiments!"

But the Baron, unable to complete his work alone, pleads with Paul to again help him. "I want you to help me. I'd thought I could work it myself—I can't." Soon the arrogance and aristocratic insolence returns: "You will help me Paul, whatever you say!" Paul agrees to help if the Baron promises to destroy his creation after he proves his experiments. The Baron agrees, but Cushing delivers the lines so deviously that viewers can almost imagine the crossed finger being held secretly behind the Baron's back.

When the Baron confronts the bandaged Monster in his laboratory, the Monster promptly picks the scientist off the ground by his neck, choking the life out of the insignificant human. Cushing, who could portray a throttled victim better than anyone else onscreen, plays the strangulated, bug-eyed, semi-conscious victim to the hilt. He will repeat this same physical talent in *Horror of Dracula*, *The Mummy* and *Brides of Dracula*. After being rescued, the Baron, rather than appear worried about his close call with death, is wild-eyed with joy as he shouts, "I did it Paul!"

Frankenstein and Paul manage to create life, but the Creature (Christopher Lee) has a damaged brain and will not obey commands in *The Curse of Frankenstein.*

The Creature escapes into the woods, and as in the Universal film, confronts a blind hermit. Paul, who is eager to destroy the unholy creation, shoots the Creature to death. Paul and Frankenstein bury the corpse, the bitter Baron saying, "I don't think I will ever forgive you for what you've done, Paul!"

Ah, but is the Creature really destroyed? Soon we see the exhumed corpse hanging suspended from a hook in the Baron's laboratory. With grim, quiet determination, the Baron obsesses and whispers, "I will give you life again."

Justine confronts the Baron, who is in the middle of creating life—and so is Justine when she informs him she is pregnant. She tells him, "You promised to marry me." To which the Baron cruelly laughs. "Pick any man in the village, it's probably him [the father]!" He then callously orders her, "Get back to your work!" When Justine threatens to expose the Baron to the authorities, he tells her, "proof, that's what authorities want." Frankenstein orders her to leave the house by morning.

Of course the spurned Justine intends to get proof, but to do that she must investigate the laboratory and the small storage room where the reanimated Creature lies. The conniving Baron knew she would go to the lab and follows her—closing and locking the door when she enters that storage room. Amid her screams the Baron's face displays an unnerving look of absolute relief. Formerly seen as simply being obsessed and committed to science for its own sake, the Baron is now revealed to be callous, evil and manipulative, murdering in cold blood to save his own prestigious reputation.

Eager to present his revived patchwork creature to Paul, the Baron demonstrates that his Creature can now obey short commands, such as sit down and stop. Paul insults the Baron by asking, "Is *this* your creature of *superior* intellect?" The Baron, outraged and defensive, responds, "There you see the result of *your* handiwork. This is *your* fault Paul [referring to the bullet in the head from when Paul first killed the Creature]. You won't win Paul. I will carry on, get another brain, and then another!"

This is the final straw—Paul threatens to go to the authorities. But the Baron counters with, "You're as much a part of this as I am." And based upon his upcoming actions, Paul does indeed understand the truth, and the threat, of these words.

The Creature again escapes from the lab, stalks the rooftop and lumbers toward the innocent Elizabeth on the eve of her wedding night ("We're not sentimental young lovers," the Baron reminds Elizabeth earlier that evening). Frantically racing to rescue his bride-to-be, the Baron gets a pistol from a glass case and fires at the Monster, who lunges at Elizabeth. Unfortunately, the bullet finds Elizabeth, and then the Creature approaches an uncharacteristically frightened Baron, who whines, "Get away from me." He throws a lamp, igniting the Creature into a blazing inferno. The pain-riddled Creature falls through the skylight into an acid tank below. The Baron is arrested for the murder.

A recovered Elizabeth waits outside the jail as Paul visits the Baron and a priest looks on. The Baron, eyes wide and excited, is eager for Paul to validate his incredible story. Paul stands by silent, refusing to lift a finger to free Baron Frankenstein. The Baron, realizing Paul's real motive for refusing to help, lunges at his former childhood tutor and tries to strangle him. The Baron's arrogance returns when he cries, "Paul, you've got to save me. I'll make you." Paul, by refusing to confirm the truth, allows the Baron to be seen as an insane murderer, who must now face the guillotine as Paul returns to the waiting arms of Elizabeth. The audience now sees that Paul may have committed the most vile, evil act of the movie by remaining silent so that the Baron will be out of the way and Paul can have Elizabeth for his bride.

Thus, sticking to a script, which revamps the 1931 Universal script, rather than returning to Mary Shelley's original novel, Peter Cushing creates a distinct persona of the obsessed, aristocratic and arrogant Baron. As enacted in *The Curse of Frankenstein*, Cushing's Baron is depicted as ruthless, self-serving and emotionally cold. He is truly a one-dimensional villain, a real "mad" scientist oblivious to those around him. Only in the film's final minutes do we feel a glimmer of sympathy for the Baron—for Paul's actions are ultimately even more evil than the Baron's.

The Revenge of Frankenstein

"He cuts 'em up, alive."
1958, Screenplay by Jimmy Sangster, Directed by Terence Fisher

After the success of *The Curse of Frankenstein* and *Horror of Dracula,* sequels were inevitable. However, Hammer's sequel to *Curse* was superior in every way, simply because screenwriter Jimmy Sangster felt free of the Universal Pictures formula and created his own version of the *Frankenstein* mythos. Also, the sequel was better able to embellish the character of the Baron, and actor Peter Cushing was, as always, enthusiastic to reveal far more of the subtleties inherent in the mad doctor's inner soul. Thus, while the first *Frankenstein* collaboration between Fisher, Sangster and Cushing was creatively stilted and confining, this first sequel allows each of these gifted artists the opportunity to creatively let down their hair.

While the Baron was primarily obsessed, aristocratic and cruel in the original entry, here the Baron displays compassion, enabling the audience to care about his character—since it is the Baron who is the returning icon, not the Creature.

When the Baron escapes the gallows, the his conspirators murder and bury the prison priest in his place. Going incognito, the Baron moves to another village and assumes the identity of one Dr. Stein, a mysterious doctor distrusted by the town's Medical Council—but loved by its citizenry. It seems Stein, a loner, refuses to join the Council, as one member intones with a degree of agitation, "Three years ago, when he first came, no one here heard of him, no one knew his background. Now he is the most popular doctor—who steals patients from us!" The verdict: Their mysterious competitor must be *made* to join this elite group.

Frankenstein (Cushing) manages to escape the gallows in *The Revenge of Frankenstein.*

Dr. Stein has become doctor to the upper class. In his office he attends to a Countess and her daughter. Her mother, who insists the girl is ill, manipulates the reticent, yet lovely, daughter. Mother complains the girl has "no vitality" and orders the doctor to "overhaul" her. The mother says her daughter experiences palpitations and dizziness and she insists the doctor to listen to her daughter's heart by placing his ear against her bosom. "You are a man, you can do a great deal for her. I have money..." The Countess' unsubtle implications are crystal clear.

The doctor uses money earned in this manner to finance a hospital for the underprivileged and needy—often inhabited by criminal elements. There the Baron is seemingly sympathetic to the needs of the lower classes, yet his true nature cleverly shines through. Examining a patient and inspecting his tattooed arm, the doctor announces, "You have to have it off." The arm is seemingly healthy, but the heartless Baron needs the arm for a perfect body he plans to create. The arm of a pickpocket, a man whose fingers are nimble and skilled, is perfect. The doctor's cold advice after breaking the grim news to his distressed patient, "Find another trade or use your other hand!"

The haughty members of the Medical Counsel, an investigative group of three, are shocked by the squalor of this free clinic. One intones, "The stench is enough to kill me." The Baron is wise enough to realize that carving off the limbs of the rich wouldn't go unnoticed, but who in power really cares about the underprivileged? Thus, his seemingly humanitarian efforts are in reality self-serving and cruel. But the Baron must remain incognito, so he creates a gentle and highly cultured persona, the external personality of a dashing, almost romantic *god* of science.

His plan is to reward his crippled and partially paralyzed assistant Karl by transferring his brain into a new, whole body, thus curing Karl of his physical infirmities. The Baron is forced to take Dr. Hans Kleve (Francis Matthews) into his confidence as the young doctor, a member of the Council, recognizes Dr. Stein as Baron Frankenstein from attending the funeral of the late Dr. Bernstein. Hans' motives are honorable, "I am in search of knowledge. I want to be the pupil of the finest medical brain in the world." The Baron, flattered by such devotion, replies, "I am not an easy man to work for. I wonder if I can trust you...Uncertainty is part of life!" Showing his young student his former wine garden laboratory located in the cellar of a building, young Hans slightly trips as the duo go down the steps. "It would be a pity to lose you!" The intent here is ambiguous: Does the Baron feel blackmailed and manipulated, or does he welcome the opportunity to become a tutor to another inquisitive mind, much like Paul Krempe was once the Baron's tutor? Frankenstein lectures Paul gleefully as resident "professor," showing him disembodied eyes and hands floating in beakers and bottles, sharing his proud secrets with his eager student. This reveals another side of the Baron.

But the Baron soon displays the inner demons that fuel his passion and his experiments. Frankenstein becomes greatly distressed when talking about his first creation. "I made it to be *perfect*. If it wasn't damaged, the name of Frankenstein, my work, would be considered a genius of science! I swore I

Hans (Francis Matthews) and Frankenstein work to build another Creature in *The Revenge of Frankenstein.*

would have my revenge!" He then shows Hans the secret behind the curtain in his lab—the upright, bandaged body of his new Creature (Michael Gwynn). The Baron beams with pride, "This is something I am proud of...this time he is perfect!"

One basic change occurs in the Baron's character: Now in public view as Dr. Stein, he hides his sarcasm and criticism under the cloak of polite manners. His tongue is just as biting, but the sting is covered with honey. For instance, when the Council members confront the Baron and tell him they have elected to have him join their prestigious order, the Baron subtly displays his loathing for them. One Council member introduces himself, "I am the President of the Medical Council," to which the Baron responds, "Congratulations," smiling politely.

Once he is offered the opportunity to join the medical group, the Baron turns angry and vicious. He proclaims that when he first came to town three years ago, he was met "with firm resistance" by the Council, whose sole purpose, according to the Baron, is to "eliminate competition." Insisting he has "grown accustomed to working alone" and that he "enjoys it," he refuses their invitation.

The Baron, except for his occasional sexual fling in *The Curse of Frankenstein,* is married to his work and has no time or patience for women. The token female in this chapter is named Margaret (Eunice Gayson), the daughter of the town minister, who insists she volunteer in the Poor Hospital. The Baron dare not insult the minister, a leading citizen, so he must put up with her intrusions. But he makes his rules perfectly clear to her, "Margaret, I must ask you to keep out of the ward when I'm on duty." Here wonderful Richard Wordsworth (the victim of *The Creeping Unknown*) plays the sweeper, sort of the titular leader of the underprivileged hospital patients, who is always eager to impress Margaret. Warning her, "He cuts 'em up, alive! Brought a new one in the other day. Locked up in the attic; I have a master key!"

This "new one" is the latest creation of Frankenstein, the result of the brain transplant between poor physically challenged Karl and the new unborn bits-and-pieces "perfect" body. As the Baron told Hans, Karl is "a very sound brain in that unfortunate body."

The Baron warns, "The brain will take time to adjust to the new body—this is only the beginning of our work!" If the brain is jarred or damaged before it has time to heal, the personality of the kindly Karl will change. These same experiments, earlier attempted on the chimp Otto, resulted in the vegetarian chimp resorting to cannibalism—eating meat, which was against its nature.

Of course, such is to be the fate of the reborn Karl when the naive Margaret, given the key to the locked bedroom door, allows the still-healing human out of his restraints. Unfortunately, assistant Hans had frightened Karl by telling him of the Baron's plans—putting Karl and his old body on display for the scientific world to question and study. Once free, the first thing Karl does is return to the laboratory and burn his old body. Unfortunately, the janitor sadistically pummels him. After repeated blows to the face and head, Karl turns monstrous and chokes the bully to death. But the damage has been done. When the Baron and Hans discover their experiment has flown the coop, Hans questions, "How did he undo the straps?" The Baron, challenging the limited thinking of his assistant, yells "Why, always why!" When Hans admits he told Karl of the Baron's plans, the Baron immediately understands the psychological implications, and retorts with his customary, "You fool!" Then the Baron aggressively states, "Sooner or later he'd need my help. Go back to the ward. Do as I tell you!"

Later the Baron attends a society party given by the

Karl (Michael Gwynn) discovers his old body in the lab.

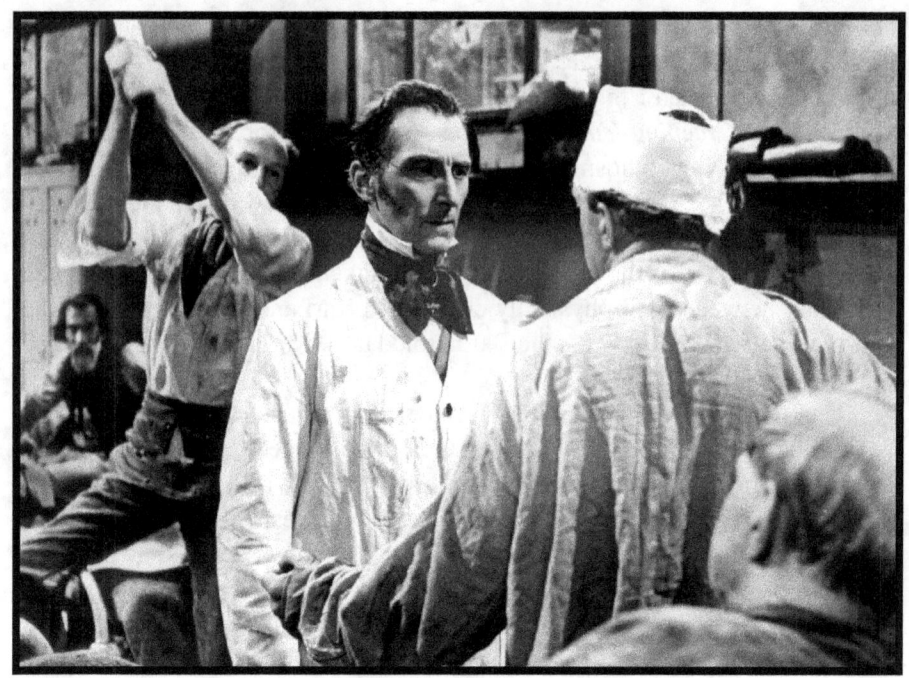

The patients take their revenge on Frankenstein.

Countess and her daughter. The Baron smiles and turns on the charm that only Dr. Stein exudes. But a party crasher ruins the festivities when the drooling, crippled maniac that Karl has become bursts through the French windows and, recognizing Dr. Stein, cries, "Frankenstein! Frankenstein! Help me!" after which Karl collapses and dies.

The war between Dr. Stein and the Medical Council now escalates with the announcement that Dr. Stein is actually Dr. Victor Frankenstein. As one Council member mutters, "This is the chance we have been waiting for!"

Hans, afraid for the Baron's life, pleads with him to flee, to start afresh somewhere else. But the Baron's pride won't allow him to run away. After being "ordered" to appear before the Medical Council, the Baron plays innocent by lying through his teeth, all with his customary believability and expertise. "Gentlemen, I deny it absolutely. There are dozens of Frankensteins. I *am* a Frankenstein. But I did not want to be handicapped by that name so I changed it...I think a little proof instead of a lot of gossip would be advantageous."

However, returning to his hospital for the poor, the Baron is greeted with utter silence, looks of hatred and suspicious eyes from those patients who had once loved and trusted the good doctor. The Baron inquires of one patient, "How's the head?" The man replies, "Keep your murdering hands off me, Frankenstein. Murderer! Murderer!" Soon bottles flung by unknown hands fly at the Baron. He is knocked unconscious when a wooden crutch beans him over the head, again from behind. The mob of patients swarms around the bloodied

Baron and they kick and stomp on him until he is near death. Hans intervenes and carries the broken, lifeless body back to the laboratory.

"Hans, it's no good...You know what to do!" the Baron desperately gasps.

Conveniently, the Baron has stitched together an exact replica of himself, ready for brain transfer in the event that he needed a new body (complete with tattooed arm, no less). During the middle of the operation when the police and members of the Council arrive, Hans produces the dead body of the original Baron—"The body must be buried in unhallowed ground!" Once they leave, Hans continues the operation, "Pray heaven I have the skill to do this."

The scene changes to London and the clinic of one Dr. Franck, the now mustachioed Peter Cushing, again dressed debonairly, a flower in his lapel. Opening the door to his study, he turns on his charm and welcomes the latest aristocratic patient.

Before, in *Curse*, Cushing was all pout and attitude. His character was consistent and clearly defined, unchanging, the same above as well as below the surface. Cushing's genius and exuberance elevated his performance well beyond a mad doctor stereotype, but as written, the script limited his ability to expand upon the characterization. Here, in *Revenge*, Jimmy Sangster's much-improved script allows Peter Cushing the latitude to subtley expand upon the Baron's character. We have the Baron pretending to be either Dr. Stein or Dr. Franck, a respected, polite and mannerly member of affluent English society. But underneath the surface, we have a not-quite-so-mad scientist, who still believes the ends justify the means. Frankenstein is a doctor who devotes his time to the free clinic for the poor—seemingly out of a sense of humanity—but in reality he is amputating perfectly healthy body parts for his man-made monster. The Baron loathes humanity, both in the larger sense (he hates the pomposity of the Medical Council, the status quo dictators of the mores of society) and the smaller sense (his disdain for Margaret, his manipulation of the Countess, the cruel mutilation of the tattooed-armed patient). Instead of immediately telegraphing his every thought and impulse, the more subtle character of the Baron is revealed through exposing and contrasting his *false* (debonair) external self to his true (cruel and heartless) internal self. At last, with *The Revenge of Frankenstein*, the character of Baron Frankenstein was coming into its own.

The debonair Dr. Franck (Cushing) is now treating society patients in London.

The Evil of Frankenstein

"Why can't they ever leave me alone!"
1964, Screenplay by John Elder (Anthony Hinds),
Directed by Freddie Francis

The image of Baron Frankenstein near the end of Hammer's *The Evil of Frankenstein* casts Peter Cushing in dashing Indiana Jones–style grandeur. After escaping cleverly from prison by tricking the prison guard, Cushing steals a horse-drawn carriage, and using a whip to motivate the horse, rides the carriage standing up, the wind blowing through his disheveled hair. Is this the image of villain?

Earlier, returning to his family chateau after 10 years in exile, the Baron becomes outraged to learn that all his family heirlooms, furniture, carpets, etc. have been cleared out and apparently sold. Later, seeing his ring on the Burgomaster's finger, the Baron causes quite a scene in a local pub by yelling for the police to "arrest that man!" while his new assistant Hans (this time played by Sandor Eles) spirits the fugitive scientist out of harm's way.

But later that evening, the Baron triumphantly invades the elegant Burgomaster's home, seething with frustration over the fact that he himself is in desperate need of money for his research and that the above-the-law burgomaster is living in high style off ill-gotten gains. "I've come for my property...my ring!" Looking around the home, the Baron's eyes bug halfway out of his head as he sees his possessions here! "My desk, my carpet—even my bed!" which at the moment is occupied by the Burgomaster's wife, a buxom blonde who seems more than a little "in the mood." In dashing rogue-hero style, the Baron escapes from the bedroom by tying a blanket to the end of the brass bed, climbing rapidly out the window, stopping momentarily to give the Burgomaster's sexy wife an all-knowing wink.

Yes, the image of the Baron has changed remarkably since his last incarnation. Jimmy Sangster, who had scripted the prior Frankenstein screenplays, was out and John Elder was in, and former cinematographer Freddie Francis replaced director Terence Fisher. Supposedly Hammer was upset at Fisher since his last Hammer horror, *The Phantom of the Opera* (1962), was not a smash hit. Compared to the original conception of the Baron in *Curse*, Cushing here plays an outlaw hero where all authority figures surrounding him are more loathsome and despicable than he ever was. Sure, the Baron dabbles in dead bodies and grave robbing, but ethically this is small potatoes compared to the grand larceny of the Burgomaster and the abuse of power by the Chief of Police. In this film, the bottom line is that the Baron is a man of dignity and determination.

And if the Burgomaster and Chief of Police aren't villains enough, enter Zoltan (Peter Woodthrope), the greedy, maniacal hypnotist. After the Baron

In *The Evil of Frankenstein*, Cushing turns into a dashing anti-hero.

reanimates his pathetic (both from the viewpoint of makeup execution and character) Monster (this was the first Hammer Frankenstein film released by Universal, so for the first time the Monster could dare to approximate Karloff's Monster concept), the Baron disappointedly discovers that the Creature's brain has been so damaged that he needs the help of the hypnotist to reach the Creature's subconscious to bring him back. The manipulative Zoltan realizes the power he can wield if he keeps the Monster under *his* own control and not under the Baron's. Zoltan threatens to leave the Creature in a dormant state, so the Baron, against Hans' wishes, agrees to Zoltan's terms.

Of course, Zoltan, who has just been run out of town by the Chief of Police, wants a little old-fashioned revenge and he puts the Monster under his direct control and sends out the Creature at night to steal gold and to kill his enemies. Thus, for the first time Hammer's resurrected "Creature" becomes a zombified killing machine that, under direct command of the evil Zoltan, blindly maims and destroys in the stereotypical Frankenstein Monster manner.

Unlike the more imaginative Jimmy Sangster, who was moving the series further and further away from the Universal 1940s image of the Monster, John Elder embraced all the weak qualities of both the Hammer and Universal series to meld into this—the most disappointing of the entire Cushing series. However, Cushing's Baron Frankenstein has been fine-tuned by the enthusiastic thespian to the point that his characterization no longer needs direction or an effective

In the finale of *The Evil of Frankenstein*, the Baron becomes the hero.

script. Cushing's Baron brilliantly survives the transition to a new (inferior) director (but brilliant cinematographer) and scriptwriter. And instead of portraying the insidious villain, Cushing's Baron here becomes the self-sacrificing hero.

Peter Cushing, as the underdog, misunderstood man of science, gains the sympathy of the audience from the opening reel. The film's best sequence, a pre-credits prelude, involves the mourning for a recently deceased peasant, laid out on a large wooden table at dusk. A large window near the table flies open, the raging wind instantly blowing out the illuminating candles near the body. Mysteriously, someone pulls the body across the table and swiftly out the window. We then see the smiling face of a grave robber, throwing the corpse over his shoulder, quickly arriving at the laboratory of Baron Frankenstein. The grave robber tells the Baron the obvious, that he has brought a body for his research, to which Cushing dryly states, "So I've observed...and so will half the county if you don't get it inside!" During the movie's credits the physically intense Baron removes the corpse's heart, declaring, "He doesn't have any more use for it" (paralleling a similar line from *Curse*).

Frankenstein orders the much younger and more virile assistant Hans to "start the wheel," the youth grunting and straining to physically start a huge wheel turning. Hans has no luck until the Baron almost pushes him out of the way and, utilizing all his strength, gets the wheel turning mostly by his own power and force of will. Thus, the movie quickly establishes the Baron as a man of dedication, perseverance and strength, values that movie *heroes* frequently display.

And to firmly establish the Baron's heroic underdog image, in the midst of his experiment the laboratory is invaded by the county priest, a stereotypical "hell and brimstone" variety clergyman. "Get rid of them, Hans," the Baron demands. However, the priest and his mob storm the lab, the priest yelling words of blasphemy and damnation, using a cane to break beakers and lab tanks, one containing the recently rejuvenated human heart. Baron Frankenstein, with a look of outrage, cries, "You realize you are trespassing, you are interrupting my work." Seeing the damage done, the Baron has to be physically restrained by Hans. "Destroyed! They always destroy *everything*!"

The Elder screenplay uses the priest to symbolize the blind hatred and fear inherent in members of society who destroy what they do not understand—assuming new knowledge to be evil knowledge. For a change we see the priest as villain and scientist/explorer as rogue hero. And actor Peter Cushing seems energized by this ever-evolving complexity.

Throughout *The Evil of Frankenstein,* the Baron constantly states, "Anything that doesn't conform...they have to destroy. They haven't beaten me. I won't let them beat me!" Sadly, at movie's end the Baron's chateau explodes and the Baron is apparently dead inside. Hans bemoans, "They beat him after all."

Zoltan (Peter Woodthrope) becomes the movie's chief villain (out of a wide variety of villains) by virtue of his manipulative and self-centered urges. Both the Baron and Zoltan are ostracized from the community, but Zoltan is a profiteer, thief and ultimately a murderer, while the Baron displays loftier virtues. Simply stated, the Baron here is displayed as a man of honor and dignity. After forcing the Baron to accept his deal that only Zoltan controls the Monster, Zoltan extends his hand and says, "Let's shake on it." Frankenstein, disdaining the opportunistic hypnotist, simply replies, "No need...I've given my word."

At the film's explosive climax, after Zoltan dies from being savagely speared by the Monster, the Creature drinks a bottle of chloroform, becomes violently ill and catches the chateau on fire. The Baron immediately tries to attend to the needs of the Creature, telling Hans and the mute servant girl to "get away from here." Displaying the best aspects of the self-sacrificing hero, the Baron wishes to save the young innocents and would rather die in the fiery inferno than see his creation suffer or harm anyone. One of Cushing's final sequences involves the dashing scientist swinging Errol Flynn–style across his lab on a chain, contradicting the standard image of mad scientist as a crotchety old man who toddles around the laboratory. No, as *The Evil of Frankenstein* establishes, the Baron, formerly the evil Monstermaker, is here shown to be the romantic, charismatic monster destroyer and ultimately the film's hero.

Frankenstein Created Woman

"Bodies are easy to come by, souls are not!"
1966, Screenplay by John Elder (Anthony Hinds),
Directed by Terence Fisher

Continuing with a screenplay by John Elder and returning Terence Fisher to the director's chair, *Frankenstein Created Woman* is an improvement over *The Evil of Frankenstein,* boasting one of the most offbeat scenarios of the entire series. John Elder, following the lead of Jimmy Sangster, creates a story which moves far beyond the Universal mythos, his major failing the first time around. Unfortunately, while the aging Peter Cushing looks wonderful as the Baron, his character has been reduced once again to being one-dimensional and his screen time has also been clipped.

Also, for the first time in the series, the subplot, involving the love between a deformed girl, Christina (Susan Denberg), and the Baron's assistant, Hans (this time played by Robert Morris), detailing how Hans (the son of a guillotined murderer) is framed for the murder of Christina's father, overrides the Baron's tale. While the story is novel, creating a strong sense of pathos, it leaves little for the Baron and his new doctor/assistant Dr. Hertz (sympathetically played by Thorley Walters in one of his best roles) to do except restore the executed Hans' soul into the resurrected Christina's body (now recreated as a blonde centerfold playmate) and watch as the soul of Hans, commanding the actions of Christina, seeks revenge on the three louts who never paid for the murder of Christina's father.

This entry does contain some wonderful sequences with the Baron, especially the film's novel beginning which establishes Baron Frankenstein as the continually resurrected star of the series (unlike the Universal series, where the Monster was constantly being *reborn*). Here, in the tense sequence, Dr. Hertz is counting down the minutes until exactly one hour has passed. The elderly, dazed doctor yells for a drink from young assistant Hans, who hands Hertz the entire bottle. Suddenly, the ice chamber door is opened and a huge metal coffin is wheeled out onto a conveyer rack. The crate lid is opened to reveal the death-like, crystallized Baron Frankenstein. Quickly, wires are attached to the Baron and then to a huge metal grid overhead. Soon electrical charges are being blasted into the Baron, quickly reviving the scientist who had been dead for one hour. "See Hans, he's alive," Hertz proudly announces. Smelling salts bring the frozen doctor to consciousness.

"Of course I'm alive. For one whole hour I was dead. It was an hour, *wasn't* it? Why has my soul remained...*why*!"

In a dramatic twist of convention, the Baron is literally resurrected, brought back to life in the film's first few minutes. By now, with this fourth entry in

Peter Cushing and Susan Denberg in a publicity shot of *Frankenstein Created Woman*

Hammer's Frankenstein series, it has been established that Cushing's Baron is the entire reason for the films.

Once again the quaint town and its closde-minded citizens become the villains, the enemy of the man of science. "He's some sort of monster in league with the devil himself," a citizen proclaims. Hans, who defends the Baron and his work, responds, "If it is a choice between him and they, I would pick *him* every time."

The other more visible villains are three young rich punks, sons of the elite of the community, who spend all their time dressed as fancy dandies drinking, partying and yet somehow they always come up short when it is time to pay their bill. The arrogance and callowness of the rich elite make this Frankenstein entry very class conscious. The Baron and Hertz are shown to be poorer than poor (with all their available cash going into the cost of their scientific apparatus), failing to even come up with the money needed to buy a simple bottle of champagne. Finally, the Baron sends Hans to the local Inn to tell the landlord to charge the champagne. Later journeying to the pub for a meal, the Baron cleverly tells one of the louts, wounded in a knife fight with Hans, who was protecting the honor of Christina, that Dr. Hertz will render first-aid for a "slight charge," just enough to pay for the meal. Thus, the Baron, who was depicted as the epitome of aristocratic arrogance in the premiere entry, is now reduced to being one of the common folk to contrast his noble endeavors to the shallowness of the rich elite.

Cushing's Baron here resembles Sherlock Holmes (Rathbone-style) and Walter's his Watson (Nigel Bruce's doddering old fool). The brilliant Baron is very impatient with those ordinary people who fail to immediately comprehend his work. "Haven't you grasped anything I've been doing these last six months?" to which the diligent, dedicated Dr. Hertz humbly responds that he is just a drunken old muddle-head. Unfortunately, the Baron's hands have been damaged (a possible tie-in to the explosive finale to *The Evil of Frankenstein*?), a fact made clear by the black gloves the Baron wears. When carrying a coffin late in the film, the Baron grunts and grimaces in pain. Earlier, while working in the lab, the Baron is unable to twist a dial and needs assistance. During the all-important surgery, Hertz admits, "The hands were mine; the skill was his!" While Cushing is constantly reminding the kindly Dr. Hertz how ignorant he is, the fact remains that the Baron depends upon Hertz's medical skills and steady hands to carry out *all* his work. The Baron's cold, cruel self-centeredness makes Hertz all the more sympathetic.

When his young assistant Hans is on trial for a murder he did not commit, Cushing speaks on his behalf in court, politely compassionate, yet looking with annoyance at his watch as if precious time is being wasted. "I am a doctor of medicine, law, physics," and when he is accused of witchcraft, declares that he would have a degree in that too if one were offered. When the court sarcastically accuses him of being a clever man, the Baron proudly retorts, "Yes I am." The Baron quickly states that Hans has been "trustworthy, diligent, quick-witted," etc. and that as a scientist he would conclude, "it is extremely unlikely that he could commit murder." When countered with the question: "Impossible?" the Baron truthfully responds, "No, not impossible."

As soon as Hans is convicted on circumstantial evidence, instead of mourning the fact, the Baron is almost exuberant, "This is our chance!" To which Dr. Hertz asks, "Is it right?" To which the Baron states, "What is right," explaining he plans to capture Hans' soul in his apparatus. As he cheerfully tells Hertz, "Bodies are easy to come by, souls are not!"

The Baron's theory is a simple one: that the human soul doesn't leave the body at the instant of death. If the soul can be contained while the body is repaired, the soul and body can later be united after the body has been "fixed." The arrogant doctor declares, "This is not supposition, it's a fact!" to which he finally summarizes, "I have conquered death!" The Baron's ego has not seen this amount of inflation since *Curse of Frankenstein.*

Later, when Christina murders two of the young louts who framed Hans for the murder of her father, the town citizenry begins to suspect the Baron's witchcraft as being the cause of this violent murder spree. "Is this why you interrupt my work! For this fantasy?" When the police announce they might have to take steps, the Baron indignantly responds, "You mean you will *burn* me?" Instantly calming himself, he now speaks to reason. "What can I do to convince you that you are wrong....How can I make you understand? The murderer will strike again unless I get to her first....It seems you beheaded the wrong man!" The police respond, "You take us for fools?" to which the Baron quickly and honestly says, "Yes!"

During the 1960s, the elderly Baron's disdain for authority made him a hero to the youth who purchased the tickets. Today, his pompous self-importance seems less heroic. yet even with all his pomposity and posturing, the audience still sides with the often too-demanding Baron.

In an abrupt finale, the Baron once again utilizes a horse-drawn carriage, this time to catch up to the murdering Christina/Hans Creature (she carries the head of her decapitated lover in her hat box and his spirit gives her murderous commands). The Baron arrives a moment too late, finding the stabbed-to-death corpse of the third hoodlum as Christina is told by the head that she can now rest, which means a suicidal leap into a raging river. The Baron slowly walks away in disgust.

While Cushing's performance is kinetic, verbally sharp and comfortable (to Cushing the character of the Baron must now seem like an old pair of broken-in slippers), the script once again lessens his importance and reduces his characterization to a one-dimensional stereotype. At least *The Evil of Frankenstein,* a far inferior film, kept the Baron front and center and pivotal to the story. Here, in *Frankenstein Created Woman,* we once again yearn for the complexities of character that the last three entries introduced and developed.

Frankenstein Must Be Destroyed

"Stupidity does bring out the worst in me!"
1969, Screenplay by Bert Batt (from an original story by Anthony Nelson Keys and Batt), Directed by Terence Fisher

After two screenplays by Jimmy Sangster where Baron Frankenstein's character was primarily evil and two screenplays by John Elder whereby the virtuous and heroic qualities of the character emerge, now the screenplay by Bert Batt invigorates the series with Hammer's finest Frankenstein script yet. Developing Sangster's conception of Baron Frankenstein rather than Elder's, Bert Batt restores the Baron as an inherently evil personality, a person more loathsome than Karloff's Frankenstein Monster could ever hope to be. And finally, Hammer has the budget to produce an "A" quality production, again directed by Terence Fisher, which features Peter Cushing in practically every scene. Many consider *Frankenstein Must Be Destroyed* to be the finest entry in the series, and while some may still prefer *Revenge of Frankenstein*, this production highlights Hammer at their creative peak.

Just as the James Bond films became famous for pre-credit sequences, which had little to do with the ensuing movie, Hammer here has fun with resurrecting Baron Frankenstein one more time. The movie unfurls with a close-up on another hatbox (a carryover image from *Created Woman*) and another ghastly decapitation. An intruder breaks into Frankenstein's subterranean laboratory (a reference to the lab in *Revenge of Frankenstein*) and gasps as he sees an "unborn" body hanging suspended in a glass case (another reference to *Revenge*). The intruder is surprised by the sudden appearance of a horrible looking fiend, who carries the hat box containing the severed head. The two struggle, damaging the lab in the process, until the intruder runs off. Suddenly, the fiend pulls the fake rubber mask from his face, revealing the dashing features of Peter Cushing. This rather silly premise of having the Baron wear a Halloween mask when committing murder becomes a strong visual image with which to introduce the returning Baron—it is almost intended as a *wink* to Hammer fans of the series.

But from this point on, the film becomes very somber and ultimately depressing, establishing a far darker, realistic tone to this entry.

The love interest is supplied by handsome Simon Ward (Dr. Karl Holst) and lovely Veronica Carlson (Anna), pawns in the manipulative game of Frankenstein. Fleeing his laboratory at the film's beginning, the Baron rents a room at the boarding house of Anna, who runs the establishment alone, using all her money to pay the expensive hospital bills of her critically ill mother. Financial help comes from Dr. Holst, Anna's fiancé, who claims, "Illegal drugs are one market where money does not dry up." Holst, in charge of drugs at the mental hospital where he works, changes the records to hide his illegal activity, all the profit going to pay for Anna's mother's medical bills.

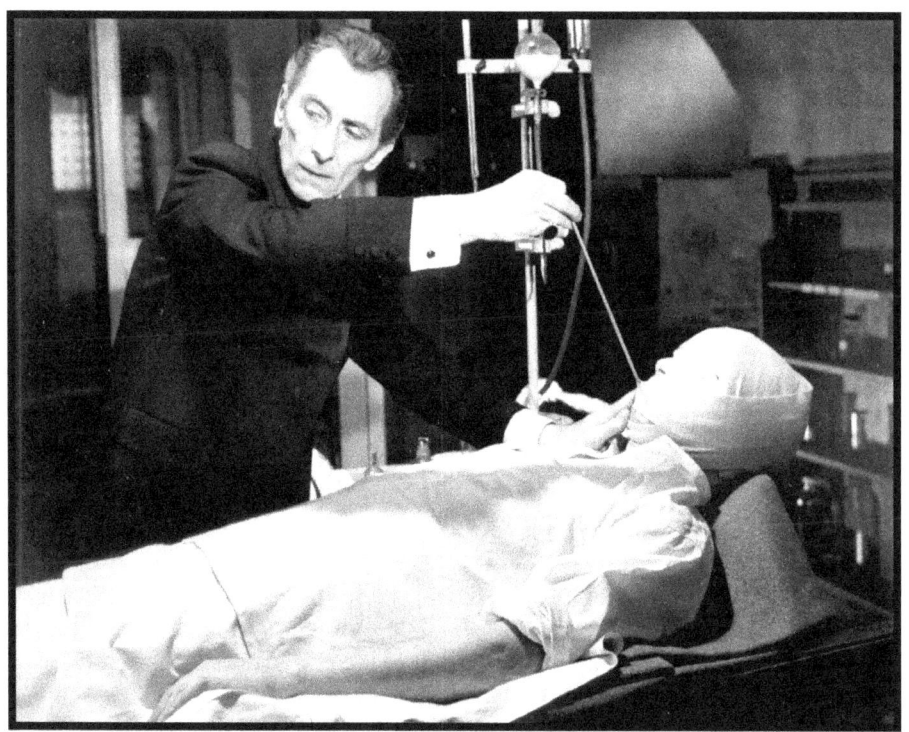

Frankenstein Must Be Destroyed creates a Baron that is inherently evil.

Unfortunately, the Baron overhears this conversation while he is outside the front door. Holst, inside, realizes he dropped a box of cocaine on the doorstep, now conveniently found by the Baron who, smiling politely, returns the box to Holst. "I found this on your doorstep…it's cocaine, isn't it?" Holtz and Anna excuse themselves, but the Baron charges to the door, turns, and declares, "*Neither* of you are going anywhere tonight. Both of you are involved in very *illegal* business!" The young doctor thinks the Baron wants blackmail money, but instead, he announces, "I want your help."

The first favor immediately occurs when the Baron has Anna eject all four of the guests staying in the boarding house. The night before, the tenants were describing the Baron as "damn surly" and as one who hardly ever manages to say one word to the others. Enter the Baron, who immediately goes to his own corner of the parlor, sitting at a desk with his back to the others. They discuss "the worst madman of the decade, Dr. Frederick Brandt," who five years earlier caused "such a furor" in the medical world with the "devilish notion" of transplanting brains. They also mention another doctor who shared the same idea, Baron Frankenstein from Bohemia. "Ran him out of his country as well." Both are referred to as "the devil's disciples."

The Baron, listening to all this talk, calmly and politely interjects, "Excuse me, I didn't know you were doctors!" The tenants immediately announce they are not. "Ah, I thought you knew what you were talking about…stupidity brings out the worst in me...fools like you." The guests all express outrage and declare their new guest to be extremely rude. Debating the use of the word "progress" as the Baron uses it, the Baron draws a parallel for them. "Man is given to invention and experiment. If that were not true, we would still be eating in caves, stringing bones about the floor, and wiping our fingers on animal skins. In fact, your lapels do look kind of greasy...Good night!!" Of course, the Baron cannot continue his experiments with these closed-minded gentlemen around.

When the Baron announces who he really is, Karl Holst proclaims, "I thought the world had seen the last of you!" And then the Baron announces his plans—to rescue Dr. Brandt from the mental hospital, cure his insanity and learn Brandt's theories on transplanting the human brain, the work of which the Baron admits has progressed further than his own. And since Karl works as a doctor in the hospital, the Baron needs his assistance to supply floor plans, supply entrance to rooms, and aid in sedating other patients during the kidnapping.

The Baron's self-professed righteous cause is preserving the brains of the great minds of the world. He claims their bodies get sick and die, the bodies are buried and rot while the mind is at the peak of its development. Brain transplants would allow the bodies to be fixed and the brain to be returned, just as his theory of capturing the human soul while the body was being repaired was established in the last entry.

Of course, after the kidnapping of Brandt from the hospital, Brandt suffers a heart attack and will die unless the Baron transplants his brain into a new body immediately. The ideal choice is a Dr. Richter, one of the chief doctors who work in the mental hospital. Karl realizes one life would have to be sacrificed: "That would be murder!" The Baron, smiling, states, "You're used to that by now," referring to Karl's earlier murder of an elderly night watchman in the drug supply storage room.

Very interesting is Frankenstein's relationship to the beautiful Anna, a person the Baron seems to enjoy terrifying. Assisting the Baron in examining Brandt after he is first kidnapped, Anna is cleaning up the superficial cuts on his face as the doctor listens to Brandt's heart. Finishing up and walking away, the Baron screams at her, "I'm not done yet!" Constantly, throughout the movie, the Baron demands that Anna make him coffee. Karl claims the Baron does not need Anna and demands he let her go. But the Baron calmly counters, "I need her—to make coffee." The ultimate outrage occurs when Anna is preparing for bed in her room, her sensuous form silhouetted under her nightgown by the lamp light as the Baron passes by her room and stops. "Please leave my room," she implores. The Baron locks the door from the inside, and she demands firmly that he give her the key, holding her robe to cover her scantily clad figure. He holds out his hand with the key in it, but as Anna pensively approaches him, he throws the key on the bed, to which she races. There the Baron savagely attacks Anna, ripping apart the back of her gown, throwing her down on the bed, he on

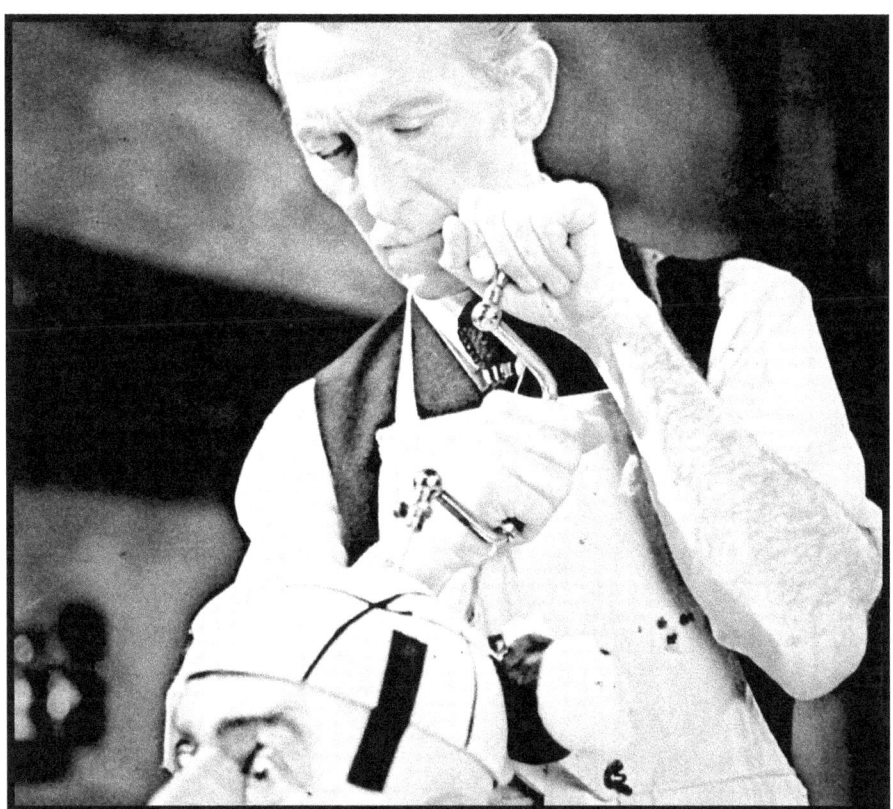

top of her. As the passive Anna squirms and screams, the Baron cruelly satisfies his sexual appetite. It is a horrifying and shocking sequence and as Veronica Carlson told us, it was quite disturbing for both actors.

The Baron's debonair and outwardly aristocratic attitude, always calm and under control when interacting in public, is sometimes less controlled internally or when around people such as Holtz, who know his real personality. This can best be seen in the sequence involving Brandt's wife, who recognizes the Baron on the street as he buys a flower for his coat lapel. Following Frankenstein to the boarding house, she knocks on the door and inquires, "Is Baron Frankenstein staying here?" Thinking cleverly and rapidly on his feet, the smiling and charming scientist goes to the front door and states, "It was my intention to call on *you* this evening. Your husband is here. It was the only way I had to save him," referring to the fact that if he had asked to experiment on her husband, she would have definitely denied him access.

Taking this woman, who has been in contact with the police, seemingly into his confidence, he continues, "It was within my power to help him. He's downstairs—he is safe." The Baron, very accommodating, very helpful, leads Mrs. Brandt into the cellar and shows her the bandaged form of her husband (unknown to her, his brain is now in another man's body). There the Baron allows her to ask her husband questions, which he can answer with a simple yes or no using his left hand. The Baron smiles, "He's cured!" Showing Mrs. Brandt upstairs, he insists, "You must never speak of this to *anyone*. You may come here anytime to visit. In one week you and he can begin a new life."

Showing the satisfied Mrs. Brandt to the front door and slowly closing the door behind her, the Baron frantically turns and shouts, "Pack! We're leaving." In other words, we once again see the difference between the cultured gentleman persona, which the Baron easily assumes, and the cutthroat, manipulative, cold persona within. And Cushing plays this ambiguity with such craft and energy.

Frankenstein shows Mrs. Brandt (Maxine Audley) her husband, although she does not know that is only his brain.

Several sequences throughout the movie show the majestic Baron sitting most elegantly in his padded chair, smoking a cigar, sipping on a delicate cup of tea or coffee, propped up in front of the fireplace. Contrasted to this elite comfort, being waited on hand and foot by Karl and mostly Anna, the beast in the Baron, lurking just below the surface, often emerges showing his savage side. Karl, planning an escape by stealing the carriage from the stables, is surprised by the Baron when he mysteriously appears and says, "What are you doing, Karl!" The two immediately fight, and while the Baron must be twice as old as the youthful Karl, the physically adept Baron wins the slugfest. Anna, inside, is confronted by the now conscious and freely walking Richter/Brandt creature. In fear, wielding a scalpel, Anna stabs the misunderstood resurrected man and, in a daze, sits on the stairs holding the bloody instrument. Returning, the Baron hears from Anna's own lips what she has done (the stab wound was not severe) and in immediate rage plunges the knife into Anna's chest, killing her instantly. Never has the evil of the Baron been delivered quite so callously and in such a cold and shocking manner.

Frankenstein is once again trapped by fire.

At the film's fiery climax, the disappointed Brandt, not happy with being reborn in another man's body, plots a fitting end for the Baron. Pulling out his notes, which he realizes are the Baron's only reason for keeping him alive, he places the papers on his desk and places oil lamps all around the house, pouring kerosene throughout. Once the Baron arrives, Brandt plays a game of cat and mouse. "I fancy I am the spider and you are the fly," he says as he sets the house ablaze and challenges the Baron to find the room where the papers are before everything goes up in smoke. Just barely finding the brain-transplant notes in time, the Baron, racing frantically out of the house, is tripped by the avenging Karl, who is then struck unconscious by Brandt, who drags the Baron, kicking and screaming, back into the flaming inferno—supposedly to both their deaths.

In sharp contrast to the dignified, eccentric, yet highly likeable Baron of the John Elder–scripted movies, Bert Batt reconstructs Baron Victor Frankenstein as a pompous, self-centered, manipulative, cruel bastard, a role performed brilliantly by Peter Cushing. Many Hammer fans sometimes wish the Hammer series had ended here on this artistic high note, but one more Frankenstein film was to follow, the final film directed by the aging Terence Fisher.

Frankenstein and the Monster from Hell

"Ten days! If I've succeeded, every sacrifice would have been worthwhile!"
1974, Screenplay by John Elder (Anthony Hinds),
Directed by Terence Fisher

By the mid-1970s, Peter Cushing looked older than his years, his body too thin, his face hollow and gaunt—he is obviously wearing a curly-haired wig for his final performance as the Baron. And while the aging Terence Fisher would never direct another film (he died two years later in 1976), this was also the final major performance for Peter Cushing in a Hammer film. And while most critics snarkily dismiss this film's importance, it is a wonderful, fitting finale to an important series.

Once again John Elder (Anthony Hinds) submits the screenplay, his finest entry in the series, returning the Baron to more sympathetic, heroic proportions, although the Baron is neither the dashing romantic hero of *Evil...*, nor the one-dimensional obsessive seeker of knowledge in *Frankenstein Created Woman*. John Elder finally got the complexities of the Baron right, submitting a script that allows Peter Cushing to add a new dimension to his faithful old friend the Baron. And while Hammer's faltering budget was beginning to show, Terence Fisher mounted a wonderful production with a creepy asylum set and superior acting by the entire cast, even the bit players. Though unjustly maligned and viewed as fluff when compared to *Must Be Destroyed*, *Frankenstein and the Monster from Hell* is one of the best entries in the series, from the point of view of overall story, acting, and Cushing's always impressive performance. The film is only compromised by the horrible execution of the Monster (here played by Dave Prowse), which rivals the ineptness of the Monster in *Evil*.

By this time in the series, the Baron's work has been published and copied by eager young apprentices, in this case Dr. Simon Helder (Shane Briant). The obsessed young scientist pays grave robbers for fresh corpses. The police search Helder's home laboratory, where they find the stolen corpse and a jar of human eyeballs. Panicking, an officer spills the eyes, to the disgust of the doctor—"You bloody fool. If only you could appreciate the difficulty in getting specimens like these!" Calmly admitting he plans to "stitch them [body parts] together to create a new man," the doctor is arrested for "sorcery" and sentenced to five years in the State Asylum for the Criminally Insane. Young Helder protests, "I am a doctor, you know. I've been involved in research...for the good of mankind," but the judge is not impressed and informs the young doctor that he sentenced, years ago, a Baron Frankenstein to the same asylum for similar offenses. At this point Simon's eyes light up.

When he arrives at the medieval-appearing asylum, the cruel guards give the cooperative surgeon an "initiation" whereby a fire hose is turned on him,

John Elder allowed Peter Cushing to add a new dimension to the Frankenstein character in *Frankenstein and the Monster from Hell.*

which injures him and knocks him unconscious. As all the inmates stand around enjoying this sadistic entertainment, the festivities are brought to a somber conclusion with the sudden appearance of the asylum's resident physician—Baron Victor Frankenstein!

"Go back to your rooms. It's all over. Quietly, don't rush." To the guards, he snaps in a firmer tone, "You will follow me..." The Baron quickly leads them to the office of the Asylum Director, a quirky, nervous sort who talks too much as though to hide his insecurity. At this point the Baron catches the Director with a half-dressed girl, obviously an inmate he has been forcing himself upon. "Don't act like an animal toward my patients!" the Baron yells. "If that happens again, I'll leave this place. The Baron is dead, remember? As resident doctor I can leave." The Director immediately reprimands the guards for their cruelty per Frankenstein's instructions. The patients really are running the asylum, as

Shane Briant, Cushing and Madeline Smith in *Frankenstein and the Monster from Hell*

it is clear that Frankenstein is in charge. The Baron complains to the Director that he has been unable to pick up his special medical supplies because past bills have not been paid. The Director agrees to rectify the situation immediately after the Baron reminds him that the asylum's budget for library books does not include rare collector's items such as the ones on the Director's desk. It is apparent that the clever Baron has dug up enough dirt on the Director that he can now call the shots. After at first refusing the brandy the Director offers, the Baron now says, "I'll take that brandy." The Director, smiling, assumes the Baron will drink with him here in his office. "No, I'll take it with me. I have work to do!" the Baron snaps.

The Baron and his female assistant Sarah (Madeline Smith), a mute girl who is called "the angel" by the inmates because of her kind and caring nature, see to Simon's wounds. Helder of course recognizes the Baron and announces that he has read his published works and has been trying to duplicate his experiments, without much success. The Baron needs an assistant to help treat the inmates because he requires "more time to devote…to my own private work." Frankenstein immediately forces the Director to sign the papers making Simon his new assistant with all privileges. As the Baron tells the Director, "He is no more insane than you or I." The irony here is that both men, the Baron and the Director, are of questionable mental health. The two main points the Baron stresses to Simon are that Baron Frankenstein is dead and buried in the courtyard out back, and that before he "passed on," "the Baron collected some notes on how this establishment is run," putting him in a position of power at the asylum where the Baron is known as Dr. Carl Victor.

The Baron makes the medical rounds with Simon, telling the young apprentice that these will be his duties tomorrow. We meet a man standing against his cell wall, his arms outstretched, who believes the he is God. The Baron declares, "He's not the first man, nor will he be the last man, who thinks he is God." Of course the obvious analogy to the Baron makes the viewer question the so-called genius and/or insanity of the Baron himself. The Baron points out a special section, claiming these are his very special patients that he will continue to care for himself. The first cell is empty, the thick metal bars are twisted and torn. The Baron claims the inmate committed suicide by jumping 30 feet and still refused to die. The Baron notes his "pure animal strength," calling the inmate a "throwback, more animal than human." Then they call upon the Professor, a man who loves playing and composing music for the violin. He composed a song called "The Angel" for Sarah, whom he claims "is more beautiful than music." The Professor is a student of pure mathematical theory—formulas are scrawled all over the walls. He claims math is "almost as beautiful as this one here," referring to Sarah. The Baron calls the Professor a genius, but claims when roused he becomes as savage as a cat (and has viciously attacked the Director in the past). Another inmate carves beautiful statues, one of an angel he gives to Sarah. "See those hands…Would you think it possible for those hands to do this sort of work?" the Baron asks Simon. Slowly it becomes apparent that the Baron uses patients in his special ward, much like his Poor Hospital in *Revenge of Frankenstein*—as a reserve for body parts needed in future experiments. However, he manages to disguise this fact for some time. Fisher's direction of the individual inmates is interesting and a highlight of the film. The twisted turnabout of having the anti-societal Baron running the insane asylum is more than just a tad ironic. His position of power is juxtaposed to all the kindly, misunderstood and sympathetic "lunatics" locked inside, while the obviously perverted and unbalanced Director is a pawn of the Baron. Elder's script seeks to have the audience question the concept of insanity, and who really here in the asylum is insane; the answer is not easy or obvious.

Simon, discovering a secret entrance used by Sarah, enters to find a beastly monster locked in a steel cell. Obviously the man who fell 30 feet to his death did not stay dead. He also notices the hands of the sculptor have been crudely sewn to the monstrous hairy limbs of this "throwback." The Baron proudly declares, when Simon notices these hands, "It is an accomplished fact, something I hope you appreciate."

Speechless, Simon slowly utters, "I've heard you were a *brilliant* surgeon," to which the Baron answers, "I was, still am, in here," pointing to his head. Still wearing the black gloves from the last John Elder–scripted *Created Woman*, the Baron slowly peels off the gloves to reveal burned, deformed hands. "They were burned in the interest of science." Thus, Sarah's crude surgery accounts for the piecemeal Monster before them. Simon excitedly announces he is not just a doctor but also a surgeon, and for the first time in a long while, the Baron's eyes light up.

During an operation, which Simon performs, the elder teacher watches Simon like a hawk ("No, never use a dirty instrument!") and is impressed as new eyes are added to his creation. At the conclusion the Baron, with an air of anticipation about him, says, "In one hour we will see!" To which Simon smiles and retorts, "Let us hope it is he who sees!" For the first time, the Baron repeats the obvious joke, laughing out loud. "I like that!" Thus, a very human, low-key moment erupts from the formerly rigid, humorless Baron. Little touches such as this one add a layer of humanity to the stuffy old Baron's character.

The only thing left, as the Baron declares, is a brain, "preferably the brain of a genius." Simon immediately fears that the Baron intends to kill the kindly old professor for his brain. "I'm not a murderer, Simon," the Baron indignantly utters. However, the next morning the Professor is found dead, having hanged himself with his violin strings. The Baron coolly proclaims, "The question of a brain has been settled." Only later does Simon find a medical record note in the Professor's violin case that claims the Professor's is "incurable." Simon obviously understands why the Baron allowed the note to fall within reach of the professor. The Baron defends himself, stating, "I was unable to cure him—could you? Then…he was incurable." Thus technically the Baron is correct when he stated he wasn't a murderer, but he is guilty of orchestrating the ultimate depression that led the Professor to kill himself, bringing the same practical results as a cold-blooded murder would have produced.

Unfortunately, although the brain transplant is successful, the desired results are not. The Baron Frankenstein of Bert Batt's *Must Be Destroyed* script would never share credit or act humbly, but the Baron of Elder's script is quite willing to give credit where due. Immediately after the operation, the Baron states, "Simon, thank you! Ten days… If I've succeeded, every sacrifice would have been worthwhile." To which Simon says, "You've done it!" The Baron corrects, "No, *we've* done it, the *three* of us," even crediting Sarah. However, during the monster's convalescence, the beast becomes frustrated while groping for his violin, which he smashes in his depression. The Baron loses patience, demanding, "You must learn to use them [his hands]. You will learn. You must practice coordination!"

Finally, the Baron admits defeat, claiming, "We failed, Simon. At least I failed… the body is rejecting the brain; the man will become a cabbage and

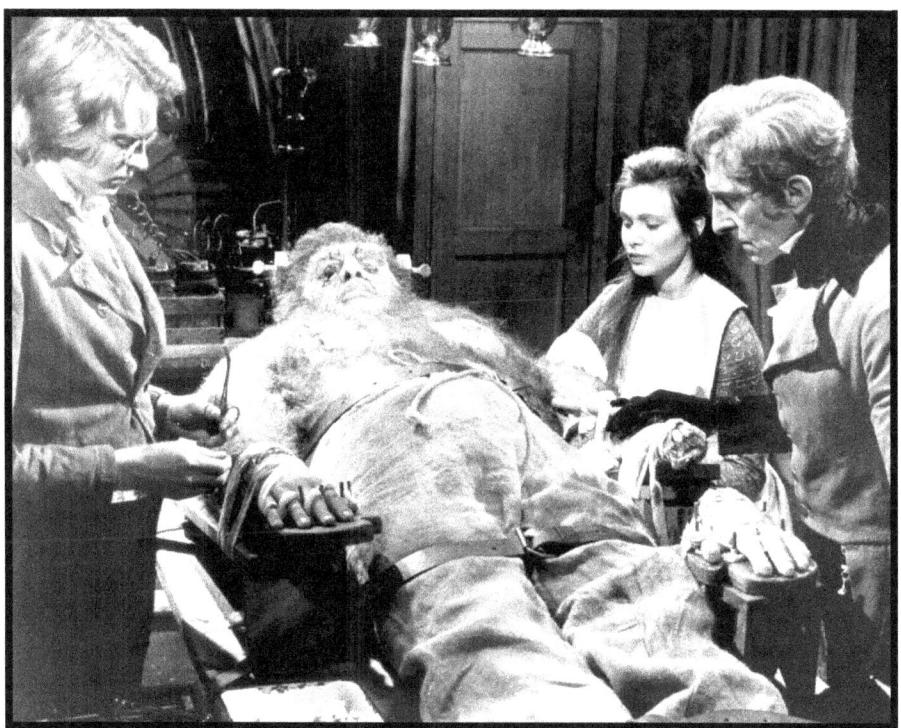

Sarah's crude surgical skills account for the mismatched Creature (David Prowse).

die." Simon tells the Baron he must be patient. Soon the Monster reverts to his old brain mentality (before the transplant), picking up shattered pieces of glass, which he uses as a weapon (something the Professor never did). Once when the glass-wielding fiend is threatening Simon, the Baron, in classic Cushing style, smashes a bottle of sleeping gas within a cloak, jumps upright upon a table, and dives onto the Monster's back. He pulls the cloak over the Monster's head, rendering the fiend unconscious as it struggles to throw the pest from his shoulders, much like a bucking bronco desires to throw a cowboy to the dirt in a rodeo. At over 60 years of age, Cushing still displays that kinetic vigor of old.

"We were both right and wrong. The body is taking over the brain... there is still a way to succeed!" the Baron proclaims. His bizarre plan is to "capture the essence of the man, that a new version of the man is born." Frankenstein plans to mate the Monster with Sarah, an idea that shocks Simon. Simon warns, "You cannot divorce science from humanity," displaying the fact that Simon is a youthful mirror image of the Baron, but a mirror image with a soul and conscience, the tragic flaw missing in the Baron's character. Adding sexist drivel, the Baron declares, "Her real function as a woman could be fulfilled." The Baron warns Simon, "Don't do anything stupid." Of course any man would try to stop this ghastly experiment!

Attempting to stab and destroy the beast before it savages its beauty, Simon is momentarily distracted by the Angel herself, and the Monster grabs his wrist and escapes. The Director and inmates see the fiend digging up graves in the courtyard, apparently wanting to see where his secondhand body parts originated. After killing the Director by slitting his throat with a piece of glass, the Monster slowly ambles down into the lower inmate cell area. The guards fire pistols and the Monster doubles over in pain. The sympathetic Angel offers her out-stretched hand for support. However, the inmates, fearing that Sarah will be injured, brutally attack and kill the beast. Entering the scene, the wounded Baron takes control. "Silence! Go back to your rooms. It's all over now. All over." Turning to the guards, he smugly utters, "*Now* you can use your hose. Make this place clean."

The final sequence is impressive, displaying a very energetic and invigorated Baron speaking to Simon. "We have a lot of work—too much reliance on surgery, not enough on biochemistry. He was of no more use to himself or us. This was the best thing that could have happened. But next time! We shall start afresh!" With that twinkle in the eye and hope in the future, the Baron, having only lost one small battle, prepares to win the war. Never discouraged, never defeated, he eagerly prepares to begin his work anew. Unfortunately, Hammer never continued the series, but at least the final screen appearance of Baron Frankenstein displays exultation and childlike enthusiasm at the thought of continuing his work, no matter how unrealistic these goals may be.

But somehow, this final impression of Cushing as the Baron is also a little sad. By now everyone in the theater realizes that the show is over for the Baron, that the escape of the Monster, the murder of the Director, and the spectacle observed by the inmates themselves cannot be easily swept under the carpet and forgotten, as the Baron assumes it will. The jig is obviously up. Investigations would expose the obvious fact that an inmate is running the asylum and that the Baron's secret position of power would be exposed. Even though he earlier threatened to simply walk out and leave the asylum, and now he expresses a similar desire to continue his work, the fact remains that the Baron, no matter how clever he might be, is reacting in an unrealistic manner. In basic terms, intelligent or not, much like the kindly Professor whose violent rages got him locked away forever in an asylum cell, the Baron is obviously insane and is acting out a dream fantasy. After a lifetime of fighting society and its confining, conservative mores and laws, the combatant Baron has finally cracked under the pressure. No longer viewed as cruel nor cold-blooded (at least as the earlier Bert Batt script depicted him), the Baron finally becomes an object of our pity, a sad, pathetic, broken man, who never achieves his cherished goals of a lifetime. On this note, the Hammer series concludes.

We must always bear in mind that the Hammer *Frankenstein* series was never concocted as a continuing series from its conception. Hammer Films,

much like Val Lewton films decades before, were sold on titles, star appeal and Monster/name recognition. Just as lack of continuity often marred the Christopher Lee *Dracula* films, the *Frankenstein*/Cushing series only contained one constant—Peter Cushing. The screenplays revolved between Jimmy Sangster, John Elder and Bert Batt. The director in five films was Terence Fisher, but Freddie Francis directed the fourth entry. Thus, when speaking of the evolving character of Baron Victor Frankenstein (aka Dr. Franck, Dr. Stein, Dr. Victor, etc.), we are not speaking of one artistic vision written and directed by the same team or same person. Instead, we are speaking of the dedication and vision of one talented thespian to imbue craft, caring and passion into a "B" film characterization that rises far above and beyond the parameters of low-budget filmmaking.

Peter Cushing, Veronica Carlson and Terence Fisher

Working with a variety of writers, more than one director, constantly changing casts, weaker or stronger scripts, the talents of Peter Cushing shine brightly and serve as a unifying artistic beacon which merges all the disparate components of the series into a unified whole. No small feat!

Whether dealing with the Baron's aristocracy and single-minded determination of Jimmy Sangster's initial script, through the creation of the dichotomy of character inherent in Sangster's second entry—whereby the genteel public-persona Baron is contrasted to the actual self-serving butcher of the underprivileged in *Revenge of Frankenstein*; whether dealing with Jimmy Sangster's vision of the Baron as dashing romantic hero or obsessive—yet somehow lovable nonetheless, self-absorbed scientist; whether dealing with Bert Batt's conception of the Baron as someone ultimately evil and cold-bloodedly cruel, committing whatever acts necessary to achieve his goals; or whether dealing with John Elder's final script whereby the Baron, obviously out of touch with reality, eagerly looks forward to the continuation of his work even though his ruse of being the resident doctor at the State Insane Asylum has been exposed; the one constant force which melds all these contrasting elements together is Peter Cushing. Cushing is an actor who spent his entire career proving that low-budget movie acting, while not Shakespeare, could be just as serious, emotional, expansive and ultimately *moving*. Whether playing the Baron as a hero or as the personification of pure evil, Cushing made the viewer care about his persona and respond accordingly. Whether committing murder, portraying the dashing romantic hero of the boudoir, or lecturing on the stupidity of the common citizen, Peter Cushing made Baron Victor Frankenstein coherent, consistent and believable, even if the opposing and oftentimes contrasting character changes in each successive script did not. For one rare time, an acting talent solidified the artistic vision of a movie series much more so than did even the writers, producers and directors involved. Meshing separate pieces from different puzzles, to use an analogy, the superlative talents of Peter Cushing allowed him to create a cohesive whole, an artistic vision that satisfied, where everything somehow fit—amazing as this might sound. He forged this vision by the sheer determination of talent and will. Peter Cushing was more than the ace up Hammer's sleeve; he was, quite simply, the entire franchise.

SCI-FI
X—The Uknown
by Ed Bansak

"Originality" is seldom the first word that springs to mind when we think of Hammer's catalogue of monsters. Given their numerous revamps of classic menaces from Hollywood's Golden Age of Horror, we are prone to overlook the studio's major *original* contribution to cinema's gallery of nightmares: that oozing, shapeless mass of creeping terror that we have affectionately come to call *the blob*. In fact, Hammer gave sci-fi cinema—in quick succession—its first blob movies: 1955's *The Quatermass Experiment* (U.S. *The Creeping Unknown)*; 1956's *X—The Unknown* (U.S. release July 1957); and 1957's *Quatermass 2* (U.S. *Enemy From Space*).

True, *The Quatermass Xperiment*, the first of this blobish trio, did not offer a species that could travel through screen doors (that distinction came with *X—The Unknown*), but Victor Carroon's harrowing transformation into a creeping monstrosity—via Richard Wordsworth's marvelous mute performance, Phil Leakey's chilling makeup and Les Bowie's wonderfully restrained special effects—surely had a significant impact upon the genesis of the prototypic *blob* movie (its "contaminated man" motif being repeated in such 1950s subgenre offerings as *The Blob* (1958), *Caltiki* (1959) and *First Man Into Space* (1959).

On the other hand, *Quatermass 2* offered a more definitive blob menace (a chain-link fence means nothing to this rascal), but it was relegated to the film's final few minutes, providing just enough time for three misbegotten masses of gelatinous matter to galumph about the set before being sent to blob heaven. Despite *Quatermass*

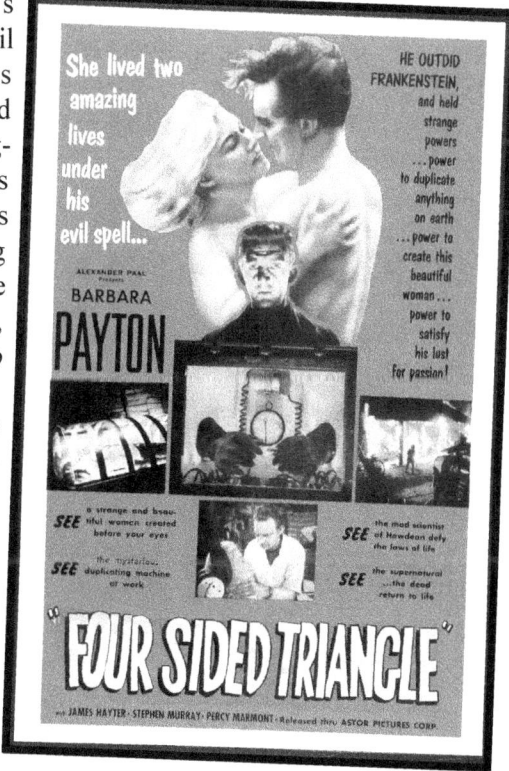

2's marginal qualifications as a Blob movie, it is, more accurately, a near-brilliant British cousin to Don Siegel's alien-doppelganger film, *Invasion of the Body Snatchers* (1956), with gestating blobbettes (if you will) substituting for pods.

If the excellent *Quatermass* adaptations have long been given their due, the overshadowed *X—The Unknown* remains an ill-begotten child in the eyes of even some of the studio's staunchest admirers, as if it were of the same humdrum quality as Hammer's desultory sci-fi efforts of the previous season, *Spaceways* and *The Four-Sided Triangle* (both 1953). Not only is *X—The Unknown* an above-average sci-fi entry of the mid-1950s, but it also has the historic distinction of being the first film to feature an ambulatory blob as its central—rather than peripheral—plot gimmick.

Taken together, *X—The Unknown* and the *Quatermass* pair were vital in paving the way for a vicious wave of other such blobbish entertainments, including 1957's *The Unknown Terror* (where fungi bubble-baths inhabit a mad scientist's cavernous basement), *The Blob* (whose titular character, cherry-red and gummy, never falls to bring on a hankering for another box of Dots), 1958's *The Flame Barrier* (here a cluster of extra-terrestrial marshmallows becomes fused to a U.S. satellite), 1958's *Space Master X-7* (with something like burnt pizza topping—Hold the anchovies!—running amuck aboard an airplane), 1958's *The H-Man* (where Japanese gangsters are transformed into fully-clothed puddles of rubber cement), *Caltiki* (in which throbbing mounds of oily lines, dating back to the ancient Mayans, begin reproducing like rabbits), *First Man Into Space* (where an astronaut's entire NASA wardrobe is ruined by an oozing alien skin rash), 1964's *The Creeping Terror* (lead non-actor, Vic Savage, being savagely victimized by a ambulating throw-rug), and 1965's *Mutiny in Outer Space* (which dares ask the perennial question, "Is there a fungus among us?"). [NOTE: Okay, I admit that I love all of the aforementioned films—easy targets all—and that I would rather watch *any* of them for the umpteenth time than be exposed to a Full Moon offering from Charles Band, but it is difficult to write about Blob movies without developing an occasional case of Gene Shalitosis—or could it be Forry Ackermania?—My apologies.]

X—The Unknown, the only film in cinema history to actually include the question "How do you kill mud?" as part of its dialogue, was Hammer's unabashed attempt to follow up their surprise 1955 British hit, *The Quatermass Xperiment*, with a film of a similar kind—a very similar kind. The earlier production, directed by Val Guest and based on writer Nigel Kneale's tremendously successful 1953 BBC television serial (*The Quatermass Experiment*), provided the most significant turning point in Hammer film history. David Pirie, in *A Heritage of Horror*, tells us:

> Within a few months [of *Xperiment's* release] Hammer had drawn up a completely new production schedule for

1956, throwing out the long-planned King Charles and the *Roundheads* in favor of two more horror/science fiction subjects *X—The Unknown* and *Quatermass 2*, and opening negotiations for the Frankenstein character. It was the beginning of a quiet cinematic revolution.

Using the *Quatermass* teleplays (the second of which had been aired on BBC in 1955) as his models, neophyte screenwriter Jimmy Sangster fashioned an intelligent sci-fi thriller in the Nigel Kneale mold. No doubt Sangster had heard that Kneale would soon be working at Hammer, collaborating with Val Guest on the screenplay of the second *Quatermass* film. Kneale had not had a hand in the screen adaptation of the first *Quatermass* teleplay, which was co-scripted by Richard Landau and Val Guest. A future collaboration between Kneale and director Guest would deliver a film version of Kneale's BBC-produced 1956 (sans *Quatermass*) teleplay, *The Creature*, a fresh, intelligent and altogether mystical interpretation of the Yeti legend—released by Hammer in 1957 as *The Abominable Snowman of the Himalayas*. Clearly, by 1956, the Hammer execs had seen the future of the British sci-fi film and his name was Nigel Kneale.

But even while the latter's arrival was being eagerly awaited, it could be said, given the derivative nature of Jimmy Sangster's original story and screenplay for *X—The Unknown,* that the spirit of Nigel Kneale had already found active employment at Hammer's Bray Studios. Sangster, whose screenwriting debut this was, rose to the occasion and turned *X—The Unknown* into an often ripping-good *Quatermass* facsimile.

True, the film has its share of flaws and is, admittedly, not of the same superior caliber as *The Quatermass Xperiment* (or its sequel, for that matter); *X—The Unknown*'s second half is seriously marred by the onscreen appearance of its peculiarly depersonalized menace, and while Dean Jagger's nice-guy scientist, Dr. Adam Royston, may be more convincing than Brian Donlevy's gruff and ill-humored Professor Quatermass, his character is also far less compelling. Such drawbacks aside, *X—The Unknown* is an intelligent, atmospheric and well-acted sci-fi thriller, one that is refreshingly adult in its approach.

Much of the credit for the film's strong first portion goes to director Leslie Norman, who joined the production early in January 1956 when its original director, Joe Walton, contracted pneumonia after a few days shooting at Gerrard's Cross, Scotland. Norman, whose auspicious directorial debut had been 1954's acutely paranoid *The Night My Number Came Up,* strove to recreate, in *X—The Unknown,* some of the same dark magic that had been integral to the success of *The Quatermass Xperiment.* Like its *Quatermass* predecessor, which would soon play in America as the similarly-titled *The Creeping Unknown, X—The Unknown* makes superior use of its natural locale, in this case offering several memorably eerie passages set amid an oppressively barren Scottish landscape, a place that would give anyone the creeps—day or night. Shot with an expressionistic bent by cinematographer Gerald Gibbs, whose camerawork would soon grace *Quatermass 2,* the film's best scenes—a scary walk-in-the-woods by two boys, a man's dark descent into an earth fissure, and two soldiers' encounter with *X* on a desolate marshland—make strong use of the "undisclosed horror" approach that had also proven vital to *Xperiment*'s success. The terrifying results speak for themselves.

Compared to some of the puerile sci-fi efforts coming from Hollywood at the time, *X—The Unknown* warrants a certain admiration.

The opening credits are unusually captivating, with some imaginative lettering effects (a black, oily pool metamorphosing into the titular X); instead of a sweeping orchestral soundtrack in the grand old sci-fi horror tradition there is absolute silence until—we begin to recognize the plaintive calls of some manner of wild bird, an eerie aural accompaniment to the haunted wasteland that is unwinding before us. A cleverly placed camera tracks a soldier's progress along a barren, puddle-infested expanse of saturated terrain, giving us our first look at the locale that is as spooky as it is provocative. The fact that it appears to be midday does not make this area any less forbidding. As the camera pulls back, we see a division of soldiers engaged in a "hucklebuckle beanstalk" [children's game where someone hides an object and the others search for it] game involving Geiger counters and previously placed radioactive samples. When one soldier discovers an aberrant source of radiation coming from the soaked ground underfoot—where no sample has been placed—a fissure opens and belches up a deadly dose of radiation. As two radiation-burnt soldiers are rushed to the hospital, so begins the series of inexplicable deaths upon which the film's mystery is based.

X—The Unknown, like so many science fiction films of its era, is structured as a mystery and, as in most early-1950s sci-fi films where scientists play detective (*The Thing, Phantom From Space, It Came From Outer Space, The Magnetic Monster, Them!, The Quatermass Xperiment*, etc.), the mystery at hand is not a "whodunit" but a "whatisit?" Because of the nature of the mystery, it is not uncommon for such films to keep their menaces offscreen until the closing reels and, of course, *X—The Unknown* is no exception. Such a plot formula opens the door for any number of horrific scenes, the most typical employing tried-and-true combinations of spooky settings, ominous sounds and unseen intruders. As Robert Bloch once said, in an article in one of the early issues of *Famous Monsters*, most sci-fi films of the 1950s were "horror films in science fiction disguise." As a horror film, *X—The Unknown* holds up its end of the bargain exceptionally well.

One radiation expert, Dr. Adam Royston (Dean Jagger), is brought into the picture, an ingeniously chilling transition—"let's not conjure up visions of nameless horrors creeping around in the night," says one of our protagonists as he drives off in his car, leaving the audience behind. This places us in a nearby section of woods where, there in the dark, we spy two children, one of them daring the other to approach the "haunted" tower in the forest in order to catch a glimpse of the old hermit rumored to live there. With considerable trepidation, the boy approaches the stark building, his crunching footsteps accenting an atmosphere ripe with apprehension, and finds himself confronted by—some terrifying presence. A static-like crackle fills the air just before the youth breaks into a run, the unseen menace presumably nipping at his heels.

Because of its "undisclosed horror" approach, *X—The Unknown*'s boys-in-the-woods sequence is a terror gem. Outside of its quotient of chills, it is disturbingly adult in its use of juvenile characters. After all, although the boy narrowly escapes, the damage has been done; he is destined to die the next day in a hospital bed, the victim of radiation burns. In Hollywood films, the likelihood that a monster would kill a child was virtually zero, and had been that way since the controversial drowning scene in James Whale's *Frankenstein.* Aside from its grim outcome, the aforementioned terror sequence is so well staged, its darkly provocative use of natural locale so fully realized, that it demands the admiration of any horror film fan. Cinematographer Gibbs wisely chose to shoot this on-location sequence during actual night and the extra trouble was well worth it; the baleful atmosphere of this startling, albeit brief, sequence anticipates the look and mood of those marvelous spooky-forest passages in Jacques Tourneur's British-produced *The Night of the Demon,* which was released in America as *Curse of the Demon* when, in 1958, it played the bottom half of a double-bill with Hammer's *Revenge of Frankenstein*.

X—The Unknown shocked audiences when a child (Michael Brooke) was killed.

The child's death brings the authorities to the fore. Joining Dr. Royston is a police official named McGill (Leo McKern). The dead boy's parents blame Royston, thinking his experiments in radioactivity are somehow the cause of the tragedy. Soon, other incidental characters become victims of the unseen crackling menace and, courtesy of the military, the town is put under a state of emergency. Of particular note is one surprisingly graphic scene where a hospital intern's face melts away from his skull, the result of his proximity to the unknown menace. The scene where two soldiers on watch (one of them played by Anthony Newley, no less) are confronted by the creature's nocturnal approach is satisfyingly gripping; moreover, its impact is not diminished by its admittedly lame provision of comic relief. Also good is the sequence where Peter Elliot (William Lucas), the obligatory younger-and-more-athletic-adult-

hero, is lowered into a fissure to investigate the source of the radiation; the shots of his descent are especially claustrophobic and his unexpectedly panicky reaction to the radiation-hungry monster is so convincing that we almost get rope burns trying to help pull the poor fool up the surface. Unfortunately, this effective set piece is nearly ruined by Sangster's ill-advised decision to have his surviving eyewitness hero spout, "I don't know what it was. It was something out of a nightmare!" Elliot's preposterously vague (and utterly unscientific) report becomes risible once we see the menace; odd as this species of monster may be, it is hardly beyond the reach of facile description. Meanwhile, Royston surmises that the radioactive creature, whatever it looks like, must come from the earth's molten core.

Alas, once we get a glimpse of the mysterious creature, the film takes a pedestrian turn. Clearly, the creature's appearance doesn't jibe with the petrified reactions of its previous victims, all of which have misled us to expect something much more horrific than mud-on-parade. Despite the inherent silliness of the concept, Hammer technicians Les Bowie and Jack Curtis, who were likely inspired by volcanic lava sequences from films like 1935's *Last Days of Pompeii* or 1940's *One Million B.C.* nicely execute the special effects for the mud monster. The only problem was that *X—The Unknown*'s radioactive mudflows, however nicely rendered, were not nearly as frightening as good, old-fashioned molten lava. Having grown up in the 1950s, with eyes glued to that wonderful showcase for old movies called television, I can plainly remember three of my greatest cinema-inspired childhood fears: molten lava, quicksand and atomic radiation. Considering that the potential was there to exploit all three such movie phobias, the creature from *X—The Unknown* is not very frightening (a regular stick-in-the-mud, as far as screen monsters go).

According to Hammer executive James Carreras (as quoted in John Brosnan's *Horror People*):

> We found that the "thing"...in *X—The Unknown* frightened nobody. They are only really terrified by something they are likely to meet in the dark on the way home from the cinema.

Although director Norman makes a last-ditch attempt to generate some suspense by mimicking the save-the-baby-from-the-lava scene from *One Million B.C.*, the film's climax is largely disappointing, with Dr. Royston finally disposing of the monster through the use of "electronic rays."

If *X—The Unknown* is not everything it could have been, it is decidedly better than it might have been. Aside from its being the first "authentic" *blob* movie, the Norman/Sangster collaboration was also the first of a long line of decidedly horrific British-produced *Quatermass* facsimiles. Leslie Norman's direction—at least in the first half of the film—exhibits a style reminiscent of the Val Lewton films of the previous decade. Of course, the same could be said of Norman's model—*The Quatermass Xperiment* also championed the less-is-more approach to terror exemplified by the Lewton films.

Without question, Hammer established the reigning trend in British science fiction cinema and the two *Quatermass* films, sandwiched around *X—The Unknown*, ushered in a "man vs. menace" sci-fi formula that was actually the cinematic equivalent of a British literary tradition founded by H.G. Wells.

Although British sci-fi films were not very popular in the decade to follow, those that were produced displayed an uncanny loyalty to the literate and subtly terrifying standards established by the Nigel Kneale films and their most immediate facsimile, *X—The Unknown*. As a result of this influence, Britain's subsequent sci-fi offerings—at least for the next 10 years—were usually more adult than their Hollywood contemporaries. Such 1956 stateside entries as *World Without End, Earth Vs. the Flying Saucers, The Beast from Hollow Mountain,* and *The Mole People* displayed Hollywood's ever-increasing tendency to pander to the juvenile trade. By the time of *X—The Unknown*'s 1957 American release (on a double-bill with Hammer's *The Curse of Frankenstein*), Hollywood's juvenile bent was no less apparent, what with films like *Beginning of the End, The Giant Claw, Invasion of the Saucer Men, 20 Million Miles to Earth, The Land Unknown, The Black Scorpion, The Invisible Boy,* and the infamously titled duo, *I Was a Teenage Werewolf/I Was a Teenage Frankenstein*. By 1958, with rock 'n' roll firmly entrenched in the collective psyche of America's youth, the trend only escalated.

It was difficult to make mud frightening.

It is no secret that the "X" used in the titles of both *The Quatermass Xperiment* and *X—The Unknown* was Hammer's way of flaunting the strictly enforced adult rating (*X for Horror*—under 17 not admitted) that the British censorship board reserved for all horror films; consequently, British sci-fi horror films, unlike their American counterparts, were fashioned for the adult market. In Britain, *X—The Unknown* shared a double-bill with Henri Georges Clouzot's horrific (and equally X-rated) French thriller, *Diabolique,* and the combination proved to be box-office gold.

Subsequent British science fiction films that owed some degree of debt to the adult approach pioneered by Hammer include such non-Hammer efforts as *Fiend Without a Face* (1957), *The Strange World of Planet X* (1957, aka *Cosmic Monsters*), *The Trollenberg Terror* (1958, aka *The Crawling Eye*, screenplay by Jimmy Sangster), *Satellite of Blood* (1959, aka *First Man Into Space*), *Village of the Damned* (1960, based on John Wyndham's *The Midwich Cuckoos*), *The Day the Earth Caught Fire* (1961, directed by Val Guest), *Children of the Damned* (1963, a sequel to *Village*), *The Day of the Triffids* (1963, another John Wyndham property), *Unearthly Stranger* (1963), *The Earth Dies Screaming* (1964), *Crack in the World* (1965), *The Night Caller* (1965), *Island of Terror* (1966), and *Night of the Big Heat* (1967). This chronology brings us full circle, as 1967 also saw the release of Roy Ward Baker's *Quatermass and the Pit* (U.S. title: *Five Million Years to Earth*).

As is readily apparent to anyone familiar with the preceding list, British sci-fi films tended to be more thoughtful, more sober and often more imaginative than their Hollywood contemporaries; even the more exploitative British outings—*The Crawling Eye, Fiend Without a Face, The Giant Behemoth, First Man Into Space*—were characterized by earnest direction, intelligent performances and sharply written screenplays. In retrospect, it makes perfect sense that Stanley Kubrick's benchmark sci-fi films, *2001, A Space Odyssey* (1968) and *A Clockwork Orange* (1971), would be British productions adapted from the works of British writers Arthur C. Clarke and Anthony Burgess, respectively.

Unlike so many of the sci-fi films made in Hollywood, Britain's genre offerings were usually thankfully free of mawkish romancing scientists. Where our movie scientists seemed to be forever distracted by curvy heroines, their British-film counterparts—even when played by aging American actors—exuded the kind of no-nonsense attitude that precluded roving eyes and the use of smarmy pickup lines. Certainly, Donlevy's Professor Quatermass and Jagger's Dr. Royston are far cries from the amorous "Hollywood" scientists epitomized by John Agar in *Revenge of the Creature* (1954), *Tarantula* (1955), *The Mole People* (1956) and *The Brain from Planet Arous* (1958). The only thing Dr. Adam Royston flirts with is radioactivity, his favorite pickup techniques require lead-lined suits, and the only curves he's really interested in are those charted by his laboratory instruments.

British sci-fi films also put a higher premium upon the establishment of a provocative atmosphere; compare Britain's *The Giant Behemoth* with Hollywood's *The Beast from 20,000 Fathoms* (1953), two dinosaur films directed by the same hand—Eugène Lourié—and you'll see what I mean. *Beast* may be far superior in the special effects department, but *Behemoth* is a richer film, pictorially, with horrific touches that put it squarely in the tradition of *X—The Unknown.* Notice that, exactly like *X—The Unknown,* the first half of *The Giant Behemoth* is primarily a number of spooky episodes, often shot in atmospheric, natural locations, all of which chronicle the progress of an offscreen menace whose proximity to incidental characters results in deadly radiation burns. Director Lourié shot the third film of his dino-trilogy, *Gorgo* (1961), in Britain as well.

This British preference for provocative on-location settings is just one more carry-over from the blueprint established by Hammer in the mid-1950s, a blueprint the studio quickly discarded once Technicolor revisionist horror films became a more lucrative venture. After 1957's Val Guest/Nigel Kneale collaboration, *Abominable Snowman of the Himalayas* (released in the wake of *The Curse of Frankenstein),* Hammer washed their hands of the sci-fi film genre, continued building period sets that would look good in color, and told aging American actors to get lost. Although *Famous Monsters of Filmland* would repeatedly announce Hammer's forthcoming adaptation of *Quatermass and the Pit,* even including a still or two from the television serial, it became increasingly apparent that the project was destined to remain in limbo with other on-again/off-again productions—remember *The Martian Chronicles* and

The Giant Behemoth is filmed in the tradition of *X—The Unknown*.

When the Sleeper Wakes—that were reported in the magazine? And so Hammer's *Quatermass and the Pit* remained on the shelf. For the next 10 years the studio's only throwback to the *Quatermass* series would be Joseph Losey's ill-fated *The Damned (*1961, aka *These Are the Damned*), which, oddly enough, starred aging American actor MacDonald Carey. Although a critical success, this black-and-white 1963 release proved to be box-office poison, reinforcing the studio's decision to stick with more colorful subjects: vampires, mummies, werewolves and man-made monsters.

When Hammer finally got around to bringing *Quatermass and the Pit* to the screen, nearly a decade had passed since its original 1958 BBC production. The times had changed and the studio with them. By 1967, with more than two dozen profitable horror films under their belt, Hammer's even-increasing reliance upon period sets had resulted in a string of lush, if somewhat studio bound, productions. By that time the studio had settled into a production formula that was often as stagy as it was sumptuous. Although Hammer made good use of exterior sets, their films had become more microcosmic in their scope, their disproportionate number of indoor scenes giving them a theatrical edge and making them feel not unlike adaptations of stage plays.

Even Hammer's interesting batch of modern thrillers, most of them scripted by Jimmy Sangster, borrowing freely from both *Diabolique* and *Psycho*, were characteristically confined to a small geographic radius—usually in-and-around a wealthy estate—with an occasional 1960s automobile substituting for a 19th-century horse-drawn vehicle. Whether for better or worse, it was evident that the studio was no longer interested in the on-location documentary–like scope that had given an air of authenticity to *X—The Unknown* and the original *Quatermass* duo. Consequently, although 1967's *Five Million Years to Earth* was graced with an intelligent, thought-provoking script and solid, credible performances, its all-color/all-studio approach seemed curiously wrongheaded to anyone enamored of the first two *Quatermass* entries. As excellent as the film may be (and there are those who consider it the best of the lot), its artificial look sets it so far apart from its earlier blood relatives that, ultimately, it is *X—The Unknown* that today seems the closer approximation of the spirit and style of the original *Quatermass* films.

X—The Unknown may not be a classic of the first order; in the long run, *Five Million Years to Earth* is the much better film, but this Knealesque excursion helped Hammer pave the way for a series of intelligent, briskly directed, and often very frightening, British-produced science fiction films. Aside from providing the world with one of the earliest *blob* movie prototypes, *X—The Unknown* also proved a significant testing ground for the writing talents of Jimmy Sangster, whose momentous next project would be preparing a screenplay for *The Curse of Frankenstein*. Formerly an assistant director, Sangster would pen the scripts for many of Hammer's most important films, including *Horror of Dracula, Revenge of Frankenstein, The Mummy, The Man Who Could Cheat Death, Brides of Dracula, Scream of Fear, Maniac, Paranoiac, Nightmare, The Nanny*, and several others. So really, not only is *X—the Unknown* a decent little film, but we can also thank it for some of Hammer's best films that flowed from the pen of Mr. Sangster.

Val Guest and Nigel Kneale: Hammer's Dynamic Duo

by Dennis Fischer

Val Guest and Nigel Kneale's production of *The Quatermass Experiment* (U.S. title: *The Creeping Unknown*) in 1955 got Michael Carreras and his father James, the owners of Hammer Films, thinking about *Frankenstein*, leading to the production of *The Curse of Frankenstein* and the full start of the Hammer horror cycle. While Hammer had tried a few marginal science fiction features before—*Stolen Face* (1952), *Four-Sided Triangle* and *Spaceways* (both 1953), all directed by Terence Fisher—*The Quatermass Experiment* was the first to combine science fiction and horror for the soon-to-be world famous company.

Val Guest, who was born in London in 1911, was a frustrated actor (*Innocents of Chicago*, 1931), who turned film journalist, first in England and then in Hollywood where he worked for *The Hollywood Reporter* and *The Los Angeles Examiner*. He returned to England and became an expert comedy man for Will Hay, Arthur Askey, the Crazy Gang and others. He started scripting films beginning with *No Monkey Business* in 1935, and became a writer-director in 1942 with the short *The Nose Has It*. He married Yolande Donlan, who starred in many of his films. Guest became a producer-director with *Penny Princess* (1952) and *The Runaway Bus* (1954), but didn't become a full-time producing hyphenate until *The Full Treatment* (1960, aka *Stop Me Before I Kill*) and *The Day the Earth Caught Fire* (1961).

His first genre project was a minor comedy known as *Mr. Drake's Duck* (1951), which starred Douglas Fairbanks, Jr., Yolande Donlan and future Dr. Who, Jon Pertwee in the story of a duck that lays eggs that are almost pure uranium. Soon the government is all over the Drake farm to discover which duck laid the atomic egg. The level of the film's coy humor may be judged by the fact that the hero's name, Drake, is a male duck.

Guest's first Hammer film was a comedy, *Life*

Opening credits of *The Quatermass Experiment* (BBC, 1953)

with the Lyons (1953), which was followed by *The Lyons in Paris* and *Break in the Circle* (both 1954).

It wasn't until Hammer decided to adapt *Quatermass*, a popular 1953 television serial by a talented Manx writer Nigel Kneale, that the talented Guest and Kneale would team up. Their creation of the *Quatermass* films have long been celebrated by science fiction and horror fans.

Nigel Kneale was born Thomas Nigel Kneale in 1922 and attended the Royal Academy of Dramatic Art. He was working as an actor when he began writing short stories and won the Somerset Maugham Literary Prize in 1950. He specialized in fantasies, many of which were collected in *Tomato Cain and Other Stories* (1949).

The Quatermass Experiment was written and produced in the summer of 1953 as a six-part serial, with each part supposedly running a half-hour, but given the difficulties of live television, each part ran from five to 10 minutes over its allotted time. This was the first science fiction program to air on British television. The production was directed and produced by Rudolph Cartier and starred the late Reginald Tate as the amiable middle-class scientist Bernard Quatermass. Unfortunately, due to the BBC's economy measures of the time, it is believed that the tape of the original production was erased subsequently, though both Penguin Books and Arrow Books (including photos) have published editions of the screenplay in England. Kneale revealed that he was still in the process of writing the last episode when it started on the air, and that he himself "played" the final creature by sticking his vegetation-covered rubber gloves through a photo blowup of Poets Corner in the final episode, and that he had selected Westminster Abbey for the finale because it would be familiar to viewers who had just watched the Coronation a few weeks earlier. A live production of *The Quatermass Experiment* was produced in 2005 for British TV. Jason Flemyng starred as Professor Quatermass.

Kneale went on to a much-complimented but little-seen serial adaptation of George Orwell's *Nineteen Eighty-Four* starring Peter Cushing in 1954, and Cushing also starred the next year as Dr. John Rollason in *The Creature,* which was later adapted into *The Abominable Snowman* (U.S. title: *The Abominable Snowman of the Himalayas*). Kneale then devised the first Quatermass sequel, *Quatermass II,* which aired in October to November 1955, and starred John Robinson as the stalwart scientist. When Hammer bought the rights to the *Quatermass* serials, they assigned Guest and American writer Richard Landau to condense Kneale's sprawling epic into a tight 83-minute feature.

Wisely, the pair concentrated on action and suspense, and this being a film, they didn't have to incorporate bridging scenes that would allow the live television actors to change costumes and switch to a different set. Also wise was

Val Guest (right) filming *The Abominable Snowman*

the decision to alter the talky ending of the original in which Quatermass literally talks the space creature to death (by appealing to its assimilated humanity to destroy itself before it propagates and destroys the whole world).

When a tax on imported films was repealed in England in May 1948, it opened the floodgates to American productions, which quickly knocked British productions out of competition. The new law required that a high percentage of American profits in Britain be reinvested in British film activity, which ended up bringing more Americans into the British film industry to take advantage of these "frozen" assets. In 1950, the government set up the British Production Fund to administer a pool of money derived from taxing cinema tickets for the purpose of subsidizing production, but with competition from television, attendance was declining at an alarming rate.

Disastrous as the situation was for British cinema as a whole, it did lead to some notable and successful Anglo-American productions such as Raoul Walsh's *Captain Horatio Hornblower*, John Huston's *The African Queen*, *Moulin Rouge* and *Moby Dick*, David Lean's *Summertime* and *Bridge on the River Kwai* and Disney's *The Story of Robin Hood* and *Treasure Island*. It also got United Artists to pick up *The Quatermass Experiment* for U.S. release and got Hammer the services of American actor Brian Donlevy, notable for his performances as heavies, especially in *Beau Geste*, *The Great McGinty* (in which he played the title role, which he reprised for a cameo in the classic *The Miracle of Morgan's Creek*), *The Remarkable Andrew* (in which he played Andrew Jackson's ghost), *The Glass Key* and *The Big Combo*.

Kneale was outraged that his sedate, middle-class British scientist was played by a forceful, dynamic, authoritarian American actor, who was notable

Quatermass (Brian Donlevy) examines the crashed ship in *The Quatermass Xperiment*.

for his drinking proclivities and bad toupees. His primary concerns were providing realistic characterization (unlike most of the science fiction films he had seen), making the reality of future spaceflight believable (this was pre-Sputnik), and taking British over-confidence down a peg or two. The Quatermass of the teleplay is a far more likeable, less driven character, who feels guilty about the consequences of his project, and ends the play exhausted.

Contrast that with the film's Quatermass, who ends the film undaunted and unbowed, acknowledging that there are risks but that they must be taken, and launching a second rocket into space. Small wonder that Kneale abuses the Guest productions every chance he gets, but as an impartial observer, I admire Kneale's genius for storytelling while preferring the changes that Guest wrought. He and Landau eliminated much of the scientific discussion of the feasibility of spaceflight in favor of launching the film with the memorable scene of a necking couple (in the usually sexless British cinema), whose late night session is interrupted by the rocket's crash and an immediate concern for the inhabitants' safety. Along the way several minor characters were jettisoned, tightening the story further.

Although the subsequent *Quatermass* films would top it, *The Quatermass Experiment* was an above-average piece of science fiction melodrama with good narrative pacing, moody monochrome cinematography by Walter Harvey (the night scenes are far superior to the typical American day-for-night material of the period), and a sparingly used but effective music. The score's tense violins, which are reminiscent of those in *Horror of Dracula*, were written by an uncredited James Bernard, who had won an Academy Award, along with partner Paul Dehn, for the 1950 gem *Seven Days to Noon* (directed by John Boulting), the story of a British scientist who tries to hold the world hostage by threatening to blow up London with an atomic bomb.

A number of sources, including the BFI, list the British title of the film as *The Quatermass Xperiment,* as that was the title on the film's poster, used to emphasize that it was given an "X" rating by the British board of censors. Four minutes were trimmed from the film for its U.S. release, perhaps for gruesomeness, though it seems quite tame nowadays and lacks any of the gore that Hammer would be notable for in later productions.

One aspect of the teleplay that was obscured in its translation to the screen is that the astronauts aboard the ship passed through something that caused their minds to meld into one and then assimilate with any other living thing it touches. While three astronauts went up in the ship, only Victor Carroon (Richard Wordsworth) returns, though with fingerprints that aren't his own. Kneale is quite adept at coming up with mysterious clues that become significant later and whetting audience's interest. The remains of the other astronauts are discovered as jelly in the bulkheads.

The film's only direct connection to this idea comes when Victor goes into a chemist's or druggist's shop and mixes up a potion which, while deadly to humans, acts as a catalyst for his transformation into the inhuman thing he becomes. Victor knew no chemistry, but Quatermass remembers that one of the other astronauts did.

Memorable scenes include Victor striking a cactus and ending up with a hand that is part human and part cactus and a scene where he literally drains the life out of a man in a hospital elevator, leaving a withered and emaciated corpse. These scenes inspired Tobe Hooper, who borrowed them for *Lifeforce*, his adaptation of Colin Wilson's *Space Vampires,* which also borrowed heavily from *Quatermass and the Pit* (U.S. title: *Five Million Years to Earth*). One of Quatermass' most impressive scenes is where the tormented monster meets the innocent young girl, vaguely reminiscent of Karloff's scene in *Frankenstein*, to which it is often compared. The young girl was played by Jane Asher, who would grow up to become Paul McCartney's girlfriend and star in *The Masque of the Red Death* (1964)*, Deep End* (1970), and *Henry VIII and his Six Wives* (1972).

In the magazine *The House of Hammer, #9,* Wordsworth recalled:

> The cactus bit was great fun. My face was covered with rubber solution and I had spikes growing out of my arm. Jane Asher

Richard Wordsworth gave a stunning performance as the doomed astronaut in *The Quatermass Xperiment* (aka *The Creeping Unknown*).

>played the little girl the monster meets. I had to lurch at her and knock the head off her doll. As soon as the scene was finished, there she was crying. Naturally I knelt down to say, "There, there," and everybody started yelling at me, "Get back, you fool!" Of course I was terrifying her. I'd quite forgotten what I looked like.

Wordsworth's mime performance, while not in a league of Karloff's in *Frankenstein*, is still well worth noting. His emaciated body and tormented, expressive face limn suffering well, and when he shambles to his feet, one does get the sense of a man fighting for control—and losing. This especially comes out in the scene with the girl when, to prevent the monster from assimilating her, he scares her away by knocking off the head of her doll. This moment immensely adds to the pathos of his character.

The Quatermass Experiment was a great success, proving for the first time that audiences would pay to see a film version of what they had already seen for *free* on TV, a fact that producers used to their monetary advantage in the '80s, '90s and on through today. Naturally, Hammer manufactured a quick spin-off—the underrated *X–The Unknown*, scripted by Jimmy Sangster. Sangster was Hammer's other premiere scriptwriter, who would later adapt Peter Key's awful Kneale imitation, *The Trollenberg Terror,* for Britain's Associated Television (ATV). The series ran for six episodes from 1956-1957. The series would be made into a film in 1958 (U.S. title *The Crawling Eye*), with Sangster again providing the screenplay.

Although *Experiment* was a good film, the collaboration between Guest and Kneale was not a happy one. Guest made extensive, though intelligent, changes including dropping one major character, Leo Pugh. The Pugh character was an old friend of Quatermass,' who almost betrays him in the final episode. On the teleseries Hugh Griffith played the role. That ending was dropped from the film and replaced with an unmanned atomic rocket wiping out the source of the alien invasion. Guest also combined some characters into the character of Inspector Lomax, who in the second film was played by John Longden, rather than Jack Warner, who had the part in the first film.

Donlevy, whom Kneale described as a "bawling bully," became the only actor to play the Quatermass role twice (Andrew Keir portrayed Quatermass in the third film, *Five Million Years to Earth*, 1967). Though there are reports that he was severely affected by alcoholism, it did not lessen his performance in the finished film. Instead, Donlevy simply seems intensely driven and dedicated. We find him yelling at his subordinates at the beginning of the film, for which he later apologizes, explaining that the funding for his atomic rocket and moon colony projects have just been cut. Once more he is quite believable as a scientist who makes things happen (and in this film he doesn't mispronounce his own name or the word "metabolic" as he did in the first film). Kneale's script switches from a lone monster that is stumbling about, to an isolated Quatermass, who must get past official barriers to uncover the horrible truth.

Kneale's story involves aliens, who control seemingly normal human beings—a basic theme in *Invaders From Mars* (1953), *Invasion of the Body Snatchers* (1956) and *It Conquered the World* (1956), as well as the subject of Robert Heinlein's 1951 novel *The Puppet Masters,* which formed the unofficial basis for Bruno DeSota's *The Brain Eaters* (1958). Kneale wrote his teleplay before *Body Snatchers,* and *Quatermass 2* (1957) was released to the states (as *Enemy from Space*) afterward, the two works didn't influence each other, but it is interesting to note the cultural differences between them.

The prime figure of British films of the mid-1950s is that of the professional male authority figure, usually a doctor, soldier, or pilot, as evidenced by the top-grossing domestic films of the period such as *The Cruel Sea* (1953), *Doctor in the House* (1954), *The Dam Busters* (1955), and *Reach for the Sky* (1956). These "men's men" roles emphasized their heroic masculinity. In the first two *Quatermass* films, Lomax and Quatermass fit into this character mold; however, in *Quatermass 2*, the world of authority has been subverted, invaded by a malignant force that has taken over the government and is adept at covering up its evil plan. Quatermass finds himself in a world where authority can't be trusted, and even Lomax realizes that he can't rely on the head of Scotland Yard because he too has the imprint of control on his wrist. Who is left to mobilize to beat this threat?

The workers of the town of Winnerden Flats naturally have been helping build the facility that feeds the invaders and helps them learn to accommodate themselves to our atmosphere. Thus, they are unsuspecting collaborationists with the invaders, which gives the film a early-Marxian political twist. Quatermass is only allowed into the aliens' facility through the assistance of Vincent Broadhead (Tom Chatto), a crusading opposition MP, who is trying to force a public inquiry into the cover story that the facility is producing artificial food. The cover story proves to be true—but the ammonia-based artificial food is for the invaders, not for humans. In one of the most memorable moments from the film, Broadhead emerges after having fallen into the food and it burns him like acid. Poor Broadhead expires as Quatermass looks on in horror.

Invasion of the Body Snatchers, *Invaders from Mars* and *It Conquered the World* have the aliens controlling local authority figures and not infiltrating the higher levels of government. The concern in all these films is how the aliens have drained off the emotions and humanity of mankind. In *Body Snatchers*, the hero once more is a doctor, who was originally intended to take his story to the people, but the tacked on frame story implies that once the authorities have confirming evidence, the FBI will take care of the problem. *Body Snatchers* was particularly effective as it appealed to both sides of the political spectrum. Critics saw the pod people as representing either communist dupes or soulless mass consumers and conformists. *Quatermass 2* (U.S. title *Enemy from Space*) hammers out the pre-1960s theme that authority can't be trusted, rendered most horrifically in the scene where the invaders (who mysteriously bark their commands over the loudspeakers in English) entice some of the Quatermass rebels to give up their strike with promised concessions. These poor dupes are then used as "human pulp" to block the pipe that's pumping deadly oxygen into the aliens' sealed environment, a fact discovered when the pipe bursts from the pressure and blood drips out.

In his introduction to the script for *Quatermass II*, Kneale commented:

> It was 1955, an unconfident time. There was much public concern about a new brand of bureaucracy, which manifested itself in the form of secret establishments: giant radars reputed to endanger human life and concealed in huge plastic pods, germ-warfare establishments behind barbed wire; atom-proof shelters for chosen administrators.

All these concerns are apparent in Kneale's screenplay, as is concern for the Empire when Anthony Eden took on Nassar at Suez in a misguided attempt to

replay WWII. This concern, on a smaller scale, also is noticeable in Kneale's screenplay of John Osborne's *The Entertainer* (1960), which equates the pathetic, fading glories of the British Music Hall tradition with the crumbling of the Empire itself.

Quatermass, the crusading scientist, is working on problems in the film that still haven't been solved: safe atomic transportation, reusable rockets and the establishment of a colony on the moon. His model for a lunar colony looks conveniently like the Shell Refinery in Essex, which was used as a location in both the teleseries and the film. This location began the tradition of setting science fiction films in old factories to give them an inexpensively achieved technological look.

Like the plague of vampirism, once Quatermass' unmanned rocket has destroyed the orbiting alien base, the controlled humans return to normal, though improbably all signs of their possession (the entry points for the takeover of their nervous systems) immediately disappear. It is amusing to note that the aliens' P.R.O. (Public Relations Officer) is played by John Van Eyssen, who would next year play Jonathan Harker in the classic *Horror of Dracula*. Hammer fans will also enjoy seeing Michael Ripper in a typical part. Future director Bryan Forbes, who directed the delightful *The Wrong Box* (1966) and *The Stepford Wives* (1975) appears in the small but key part of Marsh, Quatermass' assistant, who is taken over by one of the alien components after picking up the meteorite it arrived in. Marsh later leads the attack on Quatermass' facility in an effort to prevent the launching of the atomic rocket.

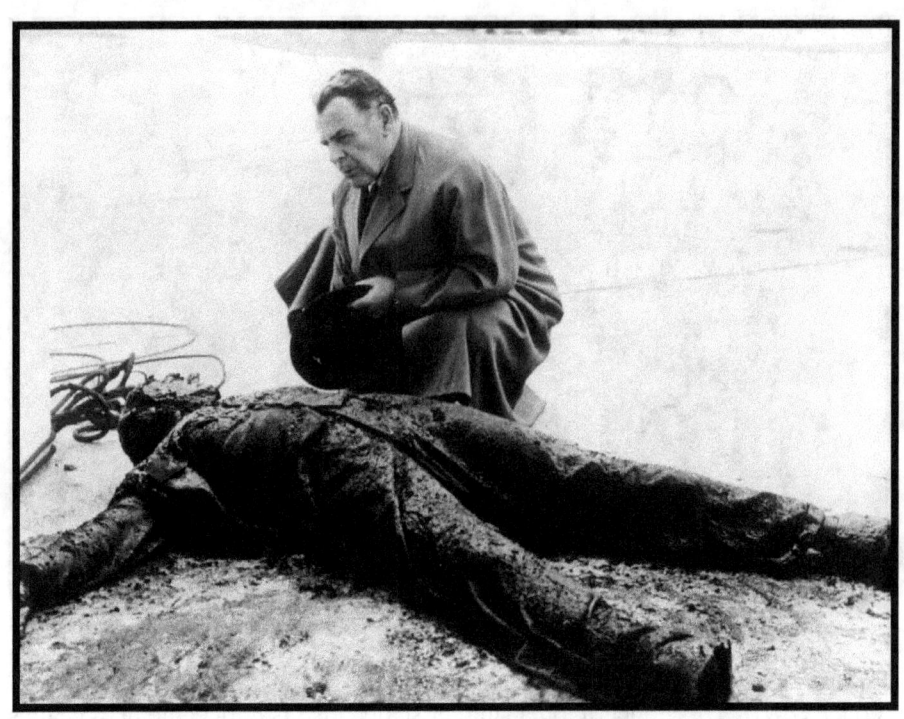

Quatermass (Donlevy) examines a burned plant worker in *Quatermass 2*.

One of the ironies the film plays on is that possessed humans, referred to as "zombies" by the villagers, make good guards but aren't considered suitable as workers and builders, hence, the workers are kept quiet by being given decent pay and benefits. When Quatermass tells them the truth, that they are manufacturing poison and supporting a deadly threat, he initially becomes the object of their wrath until a clichéd cockney barmaid (one of Guest's additions) becomes possessed, and the aliens, with their neurotic insistence on secrecy, overreact and send in masked guards to quell things. They kill a drunken reporter (again altered by Guest), whom Quatermass and Lomax brought with them in order to raise the alarm over the controlled channels of government.

Guest's direction keeps things lively. Once more he starts things with a bang as Quatermass' car is almost hit by a speeding couple—a young girl, who is driving her injured boyfriend to casualty after he was hit by a "hot" rock. Guest smartly wastes no time in getting his narrative going, the credits coming after this opening have already slammed us into the story. Though refineries aren't often interesting places to be, Guest shoots the refinery from a number of interesting angles, many of which emphasize Quatermass' entrapment in an elaborate and hostile environment.

His cinematographer, Gerald Gibbs, who also did excellent work on *X–The Unknown*, gives the film an appropriate bleak, gray look with ominous, overcast skies, littered landscapes and oppressive dark figures. In some effective shots the large white domes that hide the alien menace become a shadowy towering black with dwarfed human figures walking toward what appears to be certain doom. The scenes of the angered workers taking on the well-armed fascistic guards are given an almost documentary feel that believably captures the exploding violence and anger that the confrontation entails.

Though *Quatermass 2* was a success, Guest wasn't happy with it either. He was even less happy with his next Kneale collaboration, *The Abominable Snowman* (1957), adapted by Kneale from his teleplay *The Creature*, partly because Guest lacked the funds to make it more convincing by filming on location. The film retained Peter Cushing from the television version as Dr. John Rollason, but replaced Stanley Baker's character with Forrest Tucker, who played the ironically named Tom Friend. The theme of the story had to do with exposing man's lack of humanity by contrasting the ruthless and unscrupulous plans of Friend to exploit the Yeti to the gentleness of the supposed "monsters" themselves.

Gary J. Svehla detailed the production very will in *Midnight Marquee #29* and astutely notes the intelligence behind Nigel Kneale's screenplay. However, compared to its predecessors, *The Abominable Snowman* is slow and ponderous, concentrating more on characters' philosophical outlooks and motivations than on action, suspense or excitement. (The best Kneale scripts combine both.)

The Tibetan Lhama (played by Arnold Marle) is depicted in the cliché, *Lost Horizon*–style of the serene religious leader with a penchant for prescient powers (he's aware of who is coming up the mountain long before they are in sight). Much is made of the British expedition's racism and condescension toward the Tibetan people, except for Rollason and his wife, but such clichéd and unrealistic portrayals simply provide condescension of a fawning rather than condemning kind.

The Abominable Snowman was stupidly advertised by 20th Century-Fox in the United States with a poster proclaiming: "Demon-prowler of mountain shadow...Dreaded Man-beast of Tibet...The Terror of all that is human!" and included a box in the ad that reads: "We dare you to see it alone! Each chilling moment a shock-test for your endurance!!" Of course, Kneale's sensitive drama hardly fulfills any of these promises, leading to inevitable viewer disappointment and poor word of mouth. Additionally, Fox trimmed six minutes from the film's original running time.

In John Brosnan's *Future Tense*, Guest commented:

> We did all right with it...but it was never really a big success. It was too subtle and I also think it had too much to say. No one was expecting films from Hammer that said anything, but this one did—it had a message. Nigel had put in a lot of good stuff about man's supposed superiority over other species...but audiences didn't want that sort of thing…

For a Hammer film of that period it was quite lavish. It was more expensive than normal because of all the location shooting. We went and shot a lot of that in the French Alps—about 8,000 feet up we worked, and all roped together a lot of the time. It was something of an adventure making that picture. The rest we shot at Pinewood Studios. We used the Studios' biggest stage and built an enormous set consisting of rock, snow and a cave. There wasn't enough space to do it at Bray, though I shot some small stuff there, and we also built the Tibetan temple set at Bray, or part of it anyway—the rest was matted in together with the scenery.

Like the other Kneale projects before it, the shots of the "monster" were wisely kept to a minimum, though one close-up of a yeti's eyes and brow that suggests, in Rollason's words, "the creature's sadness and wisdom" is most people's favorite shot in the film, conveying much with a short, expressive visual. The cinematographer this time was Arthur Grant, who supplanted the superior Jack Asher as the regular lighting cameraman on much of Hammer's horror fare. Asher's Technicolor photography was superb; however, Hammer decided his rich colors and textures took too much time and decided to rely on the speedier and more economical Grant. Grant went on to photograph such Hammer classics as *The Curse of the Werewolf* (1961), *The Phantom of the Opera* (1962), *The Damned* (his best black & white work), *The Plague of the Zombies* (1966), *The Reptile* (1966), *Frankenstein Created Woman* (1967), *The Devil Rides Out* (1968, U.S. title: *The Devil's Bride*); *Dracula Has Risen from the Grave* (1968) and *Frankenstein Must Be Destroyed* (1969).

Guest, probably due to his background in comedy, knew the value and importance of keeping things moving and having a good set-up, and he applied these lessons very effectively to his Hammer film work. Still, even he was not able to entirely rein in Tucker's brash, overbearing qualities, yet the film is a serious and ambitious effort that is not without its charm, much of it provided by Cushing's portrayal of a man of dedicated intelligence and sensitivity, who learns that it is sometimes wiser not to pursue certain *truths.*

Kneale pitched the idea of a building contractor coming across a spaceship to Rudolph Cartier, who had produced and directed the previous two Quatermass teleseries, and thus *Quatermass and the Pit* was born, airing from December 1958 to January 1959. Instead of an invasion that was just starting, as in the first film, or one that had been established for a year as in the second, the third invasion takes place five million years in the past when no resistance was possible. The key discovery in the story is that Quatermass is fighting his own heredity. André Morell played the latest Quatermass, someone Kneale approved of as being civilized and debonair. The result was Kneale's greatest triumph, one of the sharpest science fiction scripts ever written, and the only one that Kneale expressed satisfaction with.

Kneale began working outside the genre when he got caught up in the Angry Young Man trend by adapting two classic John Osborne pieces into impressive films: *Look Back in Anger* (1959) and *The Entertainer*. Osborne launched the trend with his play *Long Back in Anger* in 1956, which tackled themes of modern alienation and the frustrations of the working class. The film also provided an increased frankness about sex, class, money and position, hitherto often seemingly taboo subjects.

Both the Kneale adaptations can be considered cinematic classics, though the dramatic demands of their stories ensure that they are seen far less often than the genre material I've been discussing. In *Look Back in Anger*, Richard Burton provides one of his finest film performances as Jimmy Porter, who rails against colonialism, the class system, segregation and other topics, who would like to go somewhere but can't think of any place to go that wouldn't ultimately corrupt him. It also marks the beginning of a persistent Knealean theme: that the cause of humanity is a lost one.

The Entertainer falls into the same mold, with an even finer performance by Laurence Olivier as Archie Rice, who soldiers in on his role of music hall entertainer and general rotter despite his utter despair and the pain he brings to others. England's decay is echoed in his desperation as the traditional roles can no longer satisfy. Not too surprisingly, many people found the film dismal and depressing, but there is no denying the powerful intimacy of the film's performances or the brilliant way Kneale reveals character through dialogue.

Guest returned to the genre with *The Day The Earth Caught Fire* (1961), based on the idea of Earth's climate changing due to Earth's axis shifting after atomic explosions. The film was a non-Hammer project, which Guest had been

In *Abominable Snowman* the monster was mostly kept hidden.

One of Val Guest's most interesting films was *The Day the Earth Caught Fire*, starring Edward Judd as reporter Peter Stenning.

trying to launch for a number of years, but no one was willing to risk money on a film about the bomb. Steven Pallos finally agreed and Guest also contributed money and produced. Guest, who had had a very successful collaboration with Wolf Mankowitz on *Expresso Bongo* (1960), and asked Mankowitz to write the dialogue for the film. The result is one of the wittiest and most adult science fiction films of the '60s, though one that is rarely seen.

Guest was able to gain access to the offices of the *Daily Express* by casting the paper's editor in the film and by getting owner Lord Beaverbrook's permission. The story is filtered through the viewpoint of Peter Stenning (Edward Judd in a fine performance), a reporter on the skids after his wife and child have left him. He is now assigned as the assistant to the science reporter, Bill Maguire (Leo McKern), who covers for him when he's out on a binge. By and large, the newspaper business is depicted very realistically, and we only know what the reporters are able to discover for themselves about the disaster. Indeed, verisimilitude is one of the film's strongest points, aided by Guest's insistence that it largely be shot on location.

Perhaps the main reason the film is not celebrated and acclaimed more is that it eschews spectacle, though the effects by Les Bowie are the best of his career (assisted by Brian Johnson, who would work on *When Dinosaurs Ruled the Earth, Alien* (1979) and *The Empire Strikes Back* (1980). In contrast to the more juvenile "end of the world" films of the time, *The Day The Earth Caught Fire* is far more adult and subdued. One of Guest's more interesting touches, a yellow tinting suggestive of heat, is used in the opening and closing scenes. The color tinting is missing from most modern prints of the film, although it works fine without it. Bowie uses a few matte paintings to show the Thames dry and creates a heat mist that covers Battersea park (an effect which upset the Queen, who was opening the nearby Chelsea Flower Show). But the essence of the story is more of how the characters cope with an increasingly impossible situation than in trying to dazzle audiences with apocalyptic visions.

There is also a nicely done and surprisingly sexy love story that develops between Stenning and Jeanne Craig (Janet Munro) who, at their first meeting in a "meet cute" scene, slaps him for his rudeness on the telephone. However, the bitter Stenning shapes up and shows Craig more respect at subsequent encounters, leading to a believable romance. Their relationship is complicated by feelings of betrayal when Craig reveals the secret her bosses have been covering up and Stenning feels obligated to report it to the public, a justifiable invocation of the public's "right to know."

In addition to believable workday humorous banter, provided mostly by McKern, who is quite adept at delivering it, the film offers some nice touches. For example, as the apparent end of the world approaches, a large group of youths rebel by deliberately wasting water wherever and whenever they can. The beatnik music accompanying these scenes was written by Monty Norman, who composed the famous *James Bond Theme*. Another nice bit shows cars that are altered with some kind of compartment on their tops, which is never mentioned and can be surmised to provide either needed air conditioning or an alternate cooling system for the engine.

The ending of the film leaves the resolution of Earth's fate in God's hands, as Guest pans from a *Citizen Kane*–like pair of headlines prepared at the *Express* declaring "World Saved" and "World Doomed," to the cross on St. Paul's Cathedral, all to the accompaniment of church bells. The film was slightly altered by its American distributor Universal, who cut the film from 99 minutes to 90 minutes. Actor Michael Caine appears in a bit part.

In 1963, Kneale returned to the genre with the television film production of *The Road*, directed by Christopher Morahan. Set in 1770, the Age of Reason, Sir Timothy Hassall (James Maxwell), a country squire and an irresponsible amateur scientist, seeks scientific proof of ghosts. Gideon Cobb (John Phillips), a sub-Johnsonian iconoclast, a sensualist and a bigot, who believes that machines will lead mankind to a Utopian ideal, accompanies him. Kneale's point is that the ideas represented by these two men are what lead to the horrors of our time. The play climaxes as Sir Timothy becomes an ear witness to air-attack sirens, the sounds of cars crashing and voices, while Cobb is given a vision of a road of the future and a thermonuclear blast.

The following year Kneale co-scripted with Jan Read an adaptation of H.G. Wells' *First Men In the Moon* (1964) for director Nathan Juran and special effects expert Ray Harryhausen. The film features one of the best scripts of any Harryhausen production, although the lying, cheating hero played by Edward Judd is ultimately despicable; however, in terms of enjoyable effects it ranks far behind Harryhausen's other films.

The most ingenious aspect about the production is the way that Kneale kept the story from becoming dated. A modern day United Nations moon landing uncovers evidence of a British moon landing in 1899, leading them to Bedford (Judd), who tells reporters the story of the invention of an anti-gravity paint called Cavorite, named after its inventor Professor Cavor (a delightful Lionel Jeffries), and their trip to the moon. The story ends up as *War of the Worlds* in reverse, with mankind as the invaders and the moon men as the victims of inadvertent germ warfare. The film is enjoyable, but it's played as a light-hearted adventure, a far cry from Wells' more serious intentions to use the Selenites to depict an alternative society.

Kneale's next genre project in 1966 returned him once again to Hammer. *The Witches*, known as *The Devil's Own* in the U.S., was adapted from Peter Curtis' novel of the same name. The film must be accounted a fascinating failure. Director Cyril Frankel, perhaps best remembered for *Never Take Sweets from a Stranger* (1961), lacks Guest's visual acuity and ability to build suspense scenes. While a far cry from Kneale's best screenplay, it is intelligently written, and with its plot of a secret society planning a virgin sacrifice, could have been an inspiration for *The Wicker Man* (1973) and numerous other virgin-sacrifice films.

Most film historians, despite Kneale's screenplay, have ignored the film. Our story opens with a prologue set in Africa, where Gwen Mayfield (Joan Fontaine) runs a small school and discovers a fetish [magical object] inside. Gwen is warned about witchcraft that

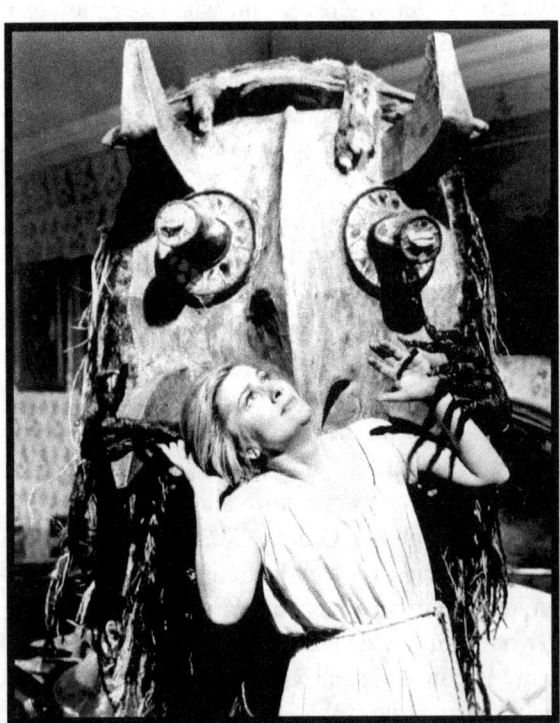

Joan Fontaine in *The Witches*

will "eat your soul," when a witch doctor in a giant mask breaks down the door, causing Gwen to have a breakdown.

Later, we find Gwen back in England applying for a position in a small private school in Heddaby, a small country village, where she becomes taken with the "nice, simple people." Kneale includes a lot of little touches to underscore the idea that things are not as they seem, beginning with the fact that Alan Bax (Alex McCowen) interviews her wearing a clerical collar, though he later admits he's not a priest or vicar. While searching for the town's rectory or its chapel, Gwen hears the sounds of a church organ but learns that it is only Bax's tape recording and that the town has neither.

It's apparent that the town keeps an eye on villager Linda Riggs (Ingrid Brett) and disapproves of her being courted by Ronnie Dowsett (Martin Stephens of *The Innocents*). Ronnie passes along his belief that Linda's grandmother is cruel to her, injuring her hand by putting it in the manglers (wringers) of her old-style washing machine. And indeed, Granny (Gwen Ffrangcon-Davies) does believe that, "the old ways served when there were no doctors, and they're still the best," which ties the film into feminist thought about women witches being natural healers with great herbal lore.

Mayfield discovers that Ronnie is gifted, if backward, and recommends he be given special tutoring. Alan Bax is willing to foot the bill for boarding school, thus separating Ronnie from Linda, but is disappointed when Mayfield convinces Ronnie's father that he would be better off being tutored by her. Shortly afterward Ronnie ends up in a coma and Ronnie's father ends up drowned in a nearby pond—after passing along gossip about Granny Riggs' casting spells.

A key scene has Gwen going to the pond and discovering the footprints of several other people near Ron's father's, but she is then terrorized by some sheep whose presence obliterate the tracks. While sheep are convincing animals to have in such an area, they simply are not scary, and the scene would have played far better if the area had been overrun by hunting dogs, or better still, wolves.

Gwen goes to Alan's sister Stephanie (Kay Walsh), a local writer, with what she's learned about witchcraft in the village, and Stephanie does nothing to deny it, instead suggesting that they collaborate on an article. However, while staying at Stephanie's house, Gwen suffers a relapse of her breakdown and remains in a coma herself for a year.

She awakens in a nursing home and is attended to by ferret-faced Dr. Wallis (Leonard Rossiter), who prescribes a trip to another home in Cornwall. Instead, Mayfield escapes and hitches a ride back to Heddaby with butcher Bob Curd (Duncan Lamont). There she quickly learns that Stephanie is the actual leader of the cult, who insists on initiating Gwen. Stephanie reveals her plans to sacrifice Linda in order to extend her own life, a ritual in which she expects Gwen to assist. Gwen learns that the victim must be a maid of less than 15 and that no blood must be spilled or the forces of evil will turn against the summoner.

Stephanie (Kay Walsh) plans to sacrifice Linda (Ingrid Brett) for longer life in *The Witches*.

Stephanie smiles in contemplation of the ceremony: "After the blow is struck, give me a skin for dancing in," clearly indicating that the victim is to be skinned Ed Gein–style.

Unfortunately, the ineptly staged climax of the witches' Sabbath is more ludicrous than wrenching, with badly choreographed villagers writhing on the floor after slurping some disgusting substance. After the warnings, it's all too easy to guess the resolution. The sight of Walsh, in her flamboyant regalia with her antler headdress lit up by birthday candles, suggests a Gloria Swanson gone to seed and is an indelible sight, though for all the wrong reasons. A horror film is truly in trouble when it turns silly instead of sinister, and *The Witches* is no exception.

Once the evil influence of Stephanie is gone, the villagers quickly return to normal, and all their past doings and allegiances are conveniently forgotten. *City of the Dead* (1960, aka *Horror Hotel*) covered similar ground in a far superior fashion. Hammer would perfect the witchcraft thriller when Richard Matheson adapted *The Devil Rides Out* (1968) for them, one of the four best Hammer films ever made. For the record, the other two top-line Hammer films, in my opinion, were *Horror of Dracula* and *Frankenstein Must Be Destroyed* and the film discussed below, though there are plenty of very good films that compete for the second tier.

Kneale's next Hammer project, *Quatermass and the Pit* (U.S. title: *Five Million Years to Earth,* 1967), is one of the greatest science fiction epics of all time. Andrew Keir, the studio's sometime-Cushing substitute, took over the role of Quatermass, who is caught between the stiff-backed officiousness of Col. Breen (Julian Glover) and intelligence of Dr. Matthew Roney (James Donald), who is ably assisted by the ever-attractive Barbara Shelley.

Kneale provided the condensation of his own story, quite satisfactorily, and production designer Bernard Robinson once more demonstrates his flare for getting the most out of minimal budget. The spaceship uncovered is far more attractive and sleek that the bell-like design from the teleseries. The Hobbs End Underground station is very convincing, and the littered London street of the finale maintains its believability on limited resources. The one flaw is the mental images of the Martian "locusts" in action, which clearly look like the stick puppet figures they are.

Roy Ward Baker does a brilliant job of generating ever increasing mystery and tension while getting effective performances from all the principals.

The Bowie Films effects are also quite impressive and effective—from objects flying around a telekinetic man, shaking tiles off the walls, to the ground undulating alarmingly under an affected individual. The spaceship gives off an unearthly glow with suggestions of capillaries to convey the idea that the ship itself is a living presence, something which Quatermass himself hints at when he notes the apparent lack of instrumentality. The arthropod aliens suggest both locusts and the "horned one" (aka the devil), especially in the giant energy image that Roney helps to destroy by simply grounding it.

What really fascinates is how Kneale builds his seemingly simple mystery into an elaborate line of speculation that ties in the origins of man, evil and prejudice in the world, coming up with the idea that the Earth might have been colonized by proxy a few years before Erich von Daniken helped to popularize the notion. By genetically altering man's simian ancestors to increase their intelligence, these aliens set the course for man's evolution. Unfortunately, these insect-like beings have regular purges of those beings that do not conform to the norm, and so imprint mankind with a hereditary fear and hatred of all who are *different* in some way.

Kneale's script also suggests that telekinesis and other psi powers are latent potentials in all human beings, instilled for the purpose of purging nonconformists from the hive. It also implies that images of evil beings, common to cultures all over the world, are simply phenomena that have been improperly observed—vestiges of clairvoyant faculties *gifted* to us by alien ancestors.

Interestingly, the true hero of the piece turns out not to be Quatermass but Dr. Roney, the excited archaeologist, who also represents restrained intelligence.

Quatermass (Andrew Keir) and Dr. Roney (James Donald) discover ancient aliens in *Quatermass and the Pit* (aka *Five Million Years to Earth*).

Even the brilliant Professor Quatermass succumbs to the power of the mob at one point. He is pulled out and brought back to normal by Roney, who reminds him that it is an act of will not to give in to hysteria and that intelligence can defeat conditioned programming. Roney ultimately sacrifices his life to save mankind.

Kneale has brilliantly provided explanations and rationalizations for things considered unexplainable. However, under all the intellectual play, he has a serious point to make—that it is only through knowledge of ourselves that we can destroy the ancient, destructive urges within us, which grow more deadly with the expansion of our knowledge and technology. Wars, witch hunts, race riots and purges—our heritage of hatred—are things we must guard against, and if such things cannot be controlled, then the "Martians" will have created a second dead planet—Earth.

Naturally, this Baker-Kneale collaboration has proven influential, particularly in Dan O'Bannon and Don Jakoby's *Lifeforce* (1985), an adaptation of Colin Wilson's *Space Vampires,* in which aliens prove to be the source of all vampire legends; and in Stephen King's novel and Tommy Lee Wallace's miniseries *Tommyknockers* (1993), which provided a big dose of *déjà vu* with its story of unearthing a spaceship and people falling under its malign influence.

Meanwhile, Guest was assigned the task of having to tie together the disparate segments of an overblown comedy, *Casino Royale* (1967), which tried to elaborately send up the Bond films while basing it (loosely it must be admitted) on one of Fleming's works. John Huston directed the first 25 minutes of the film, Robert Parrish covered the Baccarat game between Orson Welles and Peter Sellers, and Joseph McGrath, Kenneth Hughes and Val Guest all made contributions. The first cut ran an ungainly three hours and was turned into a misshapen, though occasionally funny, 131 minutes.

In July 1969, the BBC broadcast an episode of *Theatre 625*, one of Kneale's finest and least-known teleplays, "The Year of the Sex Olympics," starring Leonard Rossiter, Tony Vogel and Suzanne Neve, and directed by Michael Elliott. Despite the racy title, the story has less to do with sex than speculation of the "if this goes on" type. Kneale creates a future where everything is run by "high drive" personalities, who create televised diversions to keep the otherwise unoccupied "low drive," dim-witted lower class pacified.

In the story, Ugo Priest (Rossiter) is a TV director, who remembers the old ways and is terrified of "tension" (emotion), the force he feels that had almost destroyed the world. The world evolves around television and reality programs. However, audiences have become increasingly unresponsive to the diet of sex shows and game shows.

The purpose of the sex shows is to show sexual athletes, who are so good at making out that the average viewer, who cannot hope to attain their level of attractiveness and expertise, forgoes the act itself in favor of simply watching. Similarly, there is a game show based on gluttony as a substitute for eating. Machinery has made it unnecessary for most people to actually work, so they live their lives out watching TV. (Anyone who can't see clear parallels to today's world simply isn't paying attention.)

Taking a leaf from Aldous Huxley's *Brave New World*, Kneale inserts into the narrative an artist, Kin Hodder

Jim Danforth's special effects remains one of the only reasons to see *When Dinosaurs Ruled the Earth*.

(Martin Potter), who wants to bring his disturbing images to the masses and gum up the works. His death, however, brings a response of laughter, the first emotional response the audience has exhibited in some time (demonstrating that the audience can be shown something disturbing without creating tension, so long as what is shown is not happening to them).

This inspires Nat Mender (Vogel) and his mate Deanie (Neve) to create a new TV show based on dropping out of society and living like their ancestors, in secret hopes of a more fulfilling life for them and their child and prompting the masses to think about doing likewise. They are to be dropped on an island with no modern technology. However, the network, to keep things interesting for the viewers, stacks the cards against them. Neale should have sued the creators of *Survivor* for royalties!

"The Year of the Sex Olympics'" vision of television as numbing rather than stimulating seems right on target, as are the leads' apparent fear of the future and willingness to give it up in favor of a bleak existence, to which they return, entirely ill-prepared. Also telling are the hints of the addictive power of the medium and how it can be used for apathy control, though Kneale does ignore the effect of the have-nots being exposed to what the haves have, and the social unrest that that situation can create. Some suggest that what brought the Soviet Union down is European television showing Communists the good life they weren't enjoying under the then current system. Such thoughtful drama is entirely too rare on our airwaves.

Despite a collaboration with science fiction writer J.G. Ballard, Val Guest's next sci-fi project was the entirely brainless *When Dinosaurs Ruled the Earth* (1969), which Spielberg recently paid homage to in *Jurassic Park.* This "boobs and bronter" is more noticeable for Victoria Vetri's cleavage and Jim Danforth's painstakingly achieved special effects than for any other apparent qualities.

One shot of a village trying to capture a plesiosaur deserves its reputation as a landmark in stop motion effects as Danforth created a "reality sandwich" by putting live actors in both the background and the foreground and by having the saurian interact with the two via restraining ropes. It is a technical marvel, but it is also over with very quickly.

To eliminate dubbing in foreign markets, everything is presented in simple caveman speak and Vetri mostly runs around in an inexplicable Stone-Age bikini. Four minutes of nudity were trimmed from the British release so that the film could get a "G" rating for its U.S. release.

Guest's next project, 1970's *Toomorrow*, is better known as an Olivia Newton-John's first lead in a film before *Grease* (1978) than as a silly science fiction musical. Dying aliens kidnap the musical group Toomorrow, whose music can help save their race.

Guest himself put an injunction against showing the film when it opened because he hadn't been paid. The project is one that deserves its obscurity. While guest hoped to tackle such projects as Richard Matheson's *I Am Legend*, which he scripted, and Jules Verne's horror tale *The Carpathian Castle*, neither came to fruition. His last work for the genre was for the *Hammer House of Mystery & Suspense* TV series (syndicated in American as *Fox Mystery Theatre*), for which he directed three episodes. In *Possession* (1/12/85), a couple starts seeing images of an Edwardian murder; in *Mark of the Devil* (9/5/84), Dirk Benedict murders a pawnbroker-tattooist and starts becoming covered with tattoos; and in *Child's Play* (5/2/86), we find a family that is trapped behind a seemingly impenetrable wall.

Kneale worked with Hammer director Peter Sasdy (*Countess Dracula)* in 1972 on *The Stone Tape,* in which an electronics think tank, hoping to come up with an invention to beat the Japanese, run up against supernatural phenomena in an empty building. The important female lead was Jane Asher, the girl from *The Quatermass Experiment*. Kneale wrote it as a Christmas ghost story and its main idea is that the stone walls of a building can record a person's soul—like the metal filings on audiotape record music. Asher's character Jill Greeley dies and has her ghost imprinted on the "stone tape" in the dull climax. Lacking in complexity and depth, this is a pretty soulless production that doesn't invite reviewing.

Kneale returned to the *Quatermass* series one last time with Thames Television's 1979 production of *The Quatermass Conclusion*, directed by Piers Haggard (*Blood on Satan's Claw*, 1971, aka *Satan's Skin*). While *Quatermass and the Pit*'s title punned on the idea of Professor Quatermass confronting a "pit" as in Hell, *The Quatermass Conclusion* is a double entendre in that "conclusion" is meant both as the end of a logical progression of thought and the concluding episode of the series.

The Quatermass Conclusion appears to be the work of an embittered man with a dark view of society and social collapse. Unlike the persevering optimist of the Donlevy *Quatermass* films, John Mills plays a Quatermass who is embarrassed about the part he played in space travel because of the millions of dollars wasted on a joint U.S.-Soviet space venture. He rails against the "diseases" (economic, political, social and otherwise) spread by the superpowers that overwhelm smaller countries in their wake. Now Quatermass' only concern is locating his long-lost granddaughter who ran away sometime before.

As the miniseries begins, we are introduced to a future world where the social order has broken down and the youth of England seemingly have all gone mad. Quatermass is horrified to see dead bodies lying in suburban streets where hooligans, who want to smash in his teeth, accost him. Dr. Joseph Knapp (Simon MacCorkindale), a Jewish astronomer, drives up in a van covered in steel mesh and saves him.

Together they appear on a TV program where Quatermass blasts the U.S.-Soviet space project. He then makes an on-air plea for help in finding his granddaughter.

When an inexplicable space disaster occurs, Knapp rushes Quatermass out of the city to the relative safety of his country observatory where Knapp lives with his wife (Barbara Kellerman), two children and two assistants.

Along the way, they pass some Planet People, a group of young people dressed in Flower children outfits (or castoffs). The Planet People have formed a weird religion around the idea that the Earth has been poisoned (Quatermass concurs) and they will be beamed to another planet,

John Mills starred as Quatermass in *The Quatermass Conclusion*.

which will be their Utopia. They use pendulum-like dowsing sticks as they to find sacred sites such as Stonehenge, where they expect to begin their interplanetary journey. Unbeknownst to Quatermass, his granddaughter is one of them.

One of these sites, Ringstone Round, is nearby, and Quatermass and the Knapps are shocked to see a tremendous beam of light come down and reduce the Planet People to ashes, except for one small girl, who was outside the circle and is blinded and burned but not disintegrated.

Eventually, Quatermass solves the twin mysteries as to the increased craziness of youth and the secret behind ancient sites marked with monoliths. Five thousand years in the past, an alien machine sampled some Earthlings and found some aspect of them to be tasty. Circles of stones were erected to serve as a warning to humans to stay away. An alien machine, theorizes Quatermass, sends a signal that affects the young, lures them together in one spot and harvests them. With a team of elderly scientists, Quatermass prepares to lay an atomic trap designed to give the faraway aliens (not invaders this time) a case of nuclear indigestion.

At the finale the trap is set, only some leftover Planet People parade to the site. Quatermass sees his granddaughter among them and suffers a fatal heart attack before he can trigger the device, but the oblivious granddaughter sees what the old man is trying to do and pushes the trigger just in time.

The Quatermass Conclusion lacks the intensity and interest of *Quatermass and the Pit*. Kneale approved of John Mills as the now-aged Professor, but when a 105-minute condensation of the teleseries was prepared, he lamented that while he had written it to be condensed "here, here and here," the producers and editors decided to condense it "there, there, and there," throwing off the arc of his story. Kneale did novelize his full story for Arrow Books in 1979. Today the 105-minute version is still available on the Thorn-EMI video, while the complete series, called *Quatermass*, is available from A&E New Video in a 2-disc set running 5 hours and 12 minutes that includes "Enduring Mystery of Stonehenge." Another DVD is available from the U.K. in a PAL 3-disc DVD set, also titled *Quatermass*.

Kneale was later hired to write a screenplay for a remake of *Creature from the Black Lagoon* (1954), but Universal axed the project in favor of making *Jaws 3-D* (1983). He also scripted the original version of *Halloween III: The Season of the Witch* (1983), but his story was totally rewritten by Tommy Lee Wallace. The film retains a few Kneale elements such as an Irish toymaker Conal Cochran (beautifully played in the film by Dan O'Herlihy, who is the only good thing in the film), who is resentful of the commercialization of Samhain as Halloween. Cochran exploits that commercialization to sell Halloween masks that will turn the brains of America's children into a mass of bugs and creepy-crawlies using the ancient Celtic magic trapped inside the rock of Stonehenge. Wallace added such elements as android workers that are undetectable from human beings.

Quatermass and the Pit remains one of the all-time great sci-fi films.

John Carpenter, in an interview with this author, was asked why the original Kneale script was rejected, and he explained that it was full of the same kind of bitterness evident in *The Quatermass Conclusion* and he didn't think it would have been commercial. However, Halloween III, which exploited the Halloween name without delivering villain Michael Myers to a disappointed and resentful public, made $14 million as compared to the $47 million the original Halloween earned. Carpenter paid tribute to Kneale later by attributing his pseudonymous screenplay for *The Prince of Darkness* to Martin Quatermass.

One shouldn't expect an artist to achieve tremendous success with every project. *The Quatermass Conclusion*, while disappointing in relation to the finest science fiction film series ever produced, in still an intelligent and interesting film. What we remember Val Guest and Nigel Kneale for are their tremendous successes and the pleasure that their works have given us. If a Val Guest writes a film as unintentionally silly as *Another Man's Poison*, he also achieves both dignity and humor in the excellent *The Day the Earth Caught Fire*. If Kneale's excellent short stories such as *Jeremy in the Wind* and *The Pond* are largely forgotten and rarely anthologized, *Quatermass and the Pit* remains one of the all-time great science fiction films/stories.

Both men were serious creative artists, and together they created the films that launched Hammer horror. Their work making intelligent science fiction dramas helped pave the way for the greatest horror studio of the 1960s. Although the films had their gory elements, these were never gratuitous and helped the plot along in a logical and involving fashion. Few writers of science fiction films are as adept at characterization, social criticism and carefully laid out fantastic speculation as Nigel Kneale. Val Guest is often noted as a journeyman director, but in his science fiction films he proves he can be effective without being distractingly flashy, and that science fiction films can be vehicles of substance rather than simply dismissible kiddy fodder. While many of the sci-fi dramas of the past have been over-praised or mostly forgotten, Guest's and Kneale's finest films will continue to be revived and admired by succeeding generations.

FANTASY

Surviving the Lost Worlds of Hammer

by John Parnum

Beginning in 1957, Hammer Studios chilled audiences around the world by remaking many of the black and white universal horror films of the 1930s and 1940s. Frankenstein, Dracula, the Wolf Man, the Mummy and the Phantom of the Opera were some of the classic monsters resurrected from that Golden Age of Horror that were given Hammer's new color treatment. They pried open the vaults of other studios also in their search for exciting ideas: *The Man Who Could Cheat Death* was a Technicolor remake of Paramount's *Man in Half Moon Street* and *House of Fright* (or *The Two Faces of Dr. Jekyll*) was an unusual updating of the Jekyll and Hyde theme so brilliantly produced several decades before by Paramount and MGM. Even the 1939 *Hound of the Baskervilles* from 20th Century-Fox was adapted by Hammer, with Peter Cushing providing the definitive portrayal of Sherlock Holmes. And these adaptations always meant intelligently produced thrillers decked out in glorious color with the added never-before-beheld realism of blood, gore, discreet sex, and, later, more blatant nudity.

Then in the mid-1960s, while searching around for different story lines, Hammer rediscovered the lost world theme. Their first foray into unknown lands was a remake of the oft-filmed *She*, the story of Ayesha...that beautiful ruler of a mythical kingdom who remained young for 2,000 years until the reincarnation of a former lover returned to her. That extraordinary Frenchman Georges Méliès made the first version of the film in 1899, *Haggard's She: The Pillar of Fire*, and the 65-foot-long short has been labeled one of the screen's first science-fantasy films. Other silent adaptations followed, but the first talking *She* was produced by Merian C. Cooper, who gave it the same flamboyant treatment he did for his classic ape flick (*King Kong*, 1933). Helen Gahagan portrayed the wicked queen and, later when she ran for Congress, tried to buy up all the RKO prints, which

Jeanne d'Alcy in Méliès' *Haggard's She: The Pillar of Fire*

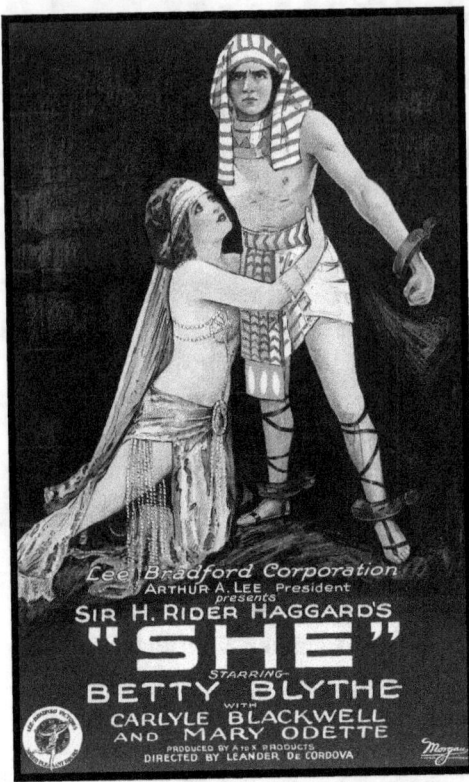

Poster for the silent 1925 version of *She*

she considered an embarrassment. So when Hammer's Michael Carreras produced *She* in 1965, the tale may have been quite an imaginative departure for younger audiences not acquainted with the 1886 novel by H. Rider Haggard.

Carreras chose Ursula Andress for the title role of Ayesha, or She-Who-Waits, and relative film newcomer John Richardson as the sun-tanned adventurer Leo Vincey for whom She awaits. Tossed in for good measure are Hammer stalwarts Peter Cushing as Leo's fellow traveler Major Holly and Christopher Lee as Billali, Ayesha's traitorous high priest. These two veteran actors are perhaps the most believable in the film, outshining the wooden Richardson and the beautiful but talentless Andress. Just watch Cushing awaken from a deep sleep when Richardson shows him a treasure map—his excited gestures for this simple feat are entertaining and truly professional.

The opening credits of *She* are exceptionally jarring, alternating between shots of lush tropical foliage with a seductive score from James Bernard and screaming natives on the warpath. It then shifts to Palestine where Leo and Holly and their valet Job (played for comic relief by Bernard Cribbins) sit in a market cafe watching the sexual writhing of an exotic belly dancer. The lovely Ustane (Rosenda Monteros), Ayesha's handmaiden, seduces Leo and kidnaps him. Ustane ultimately regrets her mission since she has fallen in love with the rugged Leo, but it is too late and he is taken before Ayesha, who tells him she has been waiting for him and that he must follow her to the ends of the Earth. Returning to Holly and Job with a map and medallion bearing his image, Leo convinces the others to cross the Desert of Lost Souls to the Mountains of the Moon where they ultimately hope to locate the hidden city of Kuma—a dream of both Leo and Holly that appears may very well come true. But Leo is having different kinds of dreams also and he continually hears the voice of Ayesha calling to him: "Will you come to me again? Everything you desire will be yours. Power. Riches." Leo asks the seductive vision, "And you?" Ayesha repeats: "*Everything* you desire!"

Ursula Andress and John Richardson in Hammer's *She*

As they cross the desert Bedouins attack them. Their camels are stolen and water bags slashed. but Leo is convinced that the Mountains of the Moon are very close. And sure enough, just over the next dune they appear. It is still several days' trek and, tired and thirsty, they stagger toward the mountains. All three drain the last drops from their canteens and toss them on the burning sands, a totally ridiculous and uncalled bit of action since the utensils would again be useful once water was located.

Ustane, who has followed them from Jerusalem, rescues them, and takes them to her people, a primitive tribe dwelling in the Mountains of the Moon. Even though Leo is wounded, the natives are fearful of him because of his resemblance to Callicrates, a former lover of Ayesha. Ustane's father and leader of the tribe, Haumeid (Andre Morell), is slowly losing authority over his people, who plan to sacrifice Leo. Just as a native prepares to pierce Leo's heart with a dagger, Ayesha's high priest Billali arrives and takes the group to Kuma. In his delirium, Leo continues to hear Ayesha's seductive promises amidst a background of violins and harps.

Leo recovers and Ayesha tells him that she has waited 2,000 years for him to return to her. In his former incarnation as her lover Callicrates, he was unfaithful to her and she stabbed him to death in a jealous rage. In order to remain young and beautiful until his return to her in a new reincarnation, Ayesha bathed in the Flame of Eternal Life. Now, since he has passed the tests set forth by her on their journey to Kuma, Ayesha is assured that Leo is really Callicrates and invites him to bathe in the flame and join her in immortality.

Billali (Christopher Lee) battles Leo (Richardson) for eternal life in *She*.

But Leo and his friends soon become aware that She-Who-Waits is also She-Who-Must-Be-Obeyed and they are forced to watch the 15 natives involved in Leo's near sacrifice hurled into a pit of molten lava. Despite her cruelty, Leo is seduced by She's power, and poor Ustane, realizing that she is a discarded love, tells Leo that she is returning to her people. In his last charitable act, Leo kisses Ustane goodbye, but they are observed by Ayesha, who sees it as her lover's second act of unfaithfulness in 2,000 years. Leo, Holly and Job are invited to the ceremonial center once more where they are shocked to see Ustane imprisoned in a wooden cage above the lava pit. When Ayesha tells Leo that he can save Ustane by plunging a dagger into her (She's) heart, he cannot do it and Holly says, "We've lost him."

As mentioned earlier, Hammer in past films was notorious for emphasizing violence and bloodshed. *She*, however, is another story—a love story, albeit a rather strange and fanciful one. We can be thankful that the lovely and enticing Ustane is not shown being lowered into the conflagration. It is enough for our sensibilities when Billali tells Haumeid that he is returning his daughter to him and then hands the shocked father a jar of ashes. This, of course, precipitates the obligatory rebellion.

In the interim, Ayesha tells Leo that it is time for him to bathe in the Flame of Eternal Life. A fiery comet plummets from the sky to the burning source, turning the flames blue and cold. Leo says he is afraid and Ayesha tells him they will enter the flames together. In other versions of *She*, Ayesha tells Leo that she will enter first and disrobes, with Leo horrified to learn that a second bathing in the flames takes away her youth and beauty, with Ayesha reverting to a 2,000 year-old corpse. In the Hammer version, Andress does not undress when she and Leo step into the flames together. Ayesha does the aging bit, of course, finally crumbling to dust at Leo's feet. And Leo, to his dismay, now finds himself immortal. The cool blue flames turn hot and red again and no longer hold their mystical powers. Holly assures Leo that the comet will return some day. "When, Holly, when?" Leo pleads. Holly reminds him that he wanted immortality at any cost, but Leo has a change of heart and promises, "When it comes back, it will find me waiting." And wait he does—at least until 1968 when Hammer filmed its tepid sequel, *The Vengeance of She*.

Watching a woman age in the matter of a few seconds is always an intriguing premise and is usually the moment eagerly waited for in such films as *The Lost Horizon* (1937) and *The Mummy's Ghost* (1944). This is probably a selfish desire of audiences to see immortals put in their places and relieving them of their gift of eternal life. In the Hammer *She*, Andress ages by degrees until she finally ends up a pile of ashes. It is interesting to note that as a victim of the fire, she not only withers away but also seems to burn—with the flames turning her fair body black as if the blue coolness were ineffective in protecting her from the heat. But then again, the Flame of Eternal Life has perpetrated other astonishing feats. In an earlier version of *She*, the flame ages Ayesha regressively by returning her to an ape reincarnation.

For the withering of Ursula, famed Hammer makeup artist Roy Ashton reported in the in the Al Taylor/Sue Roy book *Making a Monster* that Andress was only used in the early stages of the aging process. Since growing old is usually accompanied by shrinkage, emaciation and shriveling, older actresses of diminishing stature who could remove their dentures replaced the statuesque Andress.

Michael Carreras passed on the production of *Vengeance of She,* which was given instead to Aida Young, who had been associate producer of *She*. Loosely based on H. Rider Haggard's *Ayesha, Vengeance of She* is practically a retelling of the original with most of the characters interchanged. Instead of Leo's reincarnation of Callicrates being drawn to the lost city of Kuma by Ayesha, the uninspired plot involves Carol, the supposed reincarnation of Ayesha, being drawn to Kuma by Callicrates (once again played by John Richardson). Carol (voluptuous Czechoslovakian starlet Olinka Berova), instead of seeing lovely visions and hearing a seductive voice whispering "Everything you desire will be yours," is lured to Kuma by a series of noises in her head—hardly a believable motivation considering all of the dangers she encounters during the journey. High priest Men-Hari (Derek Godfrey in the Christopher Lee role) is the evil influence enticing Carol to Kuma, but is thwarted by yacht owner George (Colin Blakely) and lady friend Sheila (Jill Melford), both in comedy relief parts, and

Vengeance of She features Olinka Berova as Carol/Ayesha.

their psychologist ship guest Philip (Edward Judd), who naturally becomes enamored with Carol.

After much roughhousing and romantic interludes, Carol and Philip arrive in Kuma where Philip is imprisoned and Callicrates tells Carol to enter the Flame of Eternal Life and join him in immortality. However, Callicrates has also promised eternal life to Men-Hari as a reward for bringing Carol to him. Former high priest Za-Tor (Noel Willman) helps Philip escape with the inevitable confrontation at the Flame between Callicrates, Men-Hari and Philip over the fate of Carol. Once Callicrates realizes that Carol is not the reincarnation of Ayesha, he kills Men-Hari and jumps headlong into the fire. As it did once before, the Flame steals Callicrates' youth and he reverts to his true age—probably close to a hundred. An earthquake then destroys the kingdom of Kuma.

Of the two films, *She* is decidedly the classier. The imaginative screenplay by David Chantler moves briskly along under Robert Day's subdued direction. *Vengeance*, on the other hand, suffers from Peter O'Donnell's totally uncreative storyline. Both, of course, have beautiful and sexy female leads to send males into ecstasy, with John Richardson doing a similar job for the ladies.

The thrillers of H. Rider Haggard were immensely popular with movie audiences, especially the oft-filmed *King Solomon's Mines* in which safari leader Allan Quartermain and company find a lost tribe of Africans guarding a fabulous treasure. Michael Carreras showed a great deal of enthusiasm for a project called *Allan Quartermain Esq.: His Quest for the Holy Flower*, in which the intrepid adventurer travels to the kingdom of the Pongo People, who worship a giant white gorilla. The idea was dropped when Carreras was unable to find a partner to help him with financing.

The tribes that lived in the ruined city of Kuma and surrounding areas of the Mountains of the Moon could be considered a highly advanced civilization compared to the Rock Tribe and Shell People who inhabited the primitive landscapes of Hammer's 100th film, *One Million Years B.C.* Filmed in 1966, this prehistoric epic was a virtual remake of the 1940 *One Million B.C.*, which starred Victor Mature as Tumak and Carol Landis as Loana. While the prehistoric denizens of this first film consisted mostly of altered reptiles and animals (lizards with fins attached and elephants fitted in shag with curved tusks to represent wooly mammoths), the Hammer version was blessed with the expert craftsmanship of Ray Harryhausen, whose realistic stop-motion animation has given life to some of the screen's most fanciful creatures.

Both versions were filmed virtually without dialogue, but the Hammer flick, which was released by 20th Century-Fox, showcased that company's newfound cover girl Raquel Welch, who had created such a stir in Fox's *Fantastic Voyage* earlier that year. Raquel, as Loana of the gentle Shell People Tribe, rescues Tumak (John Richardson again) of the brutal Rock Tribe after being booted out by his father Akhoba (Robert Brown essaying the part of the tribal leader played by Lon Chaney, Jr. in the 1940 version). Tumak, having also lost his girlfriend Nupondi (Martine Beswicke), is naturally receptive to Loana's charms, but is mystified by the Shell People's peaceful ways.

Adapting somewhat to the tribe's gentleness, Tumak is finally able to display his macho image when he takes on singlehandedly an Allosaurus. Using a spear belonging to Ahot (Jean Wladon), leader of the Shell People, Tumak punctures the creature, catapulting it head over heals in a remarkable tour de force of animation. As the victor, Tumak feels he is entitled to Ahot's weapon, but the youthful leader objects. The Shell People stop Tumak from killing Ahot and then banish him from their tribe. Loana decides to leave with Tumak.

Meanwhile, back at the Rock Tribe, Akhoba is wounded in a fight with a wild boar, and his first son, Sakana (Percy Herbert), Tumak's brother, assumes leadership.

Tumak and Loana make their way back to the Rock Tribe, surviving an assault by cannibalistic ape men and a couple of Harryhausen's dinosaurs. While fleeing from a Triceratops and a ferocious Ceratosaurus (two creatures which actually did not exist in the same time span), Loana runs smack-dab into Sakana, who lustfully attacks her. Hearing Loana's call for help through the conch horn, Tumak engages Sakana in a death struggle, wounding his brother. But Tumak has learned the value of an act of mercy and spares the astonished Sakana, who himself is then banished.

Tumak and Loana then teach the Rock People many practical things, such as the art of making stone-tipped spears. But while bathing in a nearby pool, Loana is carried off by a bat-winged Pteranodon (often mistakenly referred to as a Pterodactyl) in one of Harryhausen's most amazing sequences. An extensive system of invisible wires was required to stabilize the model, and this was made more complicated when a second winged reptile, a Rhamphorhynchus, attacks the Pteranodon carrying Loana. The wings, head, body and a stop-motion figure of Loana had to be moved one frame at a time in perfect synchronization. Especially time consuming was the scene where the Pteranodon swoops down and grabs the fleeing Raquel Welch and scoops up a realistic animated model without a break in continuity. The result is one of the most exciting and smooth transitions of actress and model ever filmed and was so successful that Harryhausen repeated the action in the 1968 *Valley of Gwangi* when a Pterodactyl grabs a small boy off a running horse.

During the airborne struggle between the two reptiles, Loana falls into the sea, and Tumak, seeing the marauding Rhamphorhynchus cannibalizing the Pteranodon's nest, assumes that his love has been eaten and gives her up for dead. Loana is rescued from the sea by her tribe, but knowing that she cannot live without Tumak, she persuades Ahot and others to lead her back to the Rock Tribe. The joyful reunion with Tumak is interrupted when Sakana, now leader of a new tribe, attacks. Sakana carries off Loana once again, but is speared by Tumak, just as the ground begins to shake and volcanoes spew forth burning lava. Though the earthquake swallows up many of the tribe, Tumak and Loana and a few others survive to rebuild the human race.

Of course, other than Raquel Welch to set male hormones raging, the chief attributes of *One Million Years B.C.* are Ray Harryhausen's dinosaurs. Interestingly enough, the first dinosaur the audience sees is one of those blown up, doctored iguanas—the kind that ran rampant in the 1940 version and which have been used in stock footage in so many grade Z lost world films that followed. In his oft-reprinted book *Film Fantasy Scrapbook*, Harryhausen said, "I have never favored using real lizards pretending to be dinosaurs, but in the remake of *One Million B.C.* we felt it might add to the realism if the first creature we saw was a living specimen. I think it worked well, although there has been much criticism from animation fans." A real tarantula, greatly enlarged, was also tossed in for good measure. But the animation of the giant Archelon Ischyros, on the other hand, was so realistic that some fans felt that a real tortoise had been used.

Sometimes all the delicate time-consuming work that goes into the detailed creation of a realistic model is for naught. Stills and production sketches of a Brontosaurus confrontation whetted the appetites of animation fans everywhere, but because production time was running behind schedule, it was decided to drop this dinosaur—a real shame too since next to Tyrannosaurus Rex, the Brontosaurus is everyone's favorite guy. The production of *One Million Years B.C.* was filmed on location on the island of Tenerife in the Canary archipelago. This macabre setting with its barren landscape peppered with endless craters and three-mile-high volcano seemed an appropriate world in which the Rock Tribe and Shell People could frolic among the dinosaurs. Carreras once again produced and wrote the screenplay, consisting of grunts and unintelligible mutterings.

Raquel Welch, of course, went on to greater glories, and so for their next prehistoric epic Hammer called upon Martine Beswicke, the dark-eyed, seductive ex-girlfriend of Tumak in *One Million Years B.C.* Beswicke, a sultry Jamaican actress, hauntingly resembles Barbara Steele in both stature and looks and, interestingly enough, both are very close friends in real life. Hammer felt that Martine would be perfect as the heartless tigress queen of a lost race of Amazon women in darkest Africa in their 1968 production of *Slave Girls*. Released in the United States as *Prehistoric Women*, the film bore no resemblance to the 1950 movie of the same name in which Laurette Luez and other nubile cave women search for mates and try to ward off the advances of a nine-foot-tall ape-man played by Johann Petursson.

The Hammer *Prehistoric Women* for one thing is set in the present day and concerns the adventures of hunting scout David Marchant (Michael Latimer), who follows a wounded leopard far into the African jungles where he discovers a tribe of hostile natives worshiping the statue of a white rhinoceros. He is captured and about to be killed when he falls against the horn of the rhinoceros, causing the walls of the cave around him to rumble amidst flashes of lightning and which finally open up like something out of Ali Baba. There he discovers a tropical paradise of magnificent flora and colorful birds. But also in this Garden of Eden he finds Saria (Edina Ronay), a beautiful blonde trying to escape from a race of Amazonian women, who have held her people captive since prehistoric times (hence the title). Both David and Saria are caught and taken before Queen Kari (Beswicke).

The remainder of the film is a series of rebuffs and ruses. David spurns the advances of Queen Kari, who throws him into a dungeon where he discovers the male members of the kingdom, chained and reduced to slovenly wimps. David plays up to Kari, trying to gain freedom for himself, the other men and Saria, with whom he has fallen in love. He is imprisoned once again but is able to rout the others for their escape. They overthrow the Amazons and rescue Saria just as she is about to be sacrificed to the rhinoceros god.

In a rather peculiar ending, Saria tells David that she cannot leave with him but pledges her everlasting love. He returns to camp and wonders if it has all been a dream. Then he sees a new safari arriving and among them is Saria in modern dress. Could this be the old reincarnation theme surfacing once more? Was David really in prehistoric times and did Saria keep her promise to return to him…only millions of years later? The mind boggles.

Prehistoric Women did have a rather silly story by Henry Younger, but it certainly wasn't the stupid turgid bore that its 1950 predecessor was. Technical values were excellent and Michael Carreras, in addition to producing, also directed, giving the film all the care of past Hammer achievements. *Slave Girls* was perhaps a more fitting title since fans expected a few dinosaurs in a film called *Prehistoric Women* (although from my memory of fifth-grade history books, dinosaurs and humans never co-existed in the same era). Devoid of the superb animation that made *One Million Years B.C.* so enjoyable, *Prehistoric Women* did showcase the talent and sexuality of Martine Beswicke, and her performance alone makes the film worth viewing.

Fans, however, had only to wait another two years for the lost world denizens to be reinstated in Hammer's second stop-motion animation prehistoric flick, *When Dinosaurs Ruled the Earth*. The Canary Islands were once again picked as the locale and producer Aida Young chose the Isle of Fuertaventura for shooting since the virgin territory had never before been used in a motion picture. Val Guest's screenplay was laced with touches of humor in this violent tale of humans at the dawn of time. It consisted of only 27 words and audiences were handed fliers so they could interpret the primitive language. Whether intentional or not, some of these words were used in the original *One Million B.C.*, only with different meanings. For instance, neecha in *Dinosaurs* meant "Stop! Come back!" but in the '40s film referred to a dinosaur. Wandi meant "Where? What? Where are you?" but was the name of the child thought to have perished in the climactic lava flow in the first *One Million B.C.* The

Saria (Edina Ronay) fights Queen Kari (Martine Beswicke) for David in Hammer's *Prehistoric Women*.

many definitions of Akhoba (from "Help" to "Forgive me" to "Greetings") also include the name of the Lon Chaney and Robert Brown—the cavemen leaders in both versions of *One Million*.

Despite the often confusing dialogue, a narrator sets the scene for *When Dinosaurs Ruled the Earth*: "It was a time of beginnings...a time of fear. Man's fear lest the sun should leave him...leave him in utter darkness. A time when the color of a woman's hair condemned her to a sacrifice to the sun. A time when there was no moon." Yes, the truth be it known, blondes had less fun in those days, as Sanna (*Playboy's* 1968 playmate of the year Victoria Vetri) of the Rock Tribe was to learn when she and several other fair-haired lasses find themselves about to be offered up to the sun god just as a piece of Old Sol breaks off to form the moon. In the resulting cyclone and confusion, Sanna flees into the churning sea and is rescued by Tara of the neighboring Sand Tribe...a rather peaceful group of Neanderthals resembling the Shell People in *One Million Years B.C.*

They are quite resourceful too, for when the film opens they have just captured an angry Plesiosaurus. The interaction between the beast and the humans is a masterpiece of stop-motion animation by Jim Danforth, equaling, if not surpassing, the achievements of his mentor Ray Harryhausen. The animal's lifelike

movements are smoothly controlled, especially when it breaks loose and is finally incinerated by the Sand Tribe.

Tara (Robin Hawdon, looking very much like Ringo Starr's Atouk in the 1981 spoof *Caveman*) falls for Sanna, but his jealous girlfriend Ayak (Imogen Hassall) causes a hassle of her own and turns the tribe against Sanna when Tara is off on a fishing trip. Kingsor (Patrick Allen), leader of the Rock Tribe, still blames Sanna for the disturbance in the heavens and visits the Sand People searching for her. Feeling unwanted and threatened by both tribes, Sanna flees into the jungle where she endures such dangers as a giant serpent and woman-eating plant. To escape the latter, she must cut off her golden tresses.

Delegates from both tribes search for Sanna and encounter a prehistoric Chasmosaurus that gores Kingsor. Tara tricks the beast and it plunges off a precipice. Then Tara is carried off by a Rhamphorhyncus who drops him in its nest of hungry young in a scene reminiscent of Raquel Welch's kidnapping by a Pteranodon in *One Million Years B.C.* Jim Danforth wanted to duplicate Harryhausen's animation of the giant, winged reptile swooping down to pick up a live actor without stopping the film. Unfortunately, because the scene was shot at the base of a cliff, the Rhamphorhynchus would have smashed into the rock wall and so that idea of film magic had to be discarded.

Tara kills the creature, finds Sanna's shorn locks, and assumes the plant has eaten her. Sanna, however, has taken refuge in the shell of a dinosaur egg and is mistaken by the mother for one of its own. This turns out to be the "cute" phase of the film as Sanna plays happily with the babies and is encouraged to eat a full grown deer that the mother has killed for her. Danforth decided to create a new breed of dinosaur for this family and did not base the models on any known prehistoric beast.

Tara and Sanna are finally reunited and she grabs him by the spear (how symbolic can you get?) and leads him away to her idyllic Eden to the accompaniment of Mario Nascimbene's haunting five-note motif (he did the memorable score for *The Vikings*). But all is not well in Paradise and their romantic trysting is interrupted when the Rock Tribe captures Tara and sets him adrift on a burning raft. He escapes when a seagoing Mosasurus capsizes the raft.

The Rock Tribe continues to pursue Tara and Sanna, who stealthily try to avoid some of those doctored up lizards that appeared to have escaped from the 1960 remake of *The Lost World*. Matters become repetitious as they are recaptured and Sanna is rescued by Mama dinosaur, which still hasn't accepted Tara as a dutiful son-in-law, thus leaving him behind tied to a stake for sacrifice. But the gravitational pull of the newly formed moon causes the tide to ebb, releasing savage giant crabs that pluck up and devour as many tribesmen as they can. Tara sees a monstrous tidal wave approaching and is freed by Sanna. Together with another couple they steer a raft directly into the oncoming wave and escape the thundering wall of water. The others are drowned, and the waters rise over the forests in a scene recreated from Paramount's deluge in the 1951 *When Worlds Collide.* When the waters recede, the two couples head toward the mountains to start life anew.

Victoria Vetri is pleasing to look at and Robin Hawdon turns his caveman Tara into a real gentleman, even though at times when he grins it appears as if he is having a bowel movement. Originally considered too young for the role, Hawdon plastered a beard on his face and went back for a second casting interview and was accepted. There are some nice touches throughout the film, like the mothers of the Rock Tribe trying to darken their fair skinned daughters' blonde hair so they won't be offered up to the sun when they reach sacrificial age. In addition to writing the screenplay, Val Guest also directed the prehistoric yarn with a deft hand, and *When Dinosaurs Ruled the Earth* is probably the most satisfying of the titles discussed in this chapter.

Victoria Vetri and Robin Hawdon star in *When Dinosaurs Ruled the Earth.*

As in *One Million Years B.C.*, time and money prohibited Danforth from creating some really exciting sequences. There was to have been an attack by giant prehistoric ants that had to be omitted even though shots of the fleeing cave people had already been filmed. Also discarded was a flock of Pterodactyls being buffeted about in the wind and sent crashing into cliffs. But what is included is probably the most realistic animation of a dinosaur film to date and even equals the computer-generated behemoths of *Jurassic Park*. As Don Leifert observed in an article in the premier issue of *Movie Club*, when in *Jurassic Park* the Tyrannosaurus Rex rips down the museum banner proclaiming *When Dinosaurs Ruled the Earth*, it's almost an acknowledgement of director Spielberg's feeling threatened by Hammer's artistic achievements, or more likely a tip of the hat to an animation master who influenced him.

For their fourth prehistoric epic, Hammer pressed the salient qualities that had distinguished their Gothic remakes of classic horror films to the limits, namely, shock value and extreme violence. Audiences, who had been stunned to see ample bloodletting, decapitations, smashed brains and seductive semi-nude vampires in the late 1950s and '60s, were now treated to the most violent stone-age film yet in the 1971 *Creatures the World Forgot*. The cave people in this outing were cruel, ugly, filthy folks, far removed from the semi-civilized bikini-clad sweethearts and jock-strapped hunks of *One Million* and *Dinosaurs*. The tone of this bleak, somber film differed considerably from the tongue-in-cheek comic-book action of *Prehistoric Women*. In fact, some reviewers consider *Creatures the World Forgot* the most realistic of the four films produced. Michael

Carreras, who had written and produced *One Million,* and Don Chaffey, who had directed that film, each had similar responsibilities on *Creatures.* They threw in enough gruesome details of early man's struggle for survival, enhanced by Hammer's top-notch production values, to create a believable and exciting story for audiences. The problem is that they threw out all of the creatures. Well, the Columbia marketing gang reinstated one in their advertising: "SEE the sensational new star Julie Ege. She's a creature you'll never forget!"

Oh, there is some animal life in the film: a huge bear and a mad wildebeest that gores Mak (Brian O'Shaughnessy), leader of the Rock Tribe. And then there is the climactic struggle between Nala (Swedish bombshell Julie Ege) and a giant serpent portrayed by a rather docile python. Otherwise the plot involves two brothers, Toomak (a variation on a rather common stone-age name) played by Tony Bonner, and Rool, played by Robert John. Both vie for Nala's attentions and end up forming separate tribes. The film is a succession of bloody battles and near rapes of Nala, thereby branding *Creatures* with an R rating. A tamer version of the film shows up occasionally on television with some of the nudity trimmed and the violence toned down. In order to save on time and expenses, Carreras and Chaffey incorporated clips from *One Million Years B.C.* for the film's volcanic eruption.

Three additional dinosaur flicks were considered at one time by Hammer. The studio talked with Ray Harryhausen about a remake of *King Kong*, but at that time RKO was adamant about keeping the copyright to their classic ape film. Then, ever since the late '60s, animator David Allen had envisioned an incredible story titled *Raiders of the Stone Ring* with a WWI zeppelin blown off course near Greenland and attacked by Pterodactyls from a kingdom of lizard men. Allen asked Danforth to begin work on the lizard creatures, but the special effects wizard was called to England to animate *When Dinosaurs Ruled the Earth.* Learning about Allen's project from Danforth, Hammer became interested in the property, changing the title to *Zeppelin V. Pterodactyls*. But as Jim Danforth's animation went into overtime, Hammer became disillusioned with the process and abandoned all stop motion in future films. This also eliminated the making of a sequel to *When Dinosaurs Ruled the Earth*, which would feature the mother creature that had befriended Victoria Vetri. This third project was to have been called *Dinosaur Girl.*

Perhaps the most bizarre of Hammer's lost worlds was filmed in 1968 and released as *The Lost Continent*. Based on the novel *Uncharted Seas* by mystery thriller writer Dennis Wheatley, the film depicts what happens to a boatload of misfits when their craft gets tangled in the Sargasso Sea and they discover not one but several lost races. Earlier that year, one of Hammer's most acclaimed movies, *The Devil's Bride* from Wheatley's supernatural chiller *The Devil Rides Out*, had been released and eight years later Hammer brought his *To the Devil...a Daughter* to the screen.

Hammer's *Lost Continent* bore no resemblance to the 1951 film of the same name in which Cesar Romero, John Hoyt, Hugh Beaumont, Whit Bissell, *et al.* are led by native girl Acquanetta up a remote island plateau to retrieve a lost missile and discover dinosaurs at the top. In the Hammer version, once again produced and directed by Carreras, the story begins on board the deck of a rusty freighter adrift in a sea of derelict ships—a funeral is in progress. In attendance are armored conquistadors, capuchin monks, busty damsels, a jazz pianist and the survivors of a hurricane that has swept them into the Sargasso Sea. The captain of the freighter, a once-prominent navel officer named Lansen (Eric Porter), who has sunk to carrying illegal explosives on his dilapidated old tub, the *Carlita*, tries to fathom how they ended up in this strange situation. And thus their story is told in flashback.

In addition to the volatile cargo which will bring him a fortune when sold on the black market, Captain Lansen harbors as motley and unpleasant a batch of passengers since those who crossed the ocean in Stanley Kramer's 1965 *Ship of Fools*...no, make that more like the misfits who found themselves aboard *The Sea Wolf* captained by Edward G. Robinson in 1941. First there's Eva (German actress Hildegarde Neff), mistress of a foreign dictator, who is fleeing from the police. She is being tailed by Ricaldi (Benito Carruthers), a secret agent of the dictator, who wants to recover stolen securities from Eva. There is a deported Doctor Webster (Nigel Stock), who will commit any malpractice for the right price, and his promiscuous daughter Unity, who will throw herself at any available man. A hopeless alcoholic piano player named Harry Tyler (Tony Beckley) is probably the least offensive character on board, especially since he goes on the wagon later after taking the blame for Dr. Webster's demise when the latter is gobbled up by a shark. Good old Hammer veteran Michael Ripper is a nasty sea lawyer, who confronts Captain Lansen about the mysterious cargo labeled Phosfor-B.

The first half of *The Lost Continent* deals with the interrelationships of these disagreeable people. Unity throws herself at Harry Tyler...Eva makes a play for Captain Lansen. As unpleasant as the passengers and crew are, the audience is intrigued by their character developments, a plus for screenwriter Carreras using the pseudonym of his gardener Michael Nash. Then as a hurricane approaches and Captain Lansen refuses to change his course, the crew learns that the deadly cargo Phosphor-B explodes on contact with water and they scurry like rats into a lifeboat and are lost in the fury of the storm. The captain and his passengers also abandon ship, where they ride out the waves but can't quite seem to dispel the growing tensions among themselves.

The seaweed has clogged the engines of the *Carlita* and strangely enough seems to have a life of its own...wrapping its writhing tendrils around Captain Lansen's leg and pulling an unfortunate crewman into the sea. The ship is then carried forward through the nasty weed to a sea of lost ships. On board the

The man-hungry Unity (Suzanna Leigh) meets the woman-hungry octopus in *The Lost Continent.*

Carlita, the man-hungry Unity makes a play for Ricaldi but is attacked by a giant octopus that pops up from the side of the boat. Ricaldi chops away at the tentacle, freeing Unity, but is devoured by the beast, showing that Unity wasn't the only man-hungry creature in the area. Next, an alluring young woman, Sarah (17-year-old Dana Gillespie), approaches the ship...her bountiful breasts equaling in size the helium balloons used to transport her across the nefarious seaweed. She informs them that her pursuers want to enslave her, and sure enough, these ancient Spanish conquistadors attack the ship.

The pirates are defeated and return to their king who rules from one of the derelict ships. He is a young lad called El Diablo (Darryl Read) and a descendant of the shipwrecked Spaniards. Under the evil influence of his chief advisor, the Ku Klux Klan garbed Inquisitor (Eddie Powell), El Diablo has become a tyrant bent on enslaving the other gentle inhabitants of the Sargasso Sea.

By this time, the now sober Harry Tyler has been smitten by the mysterious Sarah, and with two crewmembers, Pat (Jimmy Hanley) and Chief (James Cossins), pursues her when she slips overboard to return to her people. Pat is eaten by a giant snail crab, which in turn is done in by a scorpion crab. Sarah and her rescuers are captured and prepared for sacrifice to giant clam monsters. Captain Lansen arrives in time with explosives and a rousing battle ensues. El Diablo tries to escape the hypnotic hold of the Inquisitor, who stabs the boy,

Critics felt the monsters in *The Lost Continent* were unrealistic.

thereby ending the flashback and returning the story to the opening funeral. Lansen's Phosphor-B is used to destroy the Hellhole of the Spaniards and burn up the living seaweed as the small band of survivors return to their now freed ship, presumably wiser and better persons for their adventures.

Despite the highly imaginative story, *The Lost Continent* was a commercial failure. Robert Mattey from the Walt Disney Studios devised the monsters, which many felt were cumbersome and unrealistic. The entire film takes on an unrealistic atmosphere, which is part of the charm of *The Lost Continent*. The acting is on a par with the professionalism of other Hammer films and the cast is persuasive in their psychological differences and their belief in the monsters when they finally appear. Most of all, *The Lost Continent* can be enjoyed on two levels: a drama involving complex characters, and an all-out fantasy finish highlighted by some of the most outlandish prehistoric mutations ever to appear in a Hammer production.

The ultimate lost civilization film was considered by Hammer in 1971 as a joint production with American International. Filmed at least three times previously, *Dante's Inferno* describes the exploits of a sadistic millionaire and what awaits him on his journey through Hell. At this period of time, Hammer was infamous for depictions of explicit sex, sadism and violence, and did not shy away from extensive nudity. Given the subject of Satan presiding over a world whose inhabitants suffered the tortures of the damned, Hammer's discarded *Dante's Inferno* would have made a Hell of a motion picture.

The Hammer Factory: Hammer Films, Corman Style

by Fred Olen Ray

When people think of cost-cutting practices in the motion picture industry, they invariably think of the low-budget antics of Roger Corman. Time and time again Corman pulled every trick in his repertoire to get films produced as quickly and economically as possible. Eyeing the potential profits as he careened recklessly through filming, he established a solid cast and crew that sped from picture to picture with dependable skills and just the right glib attitude to pull off the seemingly impossible.

Always looking for the deal, Corman spearheaded several haphazard-filming techniques that were rarely imitated, or even successful, when used by other filmmakers.

One of his most often used techniques was the filming of more than one picture on the same sets or locations as another film. Sometimes the financing for the first picture would come from outside, and when completed, Corman and his entourage would linger on for another week and shoot an even cheaper picture that he, himself, would own.

This happened when Corman made *She Gods of Shark Reef* (1956) for a private group of investors and followed it up with his self-financed *Naked Paradise* (1956). While in South Dakota he shot *Ski Troop Attack* (1960) and *Beast From The Haunted Cave* (1960) back-to-back with the same cast; in Puerto Rico they made three consecutive pictures: the color *Last Woman on Earth, Battle of Blood Island* (featuring a cast of two) and *Creature From the Haunted Sea* (all 1960).

Dementia 13 (1963) was made during breaks in the filming of *The Young Racers* (1963) and so forth. As sometimes happens, the quality varied amongst the different projects, but undoubtedly, money was saved.

One of the foremost companies to try their hand at such a procedure was Hammer Films. In 1966 they attempted to produce two sets of

The castle from *Dracula—Prince of Darkness* is disguised for *Rasputin—The Mad Monk*.

movies utilizing the same sets and some of the same personnel in an effort to economize and perhaps increase the speed with which films were released into the marketplace. The movies were *Dracula—Prince of Darkness* and *Rasputin—The Mad Monk*, both starring Christopher Lee and Barbara Shelley, followed by *The Reptile* and *Plague of the Zombies*. Like Corman, the subterfuge was disguised by sending the pictures out co-billed in a mixture of the two groups, thus *Dracula* went out with *Plague* and *Rasputin* with *The Reptile*. Corman had co-billed the Dakota lensed *Ski Troop Attack* with the Puerto Rican *Battle of Blood Island* with the same basic idea: don't get caught.

Thus the re-use of the sets was less likely to be noticed by the moviegoer. In some instances they tripped themselves up—i.e., the Tsarina's Palace exterior in *Rasputin* (aka Dracula's castle in *Prince of Darkness*) looks suspiciously like the remote country home that Rasputin is lured to at the climax. Even the churchyard in *The Reptile* looks like Dracula's castle revamped.

The re-use of the sets withstanding, the pictures must be seen as individual efforts and stand or fall on their own merits. I, personally, have always *wanted* to like *The Reptile*. The combination of elements seemed like such a sure-fire winner: foreign curse, mystical religious overtones, large-breasted reptile monster, Cornish village setting and Noel Willman. Can't beat it? Well, maybe...

The Reptile, like its partner-in-crime *Plague of the Zombies*, seems to lay bare some deep inner dread and loathing for the non-British cultures that torment them. The English seem to be punishing themselves for their attempts to subjugate people and their religious beliefs in distant lands.

While the East Indian influence is still quite thick in the U.K., they do seem to be very wary of their actual culture and customs, beyond a good lamb biriyani, mind you. The same creeping guilt also manifests itself in Tyburn's *The Ghoul,* in which Peter Cushing's son is cursed by Indians to be the flesh-eating ghoul of the title, as well as the British-lensed *Oblong Box*. What are the English so afraid of?

In *Plague of the Zombies* it is a Haitian problem that haunts the same little Cornish village. It's almost as if the under-trod are coming back to get their persecutors in the form of ethnic monsters—literally turning members of the local populace into beasts that represent their various cultural backgrounds. In each of the two films the town is plagued by a strange illness, equating death. In *The Reptile* it's the Black Death, in *Plague*, well, they just don't know, but the villagers are dropping like flies.

In both films they dig up their dead to have a second look-see. In both films Michael Ripper does some digging. Coincidence? I think not. In both films the evil originates in a far off country and centers its current activities in a large manor house decorated with art objects from that far-off country. Both films end in a big fire with the monster(s) getting their licks in on the responsible party.

The makeup for *The Reptile* is barely passable. In fact, it really doesn't extend down beyond the girl's cheeks. In a darkened cellar room or with a quick cut it looks okay, but still photographs show it for what it really is: a sort of half-done job. Whenever confronted with a question about the quality (or lack of it), makeup maestro Roy Ashton has always sidestepped, artfully pointing out that the fangs really dripped venom!

The *Plague* zombie makeup is much better, though inconsistent. The masks worn by the flaming stuntmen at the climax are laughable, but overall the work is effective (never mind that the film's most dramatic use of the undead is in a dream sequence that takes place out of context with reality).

By comparison *Plague* is probably one of the liveliest Hammer films ever made. Stuff actually happens in the movie with some regularity. John Carson makes an excellent villain and for once a true feeling of horror is squeezed out of the viewer. Like most Hammer films, the audience is way ahead of the people in the movie, waiting patiently for the film's characters to catch up with the rest of us. It's passable in *Plague* and unbearable in *The Reptile*. During the tedious course of *The Reptile* the audience almost feels like wising up the characters onscreen. The audience knows everything within the first 15 minutes and must now wait, thumbs a'twitter, while the heroes sort it all out in the slowest possible fashion. If only they'd seen the *Coming Attraction*s…

The one aspect left to our imagination is what the Reptile girl looks like, but thanks to the movie's poster, we're ahead on that game as well. It has always amazed me that filmmakers go to such lengths to keep the monster's appearance a matter of mystery and then the distributors splash its image all over the advertising materials.

And let me remind you—I really do *want* to like *The Reptile*. It's just soooo hard. At one point the young hero walks into the local pub and, by God, they're actually singing "Shenandoah!" Unbelievable!

Of the four films being discussed *Dracula—Prince of Darkness* and *Plague* probably work out best, although *Dracula* plods along at a snail's pace. What probably salvages the films are a sort of twisted, kinky weirdness that lies just below the surface of good taste.

Obviously, zombie master Clive Hamilton (John Carson) lusts after Jackie Pearce, and who wouldn't? She's inconsistently (with most Hammer heroines) non-virginally sexy and stacked (even lying flat on her back dead in the morgue she's giving that shroud a good straining). And as one of the few holdovers between the two films, Pearce goes from being monster-girl in *The Reptile* to being monster-bait in *Plague*. I think she may have been dating some Hammer exec at the time. In both films she gets killed.

Dracula, likewise, has some nasty bits up his sleeve and serving up his own blood via an open chest wound certainly must have seemed rather perverse at the time. Blood, in fact, flows freest in these films and the Black Death is nothing to sneeze at either. In *Plague* it seemed like everyone wants to get laid. A further confession of the British loathing of foreign cultures?

Most Hammer villains were at least slightly noble (Hammer treated Egyptians somewhat better). Here they wallow in their own decadence, corrupted by their exposure to non-British customs.

Rasputin, however touted, is the runt of the litter. It attempts to take on such a grandiose historical saga that it cannot hope to succeed. The sets are uncomfortably small, in many cases the actors' heads nearly scrape the ceilings. The Tsarina's palace is a barren place devoid of guards or servants or any sense of majesty for that matter. The story is noticeably scaled down to where every budgetary seam leaps out at the viewer. They dare not attempt to portray the great cities of Russia.

Christopher Lee and Barbara Shelley star in *Rasputin—The Mad Monk.*

The presence of Christopher Lee, so uncharacteristically upbeat that it becomes humorous, is the film's only highlight. Unfortunately as scripted, whether he's brooding or dancing a jig, Lee does not imbue the character with any of the complexities required to flesh out such a deviously calculating figure. Rasputin's motivations are murky and his control over the royal family is not explored. Tsar Nicholas does not even appear in the film—perhaps Michael Ripper was ill that day (too much digging?).

The picture fails miserably as a historical drama and worse as a horror picture, which it was advertised. Rasputin's supernatural healing powers are tossed off without so much as a hi-de-ho and his death scene was not nearly as dramatic as the real character's was said to be. The producers say they went to the trouble of having one of the (then still living) assassins sign off on the authenticity of the script, but they needn't have bothered. *Rasputin—The Mad Monk* could have easily been retitled *Rumplestilskin—The Mad Spinner* with equal success. It is fun, however, to watch Lee strut around like the cock-of-the-walk, thrilled silly to be anything but Dracula. It would be a wild guess, but I might be convinced that *Rasputin* was the cheapest of all the four films and certainly the least enduring.

Even in death Lee lands on the ice that cracked the skull of the young Tsar earlier (although they are supposed to be two entirely different locations), and it is the same ice that gets him willy-nilly at the conclusion of *Dracula—Prince of Darkness.*

What order the films were shot in is still hazy as conflicting reports from the actors, directors, producers and crewmembers vary. I suppose it really doesn't matter. The pictures achieved the desired result of cranking out a multiple package of films in record time at below normal cost and then foisting them

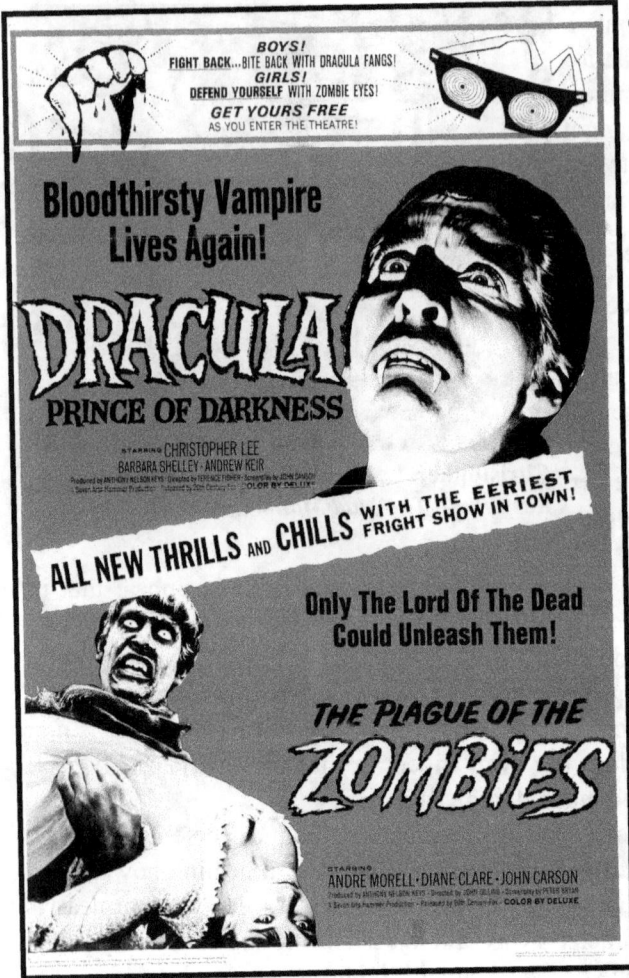

onto Hammer-hungry fans when the monster cycle of the 1960s was in bloom. Lucky boys and girls even received free *Dracula Fangs* and *Zombie Eye Protectors* when attending the promoted shock-fest. One can only wonder if the fangs dripped real venom...

Some call *Plague* and *Reptile* the Cornball (...er, Cornwall) Classics and perhaps they are, on the basis of their wildly divergent storylines and approaches (Hammer would not stray this far from home for some time to come); *Dracula—Prince of Darkness* and *Rasputin—The Mad Monk*...well, they filled the other half of the bill and had Hammer's true bona fide star, Christopher Lee. Shouldn't that be enough?

In 1970 the Hammer boys would give it one more shot with *Scars of Dracula* and *Horror of Frankenstein.* Filmed back-to-back on the same cramped sets, the illusion evaporated quickly with their release in the States on the same double-bill. Oops. At least we still got Chris Lee as part of the bargain and, while still dull in a way only Hammer could make them, they were not bad pictures entirely. At least *Scars of Dracula* gave the viewer what he paid for—a movie in which Dracula was actually an integral force as opposed to the moveable prop he had become. The return to co-filming seemed again to be one of monetary consideration, but this time instead of trying to capitalize quickly on a hot trend, Hammer seemed to be gasping their last—trying to get a shaky foothold on that same tricky ice that their monsters were always slipping under.

The Abominable Snowman

by Gary J. Svehla

As the years go by, as I watch the earlier black-and-white Hammer Film Productions once again, I've come to appreciate these monochrome Val Guest–directed productions. They are subtler than the Technicolor costume period productions and ultimately more adult-oriented. A 10-year-old back in 1960 would love Hammer's *Brides of Dracula* or *The Mummy*, but would he appreciate *Quatermass II* or *The Abominable Snowman* as much as his father would? No, these earlier Hammers were more cerebral and understated, and while as a child they seemed more slight, from an adult's perspective, these films gain in stature the more times they are viewed.

The Nigel Kneale–scripted/Val Guest–directed *The Abominable Snowman* is pure philosophy, as two great personalities—Tom Friend and Professor Rollason—lock horns in the great human debate. On one side Friend (gruff American actor Forrest Tucker) becomes the huckster-manipulator who wants to find the Yeti to exploit the find and make oodles of money. On the other side Professor Rollason (the suave British actor Peter Cushing) is interested in the

The Abominable Snowman stars Peter Cushing (second from left) and Forrest Tucker (right), whose characters lock horns throughout the movie.

mere scientific find of the century—and deciding whether human beings are the more savage species of the two. Ostensibly on an expedition to find plants, Rollason's wife is stunned and disappointed when her husband reveals his true intentions—to join the Friend expedition to search out the Abominable Snowman. The revered High Llama fosters the notion that "there is no Yeti" even though Rollason and his crew know that the Llama realizes such is not the case. And great white hunter Ed Shelley (Robert Brown), the man who supposedly is delighted with the one-on-one confrontation between hunter and prey, panics and dies from a heart attack when he is used as bait by Friend to lure the Yeti into a trap (not realizing that Friend has rendered his only rifle useless).

Incredibly well photographed (combining the village set at Bray with snow sets at Pinewood Studios intercut with actual snow sequences filmed in Switzerland) making good use of HammerScope photography, the movie has never looked better with Anchor Bay's gorgeous 35mm widescreen print. Nigel Kneale and Val Guest offer an adequate audio commentary, but many of the stories have already been told and long periods of dead space appear between respective comments. The British *World of Hammer* TV series episode offered this time out is "Peter Cushing," and an American trailer is included.

The subtlety of character interaction, along with the philosophical themes this movie discusses, all underplayed and involving, make this a top-10 on my list of all-time-favorite Hammer Productions. The Yeti is seldom seen although the real monsters are revealed to be human, but because of the well-written script and terrific ensemble performances, *The Abominable Snowman* penetrates the mind as well as the emotions. It is a movie begging to be rediscovered.

The Curse of the Werewolf

by Gary J. Svehla

Terence Fisher's 1960 *Curse of the Werewolf*, and not *The Phantom of the Opera*, was the Hammer director's first misfire, a production that wanted so desperately to deliver so much more than it did. By far the longest film in this collection, *Curse of the Werewolf* suffers from too much plot, tepid pacing and a lack of keystone sequences that became the focus of most Hammer productions. While *Curse of the Werewolf* offers some creative high points via performance, direction and cinematography, it suffers the bane of the worst Hammer offerings... the film seems overlong and boring.

The film's first act is most intriguing, featuring the wonderful Richard Wordsworth as the beggar who crashes the high society wedding party of the perverse Marques (Anthony Dawson in a wonderful supporting performance) and finds himself locked in jail, eternally. When the buxom jailer's daughter (Yvonne Romain) refuses to sexually satisfy the festering Marques, she is thrown in the jail and savagely raped by the beggar, now more beast than human. Heaving and sweaty, the jailer's daughter is returned to the Marques, but instead of sexually submitting to him, she stabs the old bastard to death. However, she is now pregnant and has the misfortune to give birth on Christmas day, thus giving birth to a werewolf. The mother dies at childbirth but the kindly Don Alfredo (Clifford Evans) and his wife adopt the young child, who is christened Leon (growing up to be the husky Oliver Reed). The period detail and perversity of performance and action maintain keen interest. Unfortunately, the middle third of the film crawls at a snail's pace, featuring a few sheep whose throats have been ripped out and a few sequences with the haunted young Leon sporting fangs after somnambulistic wanderings. Even when the now fully grown Leon leaves home to make his way in the world, the action of bonding with a buddy and find-

Oliver Reed and Yvonne Romain in a publicity shot for *The Curse of the Werewolf*.

Leon (Oliver Reed) begins to change in *The Curse of the Werewolf*.

ing work is simply the type of non-action for which Hammer deserves criticism. By the time Leon transforms into wolf, the film has simply lost viewer attention, and it does not help that most of the initial werewolf murders only show victims' reactions or outline the wolf in shadow. Terence Fisher is a master at maintaining a horrific mood and the murders are well staged. The sets are also excellent in period detail.

When the werewolf itself is shown (absolutely the best makeup execution ever by Roy Ashton and one of the best classic monsters in horror history), the film becomes a Hammer classic for about 20 minutes (and 20 classic minutes do not a classic film make). Oliver Reed's physique immeasurably helps the werewolf performance, with his hulking presence towering over the others in the cast. The use of gray fur and a partially open shirt produce a savage monster. The werewolf makeup comes to life in the carefully executed face, with lots of saliva flowing from the mouth, making the werewolf appear more animal than human. Reed (and his double?) breathes life into the makeup and brings his werewolf to startling life. Unfortunately the wolf is not seen very often in close-up, and it most deservedly should be. However, Arthur Grant's cinematography following the werewolf across Spanish rooftops ultimately making his way to the church bell tower is spectacular and gives the film a sense of depth. Even Clifford Evans' dramatic rifle shot rips into the beast's body and kicks Reed on his ass within seconds. It's a powerful sequence and seldom has a rifle shot been filmed this violently on the screen. If the movie contained more active werewolf action, *Curse of the Werewolf* might have been a classic. However, in its current overlong and dead-in-the-middle plot structure, *Curse of the Werewolf* is a generally dull werewolf movie that sports one of the best lycanthropic makeups ever executed. That's worth something, isn't it?

The Devil Rides Out

by Gary J. Svehla

By 1968, Hammer was in transition; Terence Fisher and the type of classic Gothic Hammer production that cemented the company's image (*Horror of Dracula, The Hound of the Baskervilles, The Mummy, Brides of Dracula, Kiss of the Vampire, The Gorgon*) was almost over. No longer producing films at folksy Bray studios, the old Hammer team (Fisher, Anthony Hinds, Michael Carreras, Anthony Nelson-Keys) was soon to be replaced by a new, more generic crew that would increase the budgets of Hammer films but decrease their quality (the era of *The Vampire Lovers, Vampire Circus, Lust for a Vampire, Twins of Evil*).

In many ways *The Devil Rides Out* (1968), along with *Frankenstein Must Be Destroyed* (1969), were the final two classic Hammer films produced in the old style using the old team (*The Devil Rides Out* contained a score by James Bernard, direction by Terence Fisher, production design by Bernard Robinson, etc.). Christopher Lee, as Duc de Richleau, becomes the dominant performer, turning in one of those obsessive heroic turns made so famous by Peter Cushing. As written (with a wonderful script by Richard Matheson based upon the Dennis Wheatley novel), Richleau becomes one of the strongest roles of Lee's career, showcasing a powerful, charismatic screen presence with lines of dialogue worthy of the character.

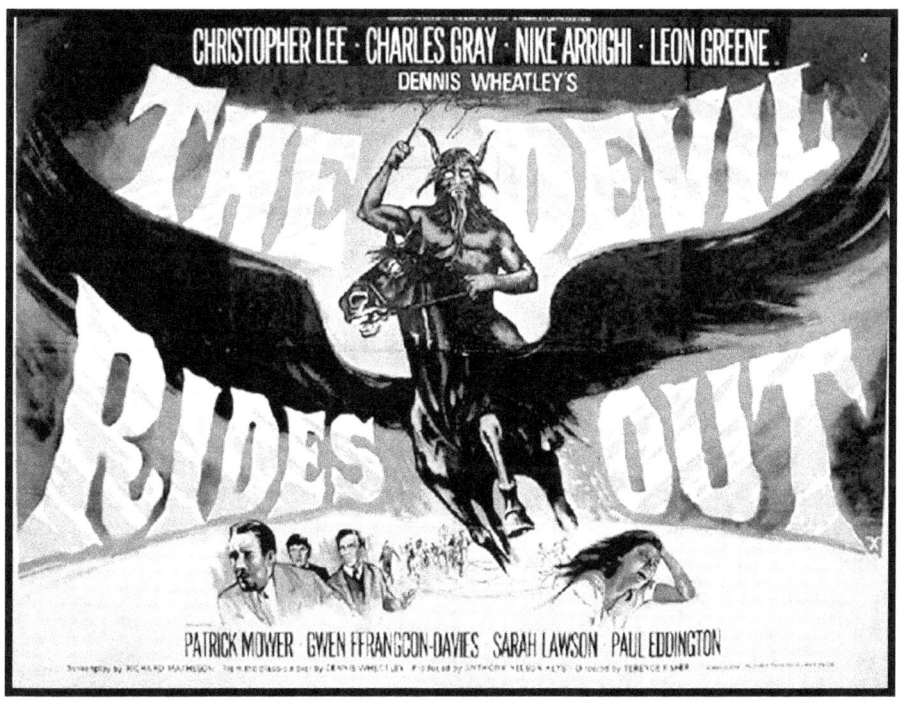

Christopher Lee as Duc de Richleau in *The Devil's Bride* with Paul Eddington, Nike Arrighi and Leon Greene

For the first half, *The Devil Rides Out* is superb, classic Hammer entertainment involving the seduction of young Simon (Patrick Mower) into a polite society of Satanists, headed by the distinguished Mocata (Charles Gray, perhaps a tad too subdued). As Richleau and companion Rex (Leon Greene) become aware of the company they find themselves amongst, a daring rescue of the spellbound Simon leads to his subsequent escape from his friends and "baptism" into the cult of evil. For a Hammer film, the pacing is energetic and non-stop, the plot contains enough mystery as the onion layers of the story slowly peel away, keeping the viewer transfixed.

But once mysterious Tanith (Nike Arrighi) and Simon are rescued from the outside initiation ritual invoking the Devil himself, the plot slows down considerably as the rescued parties are sequestered in a country estate. This leads to the double-climax involving a protective, magic circle and the satanic attacks masterminded by Mocata (with lame special effects, even for 1968), which leads to the death and then rebirth of Tanith in an ending that never quite grabs the audience by its collective lapels.

But half a great film is still to be commended, and the film's slower second half is quite good with a marvelous Lee performance to latch onto.

MUMMIES

Christopher Lee Is The Mummy; Peter Cushing Is Kharismatic

by Gary J. Svehla

After creating the complex Dracula/vampire mythos and the ongoing fictional biography of Baron Frankenstein, Hammer Films sought a new legend to explore. Dipping into the Universal monster canon once again, screenwriter Jimmy Sangster decided to reinvent the monstrous Mummy as the next Gothic installment of Hammer horror in 1959. However, instead of remaking the 1932 Boris Karloff original, Sangster turned instead to the cursed Banning family featured in the Universal mummy sequels starring Tom Tyler and Lon Chaney, Jr. With the Hammer factory placing its full creative energy into the project, those 1940s Universal productions would be bettered artistically by Hammer's wealth of talent and creativity.

Director Terence Fisher, Hammer's creator of horror mythology and its most gifted director, crafted *The Mummy* as a worthy successor to recent Hammer triumphs such as *Horror of Dracula* and *The Revenge of Frankenstein*. Of course the dynamic duo from *Horror of Dracula*, heroic Peter Cushing and devilish Christopher Lee, would return, with Lee portraying Kharis, the reanimated Egyptian high priest/Mummy, and Peter Cushing portraying archaeologist John Banning.

Although this was not the only Hammer mummy film with which Peter Cushing was associated (he would later, uncredited, recite the narration for 1967's *The Mummy's Shroud*), Cushing approached *The Mummy* knowing that he would not reprise the role of hero John Banning, as he would Baron Frankenstein and Van Helsing. The Professor and the Baron were iconic, larger-than-life characters, whereas Banning was a regular human being, an archaeologist caught in a complex mystery of revenge, so Cushing played him as an ordinary man. However, Peter Cushing would never allow *ordinary* to become *bland*.

Peter Cushing, as John Banning in *The Mummy,* uses one of his precious props.

Regrettably, perhaps because George Pastell (as evil Egyptian Mehemet Bey) and Christopher Lee have the splashy roles, Cushing's performance here is one of his most overlooked, even though Cushing's Banning becomes a synthesis of all his strengths as an actor. And, as befits the star whose opening-credit billing is twice as large as Christopher Lee's, Cushing creates a memorable hero that puts David Manners and Dick Foran to shame.

From the outset, Cushing makes John Banning an invalid—literally, at first—as he's suffering from a broken leg that needs to be properly set by a doctor. Stephen Banning (Felix Aylmer), his father and leader of the Egyptian expedition they're on, tells partner Joseph Whemple (Raymond Huntley) "that's for him to decide... I'll abide by what he says," making it clear that Banning respects and trusts his son's judgment. Cushing develops a marvelous hopping gait, using a walking cane, which allows his damaged leg to function in bouncy swoops that create a herky-jerky rhythm. Even though lame, Banning is always energetic and in a hurry.

Drawing upon another strength, when John Banning is shown an Egyptian artifact, the seal of Ananka's tomb, "Props" Cushing goes into immediate action by picking up a magnifying glass and looking carefully at the newly discovered relic. Cushing's face expresses curiosity, wonder, intensity and obsession. Moving the magnifying glass all around and changing his angle of investigation, Peter Cushing demonstrates how he can take any insignificant prop and make it meaningful in a matter of seconds. Later, after his father's murder at the hands of Kharis, John wants to sort through his father's papers to discover a motive for his murder by "person or persons unknown." Cushing exploits the library-research sequence, reading and re-reading his father's papers, limping across

the room, smoking a cigarette, pouring a drink from a decanter and finally pulling a portfolio from the library shelf. The way in which Cushing commands a sequence, making all eyes turn to him, is a credit to his artistry as an actor.

Boasting an expressive face, Peter Cushing is equally blessed with a commanding voice, and both are used to good effect in an early sequence where Whemple announces to the younger Banning that his father has just now entered what he believes to be the tomb of Princess Ananka. Banning's face lights up and the twinkle gleams in his eyes as he hesitantly inquires, "Is he quite sure... no doubt at all?" In typical fashion, Cushing uses his emotive hand to push disheveled hair back into place, smiling in eager anticipation and excitement. Grimacing in pain when he tries to move his leg to investigate, he tells Whemple to get back to the tomb to help his father, understanding full well that his limp leg would slow up the proceedings. Suddenly a horrid scream is heard bellowing from the digs. Immediately, John Banning tries to swing his leg into action, but the pain is too intense, as his face reveals. After father Stephen is found raving incoherently, bent over a sarcophagus, John Banning reveals, with deliberate enunciation, "The best of my life has been among the dead. But I never worked in a place that had such an aura of menace. There's something evil in there... I felt it." Cushing's voice can stir up the heebie-jeebies every time he speaks of *e-vil* or the "aura of menace." And Cushing never delivers his line reading sarcastically, for his primary strength as actor is making the audience believe every fantastical occurrence by nature of his seriousness and intensity.

The chief horror of *The Mummy* occurs not in vampire crypts and coffins in Castle Dracula but in the expansive, ornate Banning living room, a room lined with high French windows and library shelves. After Banning orders wife Isobel to go up to bed—"Isobel, I never asked you to do anything before, but I'm ordering you now!"—Banning opens up his gun case, prepares a rifle, and

Lee and Cushing once again face off in a battle of good vs. evil in *The Mummy*.

paces, awaiting the arrival of the Mummy. There's a suspenseful buildup, then the Mummy comes crashing through the French windows and John quickly fires off two shots that rip through the Mummy's gauze and decaying flesh. Even with his game leg, Banning rolls backwards over his wooden desk and climbs onto a library shelf to fetch a metal spear, which he thrusts downward through the Mummy, but the fiend keeps coming forward, finally engaging Banning in hand-to-hand combat, the Mummy quickly putting his gigantic hand around Banning's throat. As they struggle, disobedient Isobel suddenly appears, her hair worn down, the spitting image of Princess Ananka. Her appearance causes Kharis to stop in his tracks, his sad eyes mournfully pathetic. Slowly the Mummy turns and walks out of the house. This sequence, perhaps the most thrilling and energetic of the movie, demonstrates just how adept Peter Cushing is when it comes to acrobatic stunts and physical prowess.

In a later but equally impressive sequence, the Mummy again attacks, but this time from within the house, as Banning expects Kharis to again appear at the French windows. In a marvelous, fast-cut sequence shot from over Kharis' shoulder, Banning, momentarily terrified, turns, rifle in arm, but has no to time to fire before the Mummy grabs the rifle and again tries to choke the life out of him. With great strength, Kharis bends Banning back over a chair, until Isobel again appears, Banning screaming, "Your hair! Put down your hair!" Mehemet Bey, who is also present, commands Kharis to kill Isobel, but the Mummy's undying love for Ananka causes the creature to snap Bey's back instead, then carry the reincarnated beauty off to the swamp.

But perhaps Peter Cushing is best when he is intellectually challenged by a worthy adversary and the subtlety of his dialogue carries the full dramatic weight of *The Mummy*, suggesting the figurative nature of Banning as invalid. Such is the sequence between Banning and Mehemet Bey when Banning goes to call on his recently arrived Egyptian neighbor. The initial meeting is warm and cordial, from "Good evening; my name is Banning... hope I haven't called at an inconvenient time" to "You've come from Egypt, didn't you? I've spent many years in your country!" However, Bey soon asks about Banning's father, inquiring if he is retired, and Banning reveals the already obvious fact that his father is dead. Bey reveals his disdain for archaeology and the "desecration of tombs sealed for all time, removing the remains of kings," by putting them in the British Museum to be stared at for all eternity. Banning counters by claiming ancient Egyptians' "intelligence [was] remarkably low, believing in artificial creeds and beliefs," which leads to his insult of the god Karnack as a third-rate god: "He was insignificant, based upon ludicrous beliefs." Bey objects, "You're intolerant," to which Banning responds, calm-faced but with an obvious tinge of anger, "It occurred to me—but I dismissed it!" This causes Bey to declare, "I don't think your evil will go unpunished!" To which Banning counters, "That sounds like a threat!" Ultimately, Banning, attempting to soothe already ruffled feathers, adds, "I've only come here to welcome you. But I guess I got carried away."

Peter Cushing triumphs in *The Mummy*, a movie additionally supported by overall good acting, strong scripting, effective set decoration, cinematography and direction. Cushing demonstrates his command of his craft through a characterization that thrives on physical imperfections (his broken leg), witty dialogue (his volley with George Pastell), a nimble use of props, and effective use of energized leaps, rolls, and lunges to make his no-longer-youthful hero physically effective and, well, even dashing. Whether piercing the Mummy with a metal shaft or insulting third-rate gods such as Karnack, John Banning is a character that demonstrates all the aspects we love about Peter Cushing, an actor who never gave less than his absolute best.

Hammer Films Unearth The Mummy

by Richard Klemensen

Things couldn't have looked rosier for Hammer Film Productions Ltd. as 1959 rolled around. After the local success of the two *Quatermass* films, *The Curse of Frankenstein* in 1956 and *Horror of Dracula* in 1957 had set the film world on fire. Christopher Lee said that the head of Universal Pictures told him and other Hammer honchos that *Horror of Dracula* saved Universal from bankruptcy. With this money rolling in (although not always into their own bank account), Hammer was in demand. The last two years had seen their productions going out with Paramount, RKO, Columbia, Warner Bros. and other U.S. major studios. Universal, still basking in the glow of the huge success of the *Dracula* subject, basically opened up their coffers and offered Hammer carte blanche to do any film from their library, so it was only natural that after a *Frankenstein* and *Dracula* film, the next one in line would be *The Mummy*.

The character of *The Mummy* is the least interesting of the big three (Frank and Drac). a speechless pile of bones and bandages; it is your basic "one note" idea. Yet Universal, after the original 1932 film with Boris Karloff (moody but *oh so* slow and boring), did four definitely grade "C" sequels in the early 1940s.

Under normal circumstances, this would have been an opportunity for Hammer's resident "Gothic" producer, Anthony Hinds. Hinds, son of one of the co-founders of Hammer, Will Hinds (also know as Will Hammer on the British variety stage—and the source of the Hammer name), and a 48 percent owner of Hammer since his father's death in a cycling accident, had produced Hammer's other Gothic winners. But he had no real interest in the Mummy subject, and while involved in a United States trip to trumpet a new Columbia production deal (see section on *Curse of the Mummy's Tomb* beginning page 216), basically did not want to do the film. As Michael Carreras (son of Hammer's chief, and major stockholder, James Carreras) said: "I think you'll find—in a way—that it was Tony (Hinds) *not* wanting to do it rather then me *wanting* to do it." Michael Carreras did not care for the Gothic horrors himself, and was more comfortable with the war films and crime melodramas that were also Hammer's forte during this period. In 1959 Carreras would produce five of the eight films made that year. He had just completed *Yesterday's Enemy* when, on February 25, 1959 at Bray Studios he began Hammer's version of *The Mummy*. Carreras said:

> This was my first Gothic. But it was the one Gothic that had that sort of pretty element—this Egyptian bit. I think I like that more than the horror aspect. I've never been into the Gothic; that was Tony...but this was one that fascinated me. I wanted to work with Terry [director, Terence Fisher], too—I liked Terry

The Mummy, **Hammer 1959**

very much…and I don't think the Mummy appealed to Tony. The only thing I thought was that we ought to spend a bit more on the parade, the funeral procession. I wanted a bit more of the Egyptology and the razzmatazz…!

Terence Fisher. Is there any director's name more associated with Hammer? Any filmmaker who draws such divergent opinions on his skills? There are those who would make him an "auteur" (he wasn't). And naysayers that consider

Bernard Robinson designed the beautiful sets for *The Mummy*.

him nothing more than a journeyman and the one person least responsible for the success of the Hammer films he directed (but how wrong they are!). Fellow Hammer director, Val Guest, puts it best when he calls Fisher "an old time pro—he knew *what* he was doing." Fisher had the ability to draw the most from a script. Although he seldom had much input into any of the scripts he filmed, he just knew he would go out and make the best film he could with the materials at hand. Many scripts had only the barest bones of an idea to work from, and Fisher's direction was brilliant. One only has to look at films by other directors—*Evil of Frankenstein, Lust for a Vampire*, etc.—to make one appreciate Fisher.

Egypt, 1895. After opening the tomb of Princess Ananka, Stephen Banning suffers a breakdown and is committed to an asylum, in England. Three years later, he recovers to warn his son John that a living Mummy protected the tomb. A mysterious Egyptian, Mehemet, arrives with crates of artifacts; one of these is lost in a swamp. Mehemet reads from the Scroll of Life, and the Mummy rises from the mud. It breaks into the asylum and kills Banning senior. John Banning now recounts the legend of Ananka, and realizes that the Mummy has been reanimated in order to kill the defilers of the tomb. His uncle dismisses the idea and is killed by the Mummy. The police are called, but they refuse to believe John's story. The Mummy attacks again, but his wife Isobel, who bears an uncanny resemblance to Ananka, saves John. He decides to pay Mehemet a visit. The Egyptian is surprised to find that John has escaped death and once more dispatches the Mummy. Confused by Isobel's appearance, it kills Mehemet instead and carries Isobel to the swamp. Armed with shotguns, the police surround it. John tells Isobel to order the Mummy to release her. It does—and is destroyed in a hail of gunfire.

Terence Fisher said,

> Our Mummy never set out to be a remake of the original. Our Mummy was based upon the original idea of the actual curses. The art detail was tremendous; the hieroglyphics in the tomb—we hired technical experts. They were all historically accurate and were exact copies of the original thing. We took tremendous pains over it and it came off very well.
>
> I've had my call sheet. I know what scenes are to be shot—I know what they mean. I've thought about them within context—it could be one of the last scenes in the picture, but it could be the most important. On every day of shooting, I've sometimes made a complete overhaul of our story, so you go on the floor and you know what to do. I know exactly how many shots I've got to do, where I'm going to put the camera. In other words, once I find if the actor has the overall picture and the overall movement of the character, I then have my first physical rehearsal. I can never understand directors who say, six shots from this scene, and so and so will move from there to there to keep them in, and virtually have in their mind's eye what they think they are going to do before physical rehearsal… treating actors as puppets, then manipulating them. One of the gravest mistakes is to pre-plan to the point where an actor merely becomes a mechanical puppet with movement…it's *playing* the scene and *feeling* the scenes and movements you could not think of. You can guide actors sometimes and stop them from doing the wrong thing, but they have got to have their heads to start the chemistry of the thing going.

With a budget of around £100,000 (the original *Dracula* cost £83,000, and one year after *The Mummy*, *Brides of Dracula* would cost £120,000), Carreras and Fisher began to put their crew together. *The Mummy* was the first of the "made-to-a-price-for-outright-sale" pictures under a contract with Universal.

Many of the same people that had made the first two horrors successful were once again onboard.

Jack Asher—the king of Hammer's lighting cameramen. They said he "could paint with light." Arthur Grant and others, although very good at what they did, never matched the beauty of an Asher-lit scene. Harry Oakes, who was a camera assistant on many of these films, said:

> I think Jack Asher's photography was really marvelous. They look good, even today when we see them on television. It was one thing to work for two years on a film and win an Oscar, but another thing to work as fast as he did for such consistently good results.

Jack Asher has said:

> I did bring extra colored gelatin lighting into play, especially in the tomb scenes. I also introduced a form of air cleaning; because we were shooting on a large background for the sky, the back spotlights would immediately pick up any smoke or haze. The studio air plant was completely ineffective in clearing this. We had the painter take his high-pressure air gun filled with water into the overhead catwalks. Immediately before each shot, he would spray the air at the top of the studio. The fine particles of water would descend, bringing the smoke particles with them, leaving the atmosphere crystal clear.

Len Harris (Jack Asher's camera operator on all the great early Hammer horrors) when discussing Asher said:

> How would I compare the lighting of Jack Asher against Arthur Grant? They had different styles, really. I would say that Jack's lighting used a lot of little lamps pinpointing lights here and there, highlight here, highlight there. Arthur's was more of a general kind of lighting. They were both very easygoing in many ways. They didn't battle with the director, which is an important thing. Jack would use a gelatin film and put it over a lamp to shine on a certain part of a set to very good effect. Sometimes, he would say to me, "I hope you are getting that effect." He tended to paint the set in light and color. Where blood was featured, he would try to get a red glow into it.

Jack Asher, after lighting a set, would come over and look through the camera. His favorite saying was "What are you getting this time?"

On *The Mummy*, Bray had a very good pit (a stage where the floor boards could be lifted out and water put in, as the bog sets for *The Mummy*). You couldn't get underneath, but it was quite a good one.

Harry Oakes has two stories of the filming:

We were doing the first shot of the film. Felix Aylmer was concerned that the glasses he wore might cause glare problems. It was suggested to him to tilt his head forward and look over the top of the frames. Felix then said he thought he should ask, since they were only empty frames with no glass in them at all. Jack Asher didn't speak to him for days afterward.

Later we were going to do a scene with Peter Cushing, where he was going to blow up the tomb. Because we were at a major studio [due to the size of the sets, Hammer used a soundstage at the larger Shepperton Studios], we had a couple of effects chaps with us. Normally, for a reaction shot of an actor to a loud noise, you clap your hands or bang something like wood together. Well, for this one they set off a real charge and it was deafening. Our ears rang for several minutes afterward. Later on, toward the end of the shoot, when we were back at Bray, we were in Don Weeks' [production manager] office and he showed us the bill from a Harley Street specialist. It said, "For examining Peter Cushing's ears—20 Guineas"—which was quite a bit in those days. A Guinea was equal to one pound and one shilling.

One of the keys to the success of any Hammer period film—and *The Mummy* was no exception—was the beautiful sets designed by Bernard Robinson. Robinson had joined Hammer for the second *Quatermass* film and had stayed on to be the guiding light on most of their shoots until his untimely death in 1970. Since most of the scenes, except a few such as the Mummy striding through the coun-

The tomb explosion caused ear ringing among the crew during *The Mummy*.

Yvonne Furneaux and Christopher Lee in the impressive bog setting of *The Mummy*

tryside, were shot on soundstages, his contribution was even more important. Robinson had impeccable taste in dressing his sets and was brilliant in locating the odd bits-and-pieces to make the sets attractive. Considering he and art director Arthur Banks, who converted Robinson's plans into physical reality, had only about £15-20,000 to work with, the results were very beautiful. *The Mummy* may be the most visually appealing of any Hammer.

    Robinson's wife-to-be, Margaret, designed many of the Egyptian set pieces and accessories under the guidance of Andrew Low, the resident expert on Egyptian antiquities. A very persnickety man, Low's taste and efforts toward authenticity made the film even more interesting. Low wanted to do much of the work himself, but British trade union laws would not allow it. This was also a time when Hammer was building a number of new, standing sets on the Bray backlot. Much of the original *Dracula* set still stood at this time, although it would be leveled at the end of the year. Robinson had a structure called "the Mound" built—it was rectangular and about 70 feet long, 10 feet high and 20 feet wide. The Mound first appears when the horse-drawn cart hauling the Mummy's crate races along and the crate tips off and lands in the bog. The Mound would stand for another 10 years and is best noticed as the lead into Dracula's castle in *Dracula: Prince of Darkness*.

Obviously, one of the most important areas to be considered was the script. Jimmy Sangster, again, was the obvious choice, having done most of the previous Gothics.

"I don't remember seeing the Universal scripts. I must've seen the pictures, but I don't remember." Well, *someone* at Hammer saw the previous Universal series. As Denis Meikle points out in his book *A History of Horrors: The Rise and Fall of Hammer Film* (1947-1979): "The scenario married the first half of *The Mummy* [unrequited love that spans the centuries] to the center-section of *The Mummy's Tomb* [1942, revenge from beyond the desecrated grave] and topped it off with the climax to *The Mummy's Ghost* [1943]." Michael Carreras and Andrew Low scripted a good portion of the flashback narration. Carreras said:

> The narration—it would have been a combination [of Carreras and Low]...I think Andrew's was probably a bit highfalutin'...I'm sure I would have collaborated with him on that.
>
> The script though is functional, plays to the action well, but it is probably the least successful [and important] ingredient in the success of the film.

Roy Ashton, Hammer's resident makeup man, in charge since 1958, was given the task of creating his own version of the Mummy. Ashton remembers:

> I did a great deal of research first. I consulted the usual books on Egyptology and also paid a visit to the British Museum, where they have a mummy in a great big case: You can examine the quality of the skin and everything really guided me. In those days there was a considerable interest in the subject, since there had been an exhibition of Egyptian works in London. I think they had discovered another pharaoh in some remote grave or something. Consequently, there was quite a bit of literature available about it, with many reproductions in color. I tried to create the effect on Chris Lee's face. I cast his head in plaster, so that whatever you made on it would fit because you invariably got the exact dimensions. I started off with a zip fastener that I fixed on the model and built up from there outwards. I fabricated something I could pull in to the zipper, like a sock covered up with stripes of worn-out rag. An old handkerchief torn into shreds resembled the windings. I had to apply them one by one, until the whole head was clothed. Then, with rubber and plastic skin, I shaped the face. This operation lasted about one-and-a-half hours.

Once again Christopher Lee had to act under heavy makeup, this time as *The Mummy*.

Lee was the most patient and cooperative, even though his mask didn't have holes underneath the nose to breathe. It didn't occur to me that anything down there would scarcely be visible anyway, so he had to inhale through his eye holes, which was not very comfortable for him. When we were busy on his face he needed something to write on, as he wasn't able to talk. He was an excellent man to work with.

The haunting musical score was composed by Franz Reizenstein, born in Nuremberg, Germany in 1911 (and he died in London in 1968). Since the original 1932 *Mummy* used only stock, classical music, this was the first film of its type to have a moody original score. With the use of a large orchestra and chorus, it did just that beautifully.

Then we get to the most important part of all. The players. Peter Cushing was an obvious choice. Since his success as Baron Frankenstein, he had done four more of Hammer's period films and was right at home at Bray. There has often been a bit of interest in his character's limp—from a so-called accident during the excavation—was it simply contrived for the film or had he actually hurt his leg prior to filming? Who knows? Cushing, in a latter-day interview, joked about the poster showing the flashlight shining through Lee's body, and said it was his idea to add the thrust of the spear through Lee during the confrontation in his home—to justify the poster. None of this seems to make a lot of sense, but it is a good story.

Christopher Lee was once again buried under lots of makeup and had a not-very-good-time as Kharis. In his book, *The Films of Christopher Lee*, Lee remembers the pain of the whole thing.

> With the bandages and makeup I could hardly breathe except through the holes for my eyes. Physically, the most arduous picture I've ever done [until *The Three Musketeers* in 1974]. The things I had to do in *The Mummy* were almost beyond belief, physically—smashing through doors and a window that was real glass, dislocating my shoulder and pulling all the muscles in my neck and shoulder, carrying beautiful girls [who were a dead weight because they were supposed to be unconscious] in the mud and swamps, sometimes as far as 87 yards. The Mummy was an unstoppable automaton, but in many ways very human in his reactions, especially meeting the reincarnation of his beloved princess. A very beautiful-looking picture.

I don't think there could be much argument among *any* fans that there has never been a more effective presentation of the Mummy than that of Christopher Lee. Not Karloff, not Chaney, not Tom Tyler.

The Christopher Lee book also points out the following about the fine character actor George Pastell and his performance:

> One scene that must be mentioned is that in which Cushing and Pastell verbally duel, each of them knowing that the other sees through his pretense. The elaborate hypocrisy of the scene is worthy of Oscar Wilde at his choicest.

And some of Sangster's best work—although he was not always good at dialogue. As a rule Cushing did *not* like Sangster's scripts, and would change the lines.

Yvonne Furneaux (Isobel/Ananka) makes light of her work in the film, but her husband points out it is the film she is most often asked about (and she has a copy of it on video). Furneaux barely remembers producer Michael Carreras (or so she says) but Margaret Robinson remembers how difficult she was to apply

Terence Fisher

headpieces to because "she wanted to look beautiful for Michael." However, it should be pointed out (so as not to ruin any marriages) that Tony Hinds says it was James Carreras who was more interested in the French cuties at that time.

Furneaux is not too kind to Terence Fisher:

> Peter Cushing was the one behind it. Cushing was the one that really directed that film, between me and you. He was the brains behind it. Cushing was adorable, a gentleman and a real charmer. Not exactly Lord Byron to look at is he. And yet you'd die for him, he is so sweet.

Christopher Lee—I came across him because he had to pick me up, and he said "my God, you're heavy!" and he dropped me [laughter]. I thought the film was real rubbish and I'd never see it again [laughter]. Unfortunately, they've returned to haunt me.

Regarding Ms. Furneaux's opinions on the work of Peter Cushing and Terence Fisher, they had worked on four previous films together, they knew each other's working methods, and Cushing appreciated Fisher's willingness to accept suggestions from his performers. And knowing Peter Cushing, he would not have tolerated an incompetent director for five films. He respected Fisher as a talent and as a man, and the two would go on to work in seven more films. As Fisher says about Cushing:

> I think with Peter we have that kind of rapport. We can almost read each other's thoughts, which I've never experienced with anybody else.

This threesome were ably supported by Felix Aylmer (who had worked in such major films as *Henry V,* 1944; *Hamlet,* 1948; and *Quo Vadis,* 1951), who appear in Hammer's superb study of child molesting, *Never Take Sweets From a Stranger* (1960). Raymond Huntley, also onboard, had played Dracula on the London West End stages in 1927 (at the age of 22). Michael Ripper had his normal bug-eyed role as a poacher, and Lee claims he didn't dare even look at Ripper or he (Lee) would burst out laughing. George Pastell had another strong ethnic role in the previous year's *Stranglers of Bombay* (1959).

Before it reached the final audience, the film underwent some editing and censoring, as Michael Carreras points out:

> Was there a topless scene included in it? Every time I go to any festival or anything, that's the one question that they always want to know about—as if I've got a drawer somewhere full of cut-outs bits! But I think you are right about that parade (in the flashback): I think we had a lot of colored ladies. Maybe I might have denied it over the years where that kind of thing might have happened, but I think we *did* do it. But it just never worked—we never had a request from distributors, where they said "we won't distribute it unless it's nude..." It was just a general trend and we would also have cautiously been "having a go."
>
> The tongue cutting. Yes, I remember that. We did do that. There was this awful three-pronged instrument; that was

a censor cut. But if you were to ask me to summarize this whole thing about Hammer and "did we do this, did we do that or the other," the answer would be no, we never did. We shot what we shot, and we weren't allowed to show what we weren't allowed to show. It was never a case of "we will shoot a foreign version." I can't believe that even that parade contained more than what was finally shown: we shot it like that—but we took a "protective" with the clothes on. At the time, we might have gotten away with it. We didn't. Often we had material cut, which would appear later, and was then *interpreted* as *additional* material shot.

I guess it is not a big surprise that with all these factors working in its favor, *The Mummy* would be both a financial success—"The All Time chiller is Hot, Hot, Hot at the box offices all over the country. Breaking the all-time U-I [Universal-International] record at the Pilgrim Theatre in Boston and is topping *Horror of Dracula*..." etc.—as well as a critical triumph—something Hammer was not having a lot of at that time. It is a haunting film—a term used again and again in reviews. With so little to work with story-wise, Michael Carreras, Terence Fisher, Peter Cushing, Christopher Lee and crew had created a true milestone in the genre. Not perfect as a film—but the perfect Mummy film.

Although during the late 1950s, early 1960s, Hammer is generally remembered for its colorful Universal-International releases like *The Curse of the Werewolf* and *Horror of Dracula*, it should be noted that the vast amount of Hammer product from 1957 on was made for, and released by, Columbia Pictures. Through his involvement with Variety Club International (noted, in public, for its charitable endeavors, but a behind-the-scenes hotbed of deal-making in the entertainment industry), James Carreras became friendly with Mike Frankovich, head of overseas production for Columbia Pictures. After the success of *The Curse of Frankenstein*, Columbia was eager to get their hands on the next *Frankenstein—Blood of Frankenstein* as it was known at the time. Carreras used his leverage on that film, and in September 1957, Columbia and Hammer signed a three-picture deal that included *Revenge of Frankenstein* (the renamed *Blood*), *The Snorkel* (1958), and *Camp on Blood Island*. This involvement also leads to the "dead-at-birth" deal with Columbia's Screen Gems television arm and *Tales of Frankenstein* (ugh). In October 1958, Columbia had expanded its Hammer involvement with a deal that allowed them a one million dollar buy-in of Bray Studios (giving them a 40 percent share) and a deal that allowed for at least five Hammer films a year over three years.

Which leads to *The Curse of the Mummy's Tomb*. By early 1964, the Columbia/Hammer relationship was almost over. While Hammer had continued to produce an occasional film for Universal-International, this was also about to

The Mummy **was a critical and financial success for Hammer.**

end. *The Secret of Blood Island* would bring the contract to a close. Universal would not release another Hammer film until the 1972 paring of *Hands of the Ripper* and *Twins of Evil*, part of an arrangement with Rank that Universal was about to sever—which explains the lackluster release. Producer Anthony Hinds has said that the Universal deals were the most lucrative for Hammer, where they knew they would get their money upfront (making a £100,000 film...on delivery they would get £150,000, etc.).

It is hard to say just how interested Columbia was in their Hammer affiliation by this time. While some of the swashbucklers like *Pirates of Blood River* (1962) had been moneymakers, the majority of the Hammer releases were not of much interest to Columbia—and most were not major successes. Perhaps by this time, seeing the success Universal was having with the true Gothics like *Brides of Dracula* and *Kiss of the Vampire* (but forgetting the failure of *The Phantom of the Opera*), Columbia was in the mood for some out and out "Hammer Horrors." They got that in spades in Terence Fisher's stylish *The Gorgon* (1963) and *The Curse of the Mummy's Tomb,* which delivers the goods as an all out monsterfest.

Producer Michael Carreras had left Hammer permanently in July 1961 after finishing up the production on *These Are the Damned* (1963)—while nominally credited to Anthony Hinds, but Hinds detested director Joseph Losey and literally disappeared from the film. Carreras stepped in and finished it up. Often at odds with his father, James, Michael had felt the last straw break when his father personally cancelled Michael's *The Inquisitor* (*The Rape of Sabena*), then putting out a story about it being cancelled because of pressure from the Catholic League. *One More River*, another pet Michael Carreras project, never got off the ground. So Michael left, using his own production company, Capricorn, to launch a teen musical, *What a Crazy World* (1963) and *The Savage Guns* (1961), one of the first Westerns shot in Spain.

However, as would be his fate in later years, Michael found it very difficult to raise the necessary finances for further films. Still, he had friends within the Hammer organization—company business manager Brian Lawrence and Anthony Hinds himself. Hinds was now being forced more and more into the role of executive producer at the company's Wardour Street offices, although he would rather have been on the floor of the studio making films. By 1964, Hinds produced his last film, *Fanatic*, aka *Die! Die! My Darling!*, before giving over the producer's reins to Anthony Nelson Keys and others. He would come to depend almost totally on Hammer for his film projects.

Budgeted at £103,000, or just £3,000 more than *The Mummy* had cost almost five years earlier, Michael Carreras—using the tongue-in-cheek pseudonym "Henry Younger"—his poke of fun at Anthony Hinds' own "John Elder"—worked with director Alvin Rakoff to fashion a script with a lot of comic touches, but it was still a basic rehash of the "monster on the loose" story that was the real "Mummy's Curse" of plotlines.

An archaeological expedition has uncovered the sarcophagus of Ra-Antef, which American showman Alexander King intends to exhibit to a paying public. On the opening night, the Mummiform coffin is found to be empty. Soon, those involved start to fall victim to the vengeance of a living Mummy, who appears to be searching for pieces of a medallion inscribed with the secrets of life and death. The mysterious Adam Beauchamp is also after the medallion, and it transpires that he is actually Be, the brother of the Mummy, who is also cursed to eternal life. Having restored the medallion, Adam kidnaps Annette

Dubois, daughter of one of the archaeologists—he intends for her to join him in immortality. The Mummy will not strike the fatal blow, however, and when Adam makes for the sewers with Annette, Ra-Antef brings the roof down on himself and his brother, and Annette is able to escape into the arms of her fiancé.

It should be noted that according to British Film Union rules, Michael Carreras would not be allowed credit for three positions on a single film, another reason for using "Henry Younger," since Carreras was also producing and directing.

Shooting began on February 28, 1964 at the MGM Studios at Borehamwood. Once Michael began doing films as an independent for Hammer, he would never again use the company-owned facilities at Bray.

Although planned as the backup feature for *The Gorgon,* Michael still found the film idea interesting—he was the only one at Hammer with any real affection for the Mummy. Carreras said:

> The story had a lot of comedy in it. That wonderful Fred Clark. The circus—the banging of the drum. It was different and I liked it. The whole thing felt like fun.

Not wanting to have all the day-to-day problems of producing and directing, he brought in Bill Hill to handle the dirty work.

> The budget was so small. Bill Hill was a friend of mine, but a good producer. I said, "Bill, I want to direct it, I don't want to have the production chores. But it's got to come in on schedule, so you have to push me hard as far as the schedule is concerned. But I don't want to hear a figure, I don't want to know anything about cost." Once we'd cast it and put it to bed, 10 percent of everything saved under the budget was his (Hill's). And if it's more than 10 percent, he got a case of champagne as well.

As an independent, Carreras often used non-typical Hammer personnel. Case in point was lighting cameraman Otto Heller (with many major films and photographic prizes under his belt). Outside of Michael Ripper, the crew was definitely not typical Hammer. Still, old faithfuls like makeup man Roy Ashton were on hand. Ashton had to literally tear apart the Mummy makeup at the last moment, to make it look more massive and imposing, leaving a very patched-up look. Ashton has a story about the film:

> Dickie Owen had to walk around through an underground sewer and a whole lot of debris had to fall on his head. I warned the first assistant that they had to be aware of the extreme

danger of letting that man flounder around in water that was fairly deep: He could lose his footing and drown. "That will be all right," he said. However, I stood quite close there with a pair of scissors in my hand. And sure enough, when all the stuff came bashing down, he couldn't keep his balance and fell over. I leapt straight in and removed everything so that he could breathe freely again. He already had water in his throat.

Art Director Bernard Robinson would once again work with the Mummy. "I can't say that Bernie felt more at home at Bray than on this picture at MGM, but Bray was his home...he knew where every nail was," said Carreras. And Editor-in-Chief James Needs came onboard. Needs' in-house editing shop at Hammer disappeared several years later amid a scandal of some sort.

Lead actor Terence Morgan had achieved fame in the 1957 film *The Scamp* as a sadistic stepfather and in the early 1960s television series *Sir Francis Drake*. But as Michael said later:

> I liked him. I had never worked with him. He seemed right and was a sort of name and wasn't going to cost a lot. I think he had retired in a way and was living in Brighton and had done a bit of theater.

Ronald Howard's main claim to fame was his father, famed British actor Leslie Howard (Ashley Wilkes in *Gone with the Wind*, among many notable roles). Not exactly like-father, like-son, but Howard was competent in his male/lead/hero roles. He had also played Sherlock Holmes in a 1950s British television series.

Poor Jeanne Roland, pushed as another of the Hammer "French Cuties," was actually a Burmese-born model named Jean Rollins. Carreras had met her at a party and thought she had a wonderfully old-fashioned face.

> I thought she was quite pretty. She had never acted in her life. I used her as an ornamental piece. I said, stand here and smile. If I wave to you from behind the camera, blink, or turn left, or some such. I thought she was ornamental. That is all she was meant to be, more or less. And I thought she did it very well.

To add insult to injury, Roland was also dubbed as Annette—joining Norma Marla, the Rhodesian-born actress, whose voice was not used in *The Two Faces of Dr. Jekyll.*

Fred Clark was the obligatory American imposed on the production, who actually spent only two weeks on the film. But Carreras was very fond of him and felt he gave the film a bit of pizzazz. Clark, who for years had been doing supporting roles in both comedies and dramas, was especially good as Major Spelding in Jerry Lewis' *Visit to a Small Planet* (1960). Clark met his filmic doom in *The Curse of the Mummy's Tomb*, throttled by Mummy Dickie Owens in a very atmospheric scene shot on the fog-covered steps of a London side street. Owens, in the major role of his career, had just appeared in *Zulu* (1964)—he even had lines in addition to killing natives.

For budget reasons, except for a desert stock shot that begins the film, the whole production was done on soundstages. No exteriors. Carreras said, "It was intentional, written for that, and done for economics."

And like all previous Carreras-directed films, it was shot in the wide-screen process.

> I must say I had never directed anything with conventional lenses. From the very first thing I directed, we were testing out Hammerscope lenses, and one day somebody said to me something about lenses. And I said, "Don't speak to me about that, I've only got two, one's a 75 and the other's a 50." *Maniac* was the first time they gave me a whole box of lenses. I thought, what am I going to do with this? It was quite ridiculous. All the musicals I did were in Cinemascope. *The Steel Bayonet* was in Hammerscope. You have to be more careful in getting the setups, particularly when we had to shoot five or six minutes a day. I found that easier, if you move your camera about, you can bring 20 different people into frame in the same shot.

Carreras and musical director Philip Martell brought in a new name for the film's music in the person of Carlo Martelli (forget the Italian-sounding name, he is British through and through). Originally, Anthony Hinds had sent a letter to Carreras saying if they used Franz Reizenstein's score from the first film, they wouldn't have to commission a new one. As it was, Carreras did approve a full orchestral piece. Composer Martelli remembers:

> When I first saw the rough-cut of *Curse of the Mummy's Tomb*, I was of course told that for the flashback sequence in the middle of the film, which I think lasts about three minutes, Reizenstein's music would be used. But I was not in the remotest degree influenced by him in my score, as should be obvious to anyone who isn't tone deaf. And it didn't save money, whatever Anthony Hinds may have intended. I was paid £350 [about £3,700 today] for the job, exactly as I would have been paid had Reizenstein's music not been needed. The sessions were expensive too as I was encouraged to use a large orchestra.

Martelli later went on to score the underrated *Witchcraft* (1964), which Don Sharp directed for Lippert, starring Lon Chaney.

Hammer had been recently trying to tone down the horror in their films after painful experiences with the censors over *The Curse of the Werewolf*. Soft-peddled horrors like *The Phantom of the Opera,* or the more restrained *Kiss of the Vampire,* were the order of the day. Still, Anthony Hinds turned over three pages of British censors' instructions to Michael. Scenes showing the severing of the hands and the various deaths were called into question. Hinds recommended eight minor deletions and suggested they look again at the scenes involving the crushing of one man's skull with a blunt object and the Egyptian servant's head being smashed like an eggshell by the Mummy's foot.

A severed hand starts off the film in grisly fashion. By 1964 standards it was pretty strong stuff, which pleased the audiences of the time. It would certainly be interesting to see the censors' letter, dated February 10, 1964, which was sent to Hammer regarding this film. The secretary at the British Board of Film Censors directed it to Pamela Anderson, Anthony Hinds' secretary, but copies got to James Carreras, Anthony Hinds, Anthony (Brian) Lawrence, Michael Carreras and Bill Hill.

> I am now in a position to send you our comments about the script for *The Curse of the Mummy's Tomb*. This should be basically acceptable for the "X" category provided that it is in line with previous Hammer Productions of this kind, but there is one thing that worries us a good deal. An important point in the story is that at various points people's hands are cut off, and, according to the script, we are to see this. This is not at

Although Hammer tried to tone dowe the horror in *The Curse of the Mummy's Tomb* (with Jeanne Roland and Dickie Owen above), they still had to make censor cuts.

all a nice idea, and the most that we would accept would be the cutting off of the hands by suggestion or implication; we would not want to see trick shots, which convey the impression that the hands are actually cut off, or shots of the results. My comments on points of detail are as follows:

(Page 3, Scene 17). Here we have Dubois killed with a knife in the stomach. This may be all right provided that we do not see the knife going in. The script suggests that we are to see blood coming from his mouth. We would not like this.
(Page 3, Scene 19). Here we have the first occasion on which we are apparently to see the hand cut off. The script direction reads, "Suddenly the leader's knife enters frame and with a

mighty blow severs the hand from the wrist. Blood spurts from the wrist as the dismembered hand topples to the sand. Camera pans with the dismembered hand as the leader raises it and holds it before him. He slowly and painstakingly begins to pry the clenched fingers open, one by one." This does not appeal to us at all. Could you do this scene in some other way, which is less unpleasant and nauseating?

(Page 4, Scene 21 & 22). Here we still have trouble with the severed hand. My previous comments apply. We appreciate that in Scene 22, the shot will be under the titles, but it may well be troublesome.

(Page 4, Scene 23). The shot of the beetle on the roast pig sounds a bit disgusting. It may pass, but it seems unnecessary for the incident to appear at all.

(Page 9, Scene 34). We would not want any nasty shot of Dubois' body. The script direction says, "It is not a pretty sight. The severed arm is visible." We would not want the arm to be visible unless it was something that nobody would object to.

(Page 12, Scene 46). Here we have "the bloody stump of Professor Dubois' hand, its fingers crooked upwards." My previous comments apply. We do not like this idea. If we have to have it, it should be in a long shot and very brief.

(Page 21, Scene 63). The costume of the dance of the Arab dancer is not described. This should not be censurable.

(Page 25, Scene 68). In this scene we are apparently to see "the twisted body of the night watchman lying across an opened packing case. From the position of his head it is apparent that his neck has been broken." This suggests that we may have a very unpleasant shot. Great care should be taken.

(Page 30, Scene 78). The description of this scene suggests that we may have a violent low blow. This should be avoided.

(Page 36, Scene 93). Care should be taken with shots of the body being pulled aboard, when "a mixture of water and blood spreads out from the body." This could be very unpleasant and macabre. The shot of the body itself in Scene 94 should be reasonable.

(Page 46, Scene 114). In this scene we have another hand being cut off in flashback. My previous comments apply. We would not want to see it done, or to see shots of spurting blood of the unpleasant results.

"Not too much screaming please!" John Bray (Ronald Howard) tries to protect Annette in *The Curse of the Mummy's Tomb.*

(Page 78, Scene 182). If the Mummy is no worse than its predecessors we should have no trouble with it, but care should be taken not to make it too unpleasant.

(Page 79, Scene 189-190). We never like close shots of people being throttled. The script direction reads "his eyes bulge, his tongue protrudes…" etc. This is the kind of thing that worries us. Care should be taken with this. Would it not be possible for the Mummy to hurl the King down the steps and kill him in this way, without throttling coming into it?

(Page 79, Scene 191). It seems unnecessary for the man to hit the child as described, and I think you could get rid of it.

(Page 84-5, Scene 112). We would not want a really unpleasant shot of the mummified flesh sealing itself "as it were oozing mud." This seems a bit nauseating. Nor would we want Sir Giles killed in this way. The breaking of his back, with the effects on the sound track, would be more unpleasant than we would like. Surely there is some more conventional way in which these scenes can be shot.

(Page 85, Scene 213) Not too much screaming please!

The final scenes in the sewer are nicely realized in *The Curse of the Mummy's Tomb*.

(Page 90, Scene 232 and following). Annette is to be seen wearing a negligee, which is described as "disarranged." Since she has been subjected to violence by the Mummy we would not want any shot, which suggested that there had been some sexual impulse in the violence.

(Page 95-96, Scene 258-260) We would not want to see Hashmi's head being squashed under the Mummy's foot. Nor would we want to hear any nasty reactions from him, or to see much of the reactions from the bystanders.

(Page 103-104, Scene 275-278). These scenes, as described, are very unpleasant. We would not want a close shot of Adam's hand trapped in the door, nor of him writhing in agony; nor would we want to see the hand falling to the floor "bleeding profusely and jerking spasmodically as the nerves play out their final convulsions." This goes far beyond what we would accept. Adam wrenches the remains of his crushed arm from the crack, and falls backwards screaming into the whirling waters of the sewers. I hope you will find some other

way of dealing with Adam in this situation, in a way that is more acceptable for the cinema screen. We could have an indication of what happens with some groans, but we really do not want to see hands coming off, bleeding stumps, etc. In this kind of scene horror film material goes into disgust.
(Page 106-107, Scenes 188-292). Again these scenes are very nasty. We would not want any shots of the torn arm waving about during the drowning. Surely the wretched man could be tipped in and left to drown. The script suggests that we are to see the corpse floating about among a lot of filthy debris. I would think that most cinema audiences would object to this, but would accept the sort of sewer we had in *Les Miserables*.
(Page 108, Scene 297). We would not expect any great trouble with the Mummy's hand, but reasonable care should be taken.

Wow, we wonder how any Hammer films with even a hint of action ever got made? It is interesting that as mentioned above, Hinds suggested eight deletions and two more to be considered. Can you guess which ones they were?

In the final analysis, one can neither commend nor condemn this film. The Mummy scenes are well staged, particularly since many of them play without background music and are very effective. London fog hides the fact that some of the sets are rather threadbare and underdressed. but it is still a very colorful, nicely constructed film. Contrary to Michael Carreras' affection for Fred Clark, I find him a pain and an annoyance and was glad to see him disappear in the Mummy's grip halfway through the film.

Particularly effective are the two scenes where the Mummy bursts into the professor's home. The French windows are very reminiscent of those at Bray Studios—and both the throttling of the professor and the ineffective, but highly visual, police attempts to capture the Mummy with rope nets, are really fun to watch.

The final scenes in the sewer are nicely realized. Like most Carreras-directed films, it is better appreciated in a letterboxed widescreen version. The scenes with the Mummy, Terence Morgan and Jeanne Roland play best when you can see all that was captured by the camera.

It is not a bad film of its type. Although nothing special, you'll like it if you don't set your standards too high. It must have been great fun in 1965 to see *The Curse of the Mummy's Tomb* with *The Gorgon*, as a creepy double feature. By this time in 1966 the face of Hammer had, once again, undergone drastic changes. In July 1965, Hammer, represented by James Carreras, Anthony Hinds and Brian Lawrence, had gone to New York to sign a massive 11-picture deal with Seven Arts Productions, 20th-Century Fox, and Associated British. What this meant was that after 10 years of depending on different companies for

backing and distribution, Hammer was putting all its eggs into one basket. Seven Arts, under the guidance of Eliot Hyman and his son, Kenneth, had been the silent partners and backers for Hammer going back to *The Curse of Frankenstein*. And in their attempt to become major players in the film business they were initiating a number of film deals both in the U.S.A. and Great Britain. They would really hit the big time with their acquisition of Warner Bros. in 1968—again taking Hammer with them. Eliot Hyman made sure his friend, Jimmy Carreras, was involved.

At first, the films were very successful, represented by *The Nanny* (1965, with Bette Davis), *One Million Years B.C.*, and the duos of *Dracula: Prince of Darkness/Plague of the Zombies,* and *Rasputin, the Mad Monk/The Reptile*. But by 1967, the dew was off the rose and tastes were changing. *B.C.* took in a fortune but *Prehistoric Women/The Devil's Own* lost money, as did *The Viking Queen* (1967, a major failure). *The Anniversary* (1968) was a disappointment as was *A Challenge for Robin Hood* (1967). *The Lost Continent* and *Vengeance of She* were major flops in the U.S.A.

Hammer had high hopes for the *She* sequel. They originally signed Ursula Andress, the star of the original, then later, Susan Denberg. But Denberg's descent into the drug culture of America found her dead by the end of 1967, and Olinka Berova was signed as Ayesha.

The first of the Fox-released features, *The Devil's Bride* (*The Devil Rides Out*, 1968), again did poor business in America. Hammer's business manager, Brian Lawrence, says that by this time Fox just didn't care about these films.

In 1966, Hammer was in need of a second feature to go out with *Frankenstein Created Woman,* which had started shooting on July 4th. Four weeks after it finished filming, *The Mummy's Shroud* was in production, and using most of the same exterior sets.

We can say right up front that *The Mummy's Shroud* has a terrible reputation. Along with *The Evil of Frankenstein*, it is often used as an example of the poor filmmaking that was to be Hammer's latter day fate—or so the naysayers argue. The story is mundane and not very interesting in and of itself, but the set pieces with the Mummy and the various deaths were brilliantly conceived and executed by John Gilling, who considered the film "one of my worst" but gave it his all.

In 1920 an expedition has been financed by Stanley Preston. Archaeologist Sir Basil Walden has discovered the tomb of the boy Pharaoh Kah-To-Bey. But the tomb has a guardian, and using the sacred shroud, Hasmid calls the Mummy of Prem to life to destroy the members of the expedition. One by one, they meet a horrifying end at the hand of the Mummy, until only two remain—Paul Preston and Claire. Suspecting who is behind the deaths, Claire investigates but finds herself trapped in a museum with the Mummy. When Paul and Inspector Barrani arrive, Prem attacks. He is impervious to bullets, and blows

from a fire-axe do no harm, but during the fracas, Barrani shoots Hasmid. With his death, the Mummy of Prem crumbles to dust.

This synopsis leaves out the fact that the reading of the scroll of life really brings about the death of the Mummy, but you get the general idea. In his book on Hammer, Denis Meikle has this to say about what makes *The Mummy's Shroud* eminently watchable and enjoyable.

> With little but the obligator series of set piece murders to build upon, Gilling stages each of them with stunning visual invention: The Mummy's appearances are presaged by a variety of perceptive tricks, in the manner of the literary master M.R. James—this is evidenced in a trial of eons-old dust, spotted as a shadow on an alley wall, shown reflected in a crystal ball or in a tray of developing solution, or even as a blur in the myopic vision of Michael Ripper's Longbarrow. And the killings themselves are staged with equal aplomb: Sir Basil's skull is cracked open like an egg in a giant's hand—

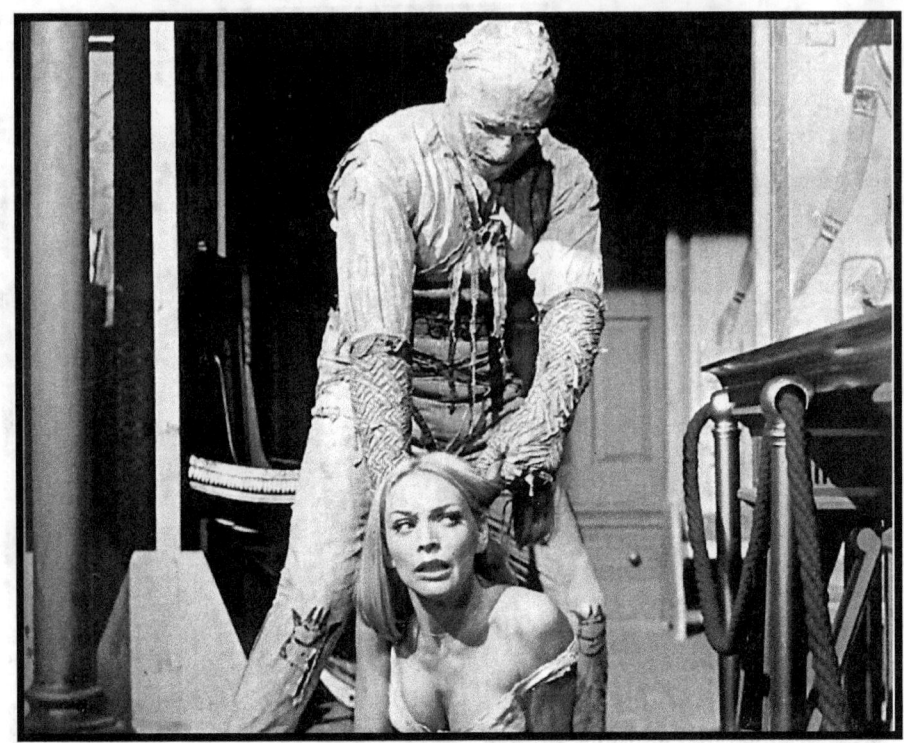

Claire (Maggie Kimberly) is attacked by the mummy (Eddie Powell) in *The Mummy's Shroud*.

Stanley Preston is smashed on a wall to leave its imprints in blood—the photographer, Barrett, is baptized in acid and fire—and the mild-mannered Longbarrow is hurled from an upstairs window, his body shattering against the side of an ornamental pool to stain the waters scarlet.

This film delivers the goods. Budgeted at £160,000, it has the sad and unique distinction of being the last film made by Hammer at their Bray Studios. With the involvement of Associated British in the Seven Arts/Hammer deal, ABPC insisted that Hammer use their Elstree Company Studio. So by the end of 1966 when this film wrapped, Hammer would start the task of vacating Bray. For so many of the studio personnel it must have been a bittersweet time. Wardrobe mistress Rosemary Barrows would end up marrying the Mummy—Eddie Powell. Makeup supervisor George Partleton, who replaced Roy Ashton at the end of 1965, would only make it through one year and three films before the doors closed. Anthony Hinds always said that firing all these people was the hardest thing he ever had to do.

For one viewing, *Shroud* is really fun. Certainly for the viewers of the time it must have seemed a lot more action-packed than the intelligent, melancholy (and slow moving) *Frankenstein Created Woman*. But *Shroud* does not hold up well to repeated viewings. Once you've seen the murders, you've really seen the best of the film.

Director John Gilling, in his last film for Hammer, ended a wonderful career with the company. The previous year he had directed, back-to-back, *The Reptile* and *Plague of the Zombies*. His work in the 1960s for Hammer had seen the script for *The Gorgon* and some of their best action films like *Pirates of Blood River*. Gilling was a tough man to work for. Hammer production manager, Hugh Harlow, called him a bully. Oliver Reed thought that a head injury Gilling suffered during World War II might have had something to do with his moods. I corresponded with Gilling during the last years of his life and found him to be an intelligent, funny gentleman. He *looked* like a lumpy farmer, but he had the heart of an artist. Gilling had accepted the direction of *Shroud* to get away from television, which he was mainly doing at the time (*The Saint*, *Department S.*, etc.). Gilling talked with me about the film:

> I wasn't very proud of *The Mummy's Shroud*. It was a rather worn out theme. I agree with you about Michael Ripper's performance [I raved about his Longbarrow]. I think Michael is a very neglected artist. I cast him with a view of introducing some lighter touches into the movie and I think these may have saved it from being a total disaster.

Actually, Ripper's Longbarrow is a sad and pitiful character that adds depth to the movie.

Ex-debutante Maggie Kimberly played the well-endowed Claire and the next year would achieve her last bit of fame when she was burned at the stake in Michael Reeve's *The Witchfinder General* (1968).

It is probably not good to dwell on *The Mummy's Shroud* at too much length. It was what it was—a programmer to support a more popular *Frankenstein* subject. While the *Frankenstein* village sets occupied one end of the Bray Studios lot, the other end had the Egyptian sets of *Shroud*. Exciting to a point, but *not* a film you would want to watch over and over. And it gives the melancholy feeling that we have seen the end of an era with Hammer's departure from Bray.

Former Dr. Watson, Andre Morell, is his normal wonderful self as Sir Basil, after his fine role in 1965's *Plague of the Zombies*. John Phillips as bad guy Stanley Preston is a little too mean to be believable. Elizabeth Sellars as Barbara Preston had worked for Hammer/Exclusive in the early 1950s. David Buck, as Paul Preston, attained some fame as a writer and playwright and was married to Hammer actress Madeline Smith, before his death in 1989. And Lord, how many people shuddered when the drool ran down the lips of old Catherine Lacey as Haiti? Dickie Owen, who was the Mummy in *The Curse of the Mummy's Tomb*, had a human role as the non-Mummy Prem in the prologue of the film. Mummy #2, Eddie Powell, would end up under makeup again as the grand inquisitor in Michael Carreras's *The Lost Continent*—and later had a small role as "The Goat of Mendes"—The Devil Himself—in *The Devil Rides Out*.

Although the series *Journey to the Unknown* failed, it did manage to spawn a board game.

The face of Hammer continued to change. The Seven Arts/20th Century-Fox deal had finished with *The Lost Continent* in 1967. Hammer had gone big-time with a 1968 television series for ABC called *Journey to the Unknown*. The series, while being a failure and only lasting one year, would prove a turning point for Hammer—with producer and Hammer co-owner Anthony Hinds deciding to leave the company. Long dissatisfied that executive duties kept him from actively producing films, he now found himself seconded to American producer Joan Harrison—Alfred Hitchcock's long-time secretary—on the TV series. Having been told he did not have the experience to produce for television, Tony found he hated being demoted and working for someone else. At the end of 1968, when the series finished, he resigned his membership in the Unions—a decision helped along by the fact that the trade unions had refused to allow needed overtime on the last days shooting the television series. Although his resignation did not officially take effect until May 1970, for all practical purposes, Tony Hinds—producer of Hammer's classic Gothics—was a part of Hammer's past.

This left company head, James Carreras, in a quandary. His strength was not in the active shepherding of the projects from inception to finished product, but in the wooing of the money men—the backslapping and schmoozing—and then bringing the funds to Hammer and turning it over to Michael Carreras or Anthony Hinds. But it was now 1970, and Hinds and Carreras were gone. Anthony Nelson-Keys, the top producer for almost seven years, was also off on his own. The people still onboard, Brian Lawrence, Roy Skeggs, etc., were businessmen, accountants, not filmmakers. To add to his problems, James Carreras' long-time partnership with Eliot Hyman was at an end. After a year of owning Warner Bros., and losing a lot of money, Hyman and his Seven Arts Group had sold out to the Kinney Corp., and Ted Ashley was now the man calling the shots at Warners. Hammer finished up their Warner contractual schedule for 1969—*Frankenstein Must Be Destroyed, Moon Zero Two, Crescendo* and *Taste the Blood of Dracula*. Except for an occasional project, their days as Hammer's "sugar daddy" were done.

Most of the other American money was fast leaving the British film industry. Totally British productions either lost lots of money or, at best, broke even. A changing face in filmmaking—and filmgoers—saw *Night of the Living Dead* (1968), *Easy Rider* (1969), etc. as the wave of the future. The British industry was a dead horse as far as most American distributors were concerned, and they were through flogging it. For Jimmy Carreras, it was time to call in a lot of favors. His long-time friendship with Bernard Delfont of ABPC (soon to be EMI) saw a long-term contract starting in 1970 with *Horror of Frankenstein*. Rank, which had never had much luck as an actual producer, also handed over the keys to the vault to Carreras, and their first film was *Countess Dracula* in 1970.

Hammer now had the real money in the industry, and with no Hinds or M. Carreras to create in-house projects, every independent producer in London beat a path to Hammer's door at 1123 Wardour Street. One such producer was Howard Brandy. It started as an ad in December 1970 issue of *Variety*.

> Howard Brandy, publicity director for the Ben Fisz–Bob Goldstein Independent, Benmar Productions, has been given leave to bow as a producer. It's for Hammer Films under its tie-up with EMI, and the feature is *Blood From the Mummy's Tomb*.

Howard Brandy remembers:

> I found the Bram Stoker story. I wasn't a big horror fan before. I just sent a letter to Sir James [Carreras], who I knew, and we met and that was it. He moved very fast on this. God, they loved it...I just verbally told him the story; it's a Mummy movie with a pretty girl, and he immediately said yes. They had a package deal going at the time with EMI, and this became part of that package. American International (AIP) picked it up in the States. What I wanted to do, what appealed to me, was doing a Mummy movie without someone stumbling around in sheets and bandages. You see the film and you'll notice that the only "mummy" is the very last shot, where the girl is wrapped in bandages.

What is strange is that in April 1970, while Hammer had been trying to develop another Mummy project, Anthony Hinds wrote a letter to writer/director Jimmy Sangster on April 17th:

> Jim Carreras has asked me to write a Mummy script. I gather that Hammer is pleased with your performance as a director;

> if you have been bitten by the bug and fancy doing some more of it, maybe you'd like to work on the script with me. You will appreciate I have no influence at Hammer anymore, so this is not a contract.

But by April 22, it was all a moot point when James Carreras wrote to Sangster and Hinds:

> I have today told Tony Hinds that there is very little interest in a Mummy subject. Under the circumstance, therefore, we will have to forget it.

Such was life at times. But by later in the year, things had definitely changed.

With a starting date of January 11, 1971 on the soundstages of EMI's studios at Elstree, the crew on hand was certainly not (again) typical of Hammer. Brandy, along with Fine and Style (the Carmilla films), were among the first of the "hired gun" producers coming along to do the films Hammer once did all by themselves. Seth Holt, a fine director of such Hammer hits as *Scream of Fear* (1961) and *The Nanny*, hadn't worked in two years and was eager to do something special with his first "horror" film. Christopher Wicking, after several projects for AIP-British and Amicus, was brought on board with Holt to script his first film for Hammer. Wicking talked about his involvement in the project with Kim Newman in *Shock Xpress*:

> It was one of the very last films that the Colonel, Sir James Carreras, actually personally brought into the stable. He said, "Of course, we can't call it *The Jewel of the Seven Stars*, we have to call it something else." I was pleased to be getting the deal. He [Carreras] did something I'd once seen Tony Tenser [of Tigon Pictures] do, like putting down all the words that would be right for the title. So we put down all the words to do with the Mummy pictures, you know, "blood" and "tomb," and it all turned into *Blood from the Mummy's Tomb*, and we really didn't think anyone would use it. But they did. We should have fought for the original title. It became more and more like a Mummy film as it went along. Then Seth Holt got involved, and he and I worked on it every day for months, and when it went into production, it was supposed to go in March. Something else had dropped out of the production line and they said to us, could we go in January? We said we didn't want to, but we thought they might cancel it altogether if we didn't go now, so we'd worked on maybe two-thirds of the

Valerie Leon as Queen Tera in *Blood From the Mummy's Tomb*

screenplay that Seth had seen. I then had a falling out with Howard Brandy, the producer, and was barred from the set, so I'd work with Seth in town after he'd finished work, about what he'd shoot tomorrow. And the idea was that after he'd finished shooting, he'd get together with Ossie Hafenrichter, who'd cut all Seth's films, and put it together. The system at Hammer is that they were cutting it together as they went along, and a week after the film was finished you'd have a rough cut. But they weren't doing that because that wasn't the way Seth worked, and he died a week before the end of shooting. So there were piles of meaningless, to anyone else, footage. I might have known what some of it was supposed to be, but I wasn't asked to come and look at it. But the shape of it was different in the end. We weren't having any flashback, but undoubtedly it's got a very strange atmosphere. I felt very guilty [when Holt died] since I suggested him.

Michael Carreras, who shot the extra week, said he was sitting there on the first day wondering what in heaven's name to do, and it was as if the ghost of Seth came by and suffused him with the vision of what it was supposed to be. I don't know if that's true.

Producer Brandy has a differing opinion of Wicking's involvement:

> We tried to get the script in shape; he [Seth Holt] rewrote most of it. We had a writer named Christopher Wicking on that, who was entirely unprofessional. He turned in a very sloppy draft, which was unusable. It was zero, nothing—it was my idea to call the hero Tod Browning as an in joke; Wicking, the writer, refused to do that. And he'd say, "I won't do that," when we asked for changes. Seth said "Don't worry. I'll rewrite it." So he did—he gave it [the script] whatever merit it had. Wicking was just unavailable. We tried calling his flat and he'd pulled the plug on the phone.

Time and tides affect people's memories, and what was obviously a difficult situation between Wicking and Brandy affects both views. Perhaps Holt was trying to smooth over the two's feelings and would spend his evenings working with Wicking, bringing the script in to Brandy each morning. Michael Carreras, taking over as managing director of Hammer on January 4th, 1971, had taken Holt to dinner because he found the script confusing. Carreras said:

> "Tell me the story," I said to Holt, which he did. I had reservations but I had complete faith in him so I said, "Go ahead." He went ahead with the project and died.

Professor Fuchs has discovered the burial tomb of Tera, Queen of Darkness—in it he finds her mummified body, but her right hand is severed at the wrist. On the hand is a ruby ring—the Jewel of the Seven Stars. In the tomb they also find a statue of a snake, a mummified cat and the skull of a jackal. The artifacts are brought to England and divided among the members of the expedition, who then go their separate ways. Fuchs enshrines Tera's body in the cellar of his home and gives the ruby ring to his daughter Margaret. When she wears it, she feels a psychic affinity with the dead Queen—for whom she is a living double. The other three members of the team suddenly fall victim to some supernatural force. In the meantime, Margaret has come under the influence of evil schemer Corbeck. Corbeck desires the power trapped in Tera's tomb and plans to conjure up Tera's spirit in Margaret's body. As he reads from the scroll, Fuchs tries to intervene. a struggle ensues, and in the confusion, Margaret plunges a dagger into Tera's heart. The vault collapses—and only Margaret survives. Or does she?—as she lies in the hospital swathed in bandages, only the eyes are visible.

With a director and script (sort of) on hand, production designer Scott MacGregor set about putting together his materials. Never quite the stylist of Bernard Robinson, MacGregor was still a consummate craftsman. He made a beeline for Bray Studios, now vacated by Hammer, where he picked out some of the architecture and statuary that had been created for the original *Mummy*, saving a lot of money. He also revamped some of the interior Elstree sets that were initially built for *Taste the Blood of Dracula* in 1969 and had been used in different forms for the four 1970 productions at EMI, starting with *Vampire Lovers* and ending with *Lust for a Vampire*.

As we said before, Michael Carreras was once again onboard, officially, as Hammer's managing director, doing the day-to-day work that had once been the domain of Anthony Hinds. Having first refused the role of executive producer, he was surprised when his father gave him this opportunity to influence the direction of Hammer. One of Carreras' first moves was to appoint Roy Skeggs as production supervisor. In April 1971 he cancelled Hammer's contract with Jantale films, which had done *Twins of Evil,* which completed the Carmilla trilogy. They would never get to film *Vampire Virgins,* which was on tap for a fourth in the series, along with another prehistoric epic and a project by Josephine Douglas, producer of *Dracula A.D. 1972* and James Carreras' mistress at the time. Which did nothing to cement father/son relationships.

Next came casting the film. Howard Brandy remembers:

> Seth and I had cast Amy Grant as the girl. She'd played with the Royal Shakespeare Company, was a wonderful actress and really had something about her. Beautiful, brilliant actress. And I get a call from Sir James—"Who is Amy Grant?" I explained and he said, "You don't quite understand. We need someone larger than life for this." He meant Valerie Leon...We had tested Valerie Leon and we didn't think she was going to work out. We'd tested the actresses with one of the speeches from the script, which we gave them beforehand to memorize as a courtesy. In the meantime, because we were seeing so many, Seth had cut the speech down, taken some lines out during the reading. When Valerie read, she invariably went back to the original speech. She couldn't seem to adjust to the shortened version.
>
> Now, I just saw her on TV; they ran the James Bond film *Never Say Never Again* and she looked fabulous. But Seth and I, at the time, didn't think she could do the part. We told Sir James we just didn't think Valerie could do it and he

said, "You guys are the movie geniuses here—*you* make her an actress!" He felt very strongly that she had star appeal. In Valerie's defense, she was a lovely, lovely girl, who worked very hard. In the end, we had to revoice her completely. Even then, the bad luck that plagued us on the movie kept up. This sweet, middle-aged lady, a voice actress, came in to redo Valerie's part, sat down in a chair, and the chair collapsed! We couldn't get away from it. Another accident. Just bizarre.

The casting problems continued. Peter Cushing was a given and did the first day of filming. Valerie Leon commented:

Peter Cushing and I actually worked together, we did shoot a scene. We shot the scene when he gave me the ring right at the beginning of the film. It was really sad when he had to drop out. Not only is he a very nice man, but obviously better known than Andrew Keir.

After that first day, Cushing went to producer Brandy, who remembered:

It was a miracle that *Blood From the Mummy's Tomb* makes any sense at all. All the stuff added up, it was just one problem after another. Peter Cushing came to me just in tears. His wife, who he loved and adored, was very ill. He had to leave. I think she died the next day or something. So, of course, we had to replace him. Andrew Keir was cast by the fellow who's now the owner of Hammer, Roy Skeggs. He was the heart of the film as far as I'm concerned—he helped put it together. Keir was very quick and talented.

Michael Carreras ended up ringing Keir on a Friday night, saying that they were in trouble. Keir told him to leave the script at the studio gate. As Keir was living in Wales, he traveled overnight, learned the script and started on Monday. Keir felt the script was written for Cushing and that it didn't work for him.

But troubles or no troubles, the film was underway. With a typical budget of the times of £200,000 (around $400,000), it was a very nice-looking picture. While not the best actress, at least Leon was physically perfect for the part. And I think James Carreras' views on the larger than life qualities needed were borne out. Leon is Tera. I haven't a clue who Amy Grant is, but it is hard to visualize anyone other than Leon in the part.

Mark Edwards was another unknown—but the actor chosen had to be tall, since Leon is something of an Amazon at six feet tall. They didn't need an "Alan

Ladd-clone" to be her boyfriend. One other bit of info—the shot of Leon getting out of bed with Edwards, and exposing her bare bottom as she runs across the room, is not her, but one of the three doubles who stood in for her during the filming—that shot was cut from American prints.

But five weeks into the filming, another disaster occurred. Seth Holt, who had secretly amused the crew with a constant case of hiccups, suddenly died of a heart attack. Howard Brandy said:

> Seth Holt died halfway through the filming. That was a shock, and it was very eerie to watch the dailies afterward and hear his voice on the track giving directions.

Michael Carreras was left with the task of picking up the pieces. He arranged two days of shooting pickup shots, etc., for director of photography Arthur Grant. And he started going over what had already been shot.

Brandy said:

> Seth didn't keep editorial notes, he had it all in his head. He's shooting certain things and I'd ask him, "Why are you shooting that?" He'd say, "Don't worry, I know what I'm going to do with that. I can't wait to get my hands on this in the editing room." [Holt was a brilliant editor who had cut many of the great Ealing comedies of the 1950s.]
>
> So when he died, it was a mess. Michael Carreras and I looked at the dailies, a rough assembly, and there seemed to be things missing and things that were shot that didn't seem to fit. Seth was the only one who knew how he was going to put it together and he was gone. Brian Hutton, the director, is an old friend, another New Yorker. He came in when we were looking at the dailies and said, "Boy, you're in a lot of trouble."

Michael Carreras commented:

> On the sequences I inherited, he [Holt] had done no intros or exits, but had gone instead straight into the master sequence. There was a blockage. I had to take over the picture from a man for who I had enormous regard and had to assemble the material myself. I read the script and the production office crossed out the scenes that had supposedly been shot. I came in on one Sunday night—Seth had died on a Saturday—ran all the material and made several decisions as to how to re-edit it.

When the sequences were finally all put together, I ran them through the following day and then went in on the Monday and said to everyone that the picture must go on regardless of what happened. I spent most of the time in the cutting room. When we put the sequences together, everything was done in the master scene and there was all the coverage you could want *in the scene*, but nobody ever came in or went out. So, in addition to taking over the picture and finishing all the scenes that were not filmed, I also had to pick up the three dozen or so scenes and make them work.

It was not Carreras's idea, originally, to direct the film. He struggled to keep production going through what should have been the sixth and final week. He offered Don Sharp the chance to direct it, with the provision that he could start over again if he agreed. Sharp turned it down, and by week seven Michael had no choice but to do it himself. He was also having some problems with the crew. After firing editor Oswald Hafenrichter and replacing him with his own editor, Peter Weatherly, he found some of the other crewmembers turning in their resignations. Holt had created a fierce loyalty in them. With the pressure of a tight shooting schedule, even star Valerie Leon was not allowed to go to Holt's funeral:

> I had worked with him back in 1967. He was an extraordinary man and very helpful. I remember distinctly the day of his funeral, I was not allowed to go and I remember being quite tearful.

All the pressure caused Valerie Leon to become ill.
Brandy said:

> We had to use her double; that's not Valerie in the scene where her father is standing over her and she's seen on the ground.

Michael Carreras was finally forced into the director's chair. He said:

> I looked at the material and couldn't find anything that tied in with what he [Holt] had told me, but there was one marvelous sequence with an elderly lady with a cat; that was a scene that told the whole story for me. So all I actually did was to try and relate all the material that had to be shot with that one scene.

Brandy spoke of the editing:

All the stuff, the editing. I'm very proud of. All these little touches. We used everything we could. There were three people, who get killed in the story, and we had footage of two of the three of them. So we integrated it all.

What is amazing, when all is said and done, is that the film *did* turn out fine. Comparisons were made at the time of release between it and the films of Val Lewton. Keir and Leon turned in good performances. James Villiers made a career out of the sneering upper crust British villain. The music by Tristram Carey was moody and effective, making up for his debacle on *Quatermass and the Pit* in 1967, where stock music and bits and pieces from other composers covered up the fact he couldn't handle the job.

AIP turned out a nice double feature with *Blood…* and *Dr. Jekyll & Sister Hyde*, although both films took some severe editing. In addition to the aforementioned "nude/not nude" shot of Valerie Leon's butt, there were slashed throats and other bits of gore that hit the cutting-room floor—no exposed Martine Beswicke's breasts in *Dr. Jekyll & Sister Hyde*. Like many, if not most of the EMI-backed Hammer films of the 1970s, it probably did not make a lot of money. Certainly, Brandy didn't come out of it rich:

> It took a year out of my life to do this, start to finish. As this editing was going on and on, I went to Brian Lawrence

Valerie Leon and Andrew Keir in *Blood From the Mummy's Tomb*, which turned out to be one of Hammer's better later efforts.

> [Hammer's business manager] and asked, "How about a little more money? This is going on a lot longer than I'd planned." He said no. He was right, of course. We'd made a deal for a certain amount. But I didn't think it'd take a year to make the movie.

In looking at the Hammer product of the '70s, *Blood From the Mummy's Tomb* (1971) was one of their better films. Brandy agrees:

> I think it's a good movie, for all the problems. Bob Solo, who's a buddy and a fellow New Yorker, who made a big remake with Charlton Heston [*The Awakening*], said to me, "Boy, is your picture a stiff." I laughed and said yeah, well, I'm not even going to watch yours!

The Mummy, 1959

Brandy's main claim to fame today is as the publicity man for the legendary cartoon producer Jay Ward (*Rocky and Bullwinkle*, etc.). He continued to push projects in England and once had Hammer interested in *Victim of His Imagination*, a story based on the life of Bram Stoker. A poster for this project, painted by Roger Dean (around 1970 & '71) appears in *The Hammer House of Horrors* book from Lerrimer Press. As an aside, Dean was commissioned by Brandy to do a series of drawings for other projects. According to the book *Roger Dean—Views,* he was asked to depict the characters in *Victim* as Donald Pleasance and Christopher Lee, but as they had not agreed to be involved, Dean couldn't make them too realistic. Dean did not like the style and stopped designing posters.

Hammer's *Mummy* never received the respect that the *Frankenstein* and *Dracula* series did. And actually it did not deserve it. But *The Mummy* is the best film of its type ever done, and that includes the old Universal series. The other three deliver what they promise, in varying degrees. *Curse* and *Shroud* are programmers but very lively. *Blood* takes an entirely different (and successful) approach. For a guilty pleasure, you can't go too far wrong here.

Special thanks to Michael Carreras and Howard Brandy. A special note of thanks to Denis Meikle for providing the synopses, cast and credits.

PSYCHOS

The Phantom of the Opera

by Gary J. Svehla

Hammer's 1962 production of *The Phantom of the Opera*, the first commercial fiasco directed by Terence Fisher, was the proof that not everything that Hammer touched turned to gold. And insiders say that because of the financial nose-dive at the box-office; Terence Fisher was not given new projects by Hammer, who thought that their maestro lost his golden touch. To be honest, *The Phantom of the Opera* is an adequate chiller and sports a superb cast. Herbert Lom, before his success with the *Pink Panther* movies, plays the phantom and does a superb job. The scenes in his underground lair, in sequences where he plays dramatic, spooky music on the organ, are classic. Supporting characters include Patrick Troughton and Michael Ripper. Edward de Sousa, soon to star in *Kiss of the Vampire*, plays the male lead. The rather bland Heather Sears

Herbert Lom as the Phantom battles Edward de Sousa in *The Phantom of the Opera.*

Christine (Heather Sears) is saved from the falling chandelier by the Phantom in Hammer's *The Phantom of the Opera*.

plays the heroine, the love object of the obsessed phantom. Michael Gough plays a sinister villain to utter perfection and the always-reliable Thorley Walters is much more subdued than he usually is.

The film's climax, where Heather Sears, alone on stage, is ready to be crushed by the dangling chandelier, is very tense and well photographed. For simple dramatic effect, Herbert Lom tears off his mask revealing his scarred face, and he darts down upon the stage majestically just in time to push Sears out of harm's way before he is crushed by the shattering glass and metal. A nice climax to an obviously artier Hammer production, a movie that attempted

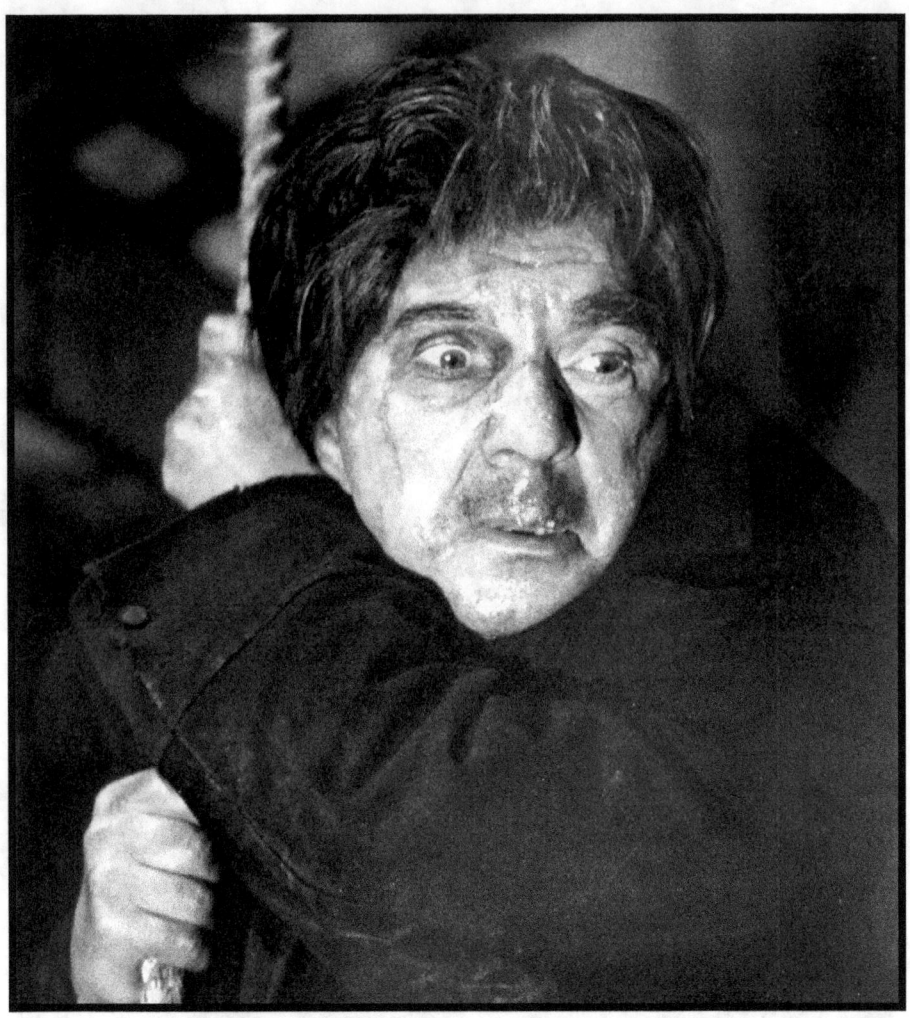

to push the romance and angst forward and subdue the horror quotient. The sets are marvelous and the cinematography by Arthur Grant is first rate. But this *Masterpiece Theater* approach to Hammer horror was a compromise no one enjoyed. The fans of *Brides of Dracula* and the other Gothics found *The Phantom of the Opera* too talky, too slow and too tame to interest them. And the production, hampered by (and actually transcending) a low budget, did not have the spectacle to rope in the more mainstream movie fan. So while Hammer was obviously trying to move subtly from exploitation to literary drama, the experiment was less than successful, and *The Phantom of the Opera* proves to be a Hammer production that fails because it tries to be too many things to too many people. Still, the production has moments of tension and horror and Herbert Lom becomes a quite sympathetic Professor Petrie, who loses his life's work to a money-grubbing entrepreneur and eventually sacrifices everything for the love of the beautiful singer Christine (Sears).

Paranoiac and Nightmare

by Gary J. Svehla

Freddie Francis, one of cinema's most creative cinematographers, was unfortunately not one of its best directors; however, *Paranoiac*, a seldom-seen Hammer psychological thriller, is one of Francis' best efforts and is one Hammer treasure waiting to be rediscovered. Its widescreen black-and-white presentation is flawless, showcasing a pristine print featuring superb cinematography by Arthur Grant (with much influence by Francis himself). The dynamic musical score by Elisabeth Lutyens (notice how the Universal Hammers did not feature many musical scores by James Bernard) helps to punctuate the excellent script by Jimmy Sangster (certainly one of his best).

Paranoiac was released in 1963 and follows in the creative wake of Alfred Hitchcock's *Psycho*, released three years earlier in 1960. The complicated plot involves family grief and madness over the deaths of parents and the suicide (or was it?) of younger son Tony. The family is spiritually ripped apart when sister Eleanor (Janette Scott) begins to see visions of the now adult Tony and questions her own sanity.

Equally traumatized brother Simon (Oliver Reed, fresh from his success in *Curse of the Werewolf* and *Night Creatures* for Hammer) buries himself in guilt over the death of his brother Tony. Oliver Reed's screen persona was created by this movie. He plays the deeply romantic and troubled young man (and

Janette Scott gives a fine performance in *Paranoiac*.

beds the French housekeeper, the sensual Liliane Brousse), who has a cigarette or drink in hand in virtually every scene (and in most he holds both). Reed's persona of the hard-boozing, self-centered hedonist was created right here. And his performance smolders as he descends into effective over-the-top insanity. In his most delicious sequence, for a few glorious seconds, Reed descends the family stairs cackling, eyes rolling in what otherwise might be considered a ridiculous interpretation of insanity. But for these wondrous seconds the descent (quite literally) into madness works.

Reed does not believe that his French lover is planning to stick around after she dared to leave him only a night before, but he makes love to her by the family duck pond. In a very interesting point-of-view shot, we see Simon bend Francoise's head back into the water. And then we see Francoise's point of view as the camera, underwater, looks up at the crazed Simon holding her head underwater until she drowns. At the appropriate moment all the ducks, in unison, make a sound approximating Bernard Herrmann's *Psycho* music score, creating a wink juxtaposed to one of the more creative murders in screen history.

But the sequences of true horror are reserved for the mysteries to be revealed in the deteriorating organ cottage that sits outside the main estate house. Inside Simon, in a daze, plays his organ creating frantic music that mirrors his emotional state. When returning brother Tony (or an imposter?) and Eleanor interrupt Simon, they encounter the terrifying form of a choir-robed figure sporting a smiling stone mask, and the figure is holding a metal hook to be used as a weapon. Before long a decaying corpse is discovered behind the organ pipes that reveals the ultimate secret of the family that holds more than one skeleton in its closet.

The plot keeps the audience guessing, the surprises abound, the performances teeter on the edge, and innocent and not-so-innocent people deceive the unwary. In a sense the film is little more than an exercise in technique and style, but with such well-drawn characterizations and performances (especially Oliver Reed and Janette Scott), *Paranoiac* becomes a movie that grows more intense and interesting as time goes on.

Unfortunately, lightning does not always strike twice, as now writer/producer Jimmy Sangster and director Freddie Francis teamed up for *Nightmare*, which was similar in style to *Paranoiac* but contains little of its predecessor's charms. *Nightmare* opens with its defining sequence, a vivid black-and-white widescreen horrific dream (Francis always likes to work in widescreen, and black-and-white became a requirement in the wake of Hitchcock's *Psycho*) featuring lovely Jennie Linden (as Janet) imagining herself, nightgown garbed, roaming the dank corridors of a mental institution, hearing the voice of her mother, as Janet tries to find the padded cell where she has been confined. Once Janet enters the cell and the door slams behind her, the obviously insane mother states, "Now they got us both, as it should be!" This opening sequence, beneath the credits, is mesmerizing and sets the tone for the psychological drama to follow. Janet, a student at a private girls' school, wakes up screaming in the middle of the night, and before long, she is asked to remove herself from the school in order to seek out treatment. A sympathetic teacher drives her to her foreboding estate home, where the nightmares continue. In the middle of the night, a strange female figure, with a large facial scar, silently stalks the young girl, who soon believes that she too, like her mother, is going insane. Janet follows the strange woman to a bedroom where the woman lies dead, a knife in her chest, as a fully decorated birthday cake glows alongside the bed. In sheer terror, Janet runs out of the room. When the housekeeper catches up with her, Janet is out of her mind, laughing hysterically, and is soon confined to bed and medicated by the family doctor. The next night the same nightmares again occur

Janet (Jennie Linden) is slowly being driven insane in *Nightmare*.

with the same woman found dead with a knife in her chest. This time Janet is sent over the edge. But when the scarred woman appears at Janet's birthday party, the distraught girl picks up the huge knife lying next to her cake and plunges the blade into the woman's chest. In the next sequence Janet is being lifted out of her home on a stretcher to be taken to the asylum. However, this same strange and unidentified woman is standing at the window glaring downward as Janet is being carted off. Inside people are cleaning up as the scarred woman lifts a lifelike plastic mask off her face to reveal Grace inside (the woman sent to take care of Janet as she mends). Janet's lawyer guardian Henry (David Knight) and his wife Grace (Moira Redmond) are in cahoots to drive the poor girl insane, and they have succeeded.

So far the movie has been excellent, very suspenseful and mysterious in a stark visual sense, and the poor, pathetic Janet has been the catalyst holding the audience's sympathy and concern. However, now with her committed and out of the picture, the second half of the film involves mysterious parties who pull the same pranks on Janet's tormentors. Thus, the film's second half repeats the gimmick of the first, but the victims are evil and unsympathetic, so while our hearts went out to the poor victimized student, we secretly wish that Henry and Grace die horrible deaths in the film's second half. What we have here is half a wonderful film, and while the film's second half is not bad, it lacks the originality and emotional involvement provided during the first half. Freddie Francis' direction and the stark composition of the film are plusses that elevate the film above the generic.

To the Devil... a Daughter

by Gary J. Svehla

Opinions certainly change in 35 years. Back in 1976, when *To the Devil... a Daughter* was released, I felt Christopher Lee's finest later performances were in *Rasputin—The Mad Monk* and *The Wicker Man*. While I agree that Lee is mostly stellar in *The Wicker Man*, his character is undermined by its foolish cross-dressing, prancing and dancing and silly-sung climax. Rasputin, one of his best performances that tried to stretch beyond his horror film persona, is interesting yet flawed. Lee tends to create a larger-than-life caricature and delivers a performance way over the top, bombastic throughout when it needs to be subtle. His Rasputin does have some marvelous sequences, but overall, the characterization does not stand the test of time.

However, *To the Devil... a Daughter*, sadly the final film Hammer ever released, co-stars Christopher Lee as Father Michael, a renegade priest (of a religion that worships Astaroth, or Satan), and while I did not think much of the movie upon its initial theatrical release, the DVD release totally changed my mind. While the film is very flawed, especially its final five minutes or so, the performance by Christopher Lee is one of his best—Hammer or otherwise. In the film's opening moments, Father Michael is excommunicated from the Christian

Christopher Lee is Father Michael in *To the Devil... a Daughter*.

The bizarre *To the Devil... a Daughter* is based on a Dennis Wheatley story.

church, and the film picks up his life two decades later as he now uses the black arts to resurrect the power of Satan. His 17-year-old "nun" Nastassja Kinski, in her first major role, will be used sexually for satanic purposes. She is rescued from Michael's henchman by her biological father (Denholm Elliott) and placed in the care of friend and occult author Richard Widmark (sleepwalking through a role tailor-made for Peter Cushing, in healthier days), who does not understand the evil inherent in the innocent-appearing young girl. Father Michael, wearing the mask of Astaroth, ritualistically impregnates a woman, who will give birth to a monstrosity nine months later. Once her labor begins, Father Michael ties the unfortunate mother to the bed and binds her legs together, bending her legs at the knees so vaginal birth is impossible. As the woman writhes in pain, director Peter Sykes juxtaposes sequences of the sleeping Kinski writhing (but hers is more orgasmic) and thrusting her bare legs halfway back over her head, showing more than a few pubic hairs in the process. Ultimately, the doomed pregnant woman delivers her baby almost *Alien*-style (hmm, did Ridley Scott see this movie?), with the baby bursting forward through the woman's abdomen, leaving the mother a blood-soaked mess, and she soon dies. Using many interesting camera angles, the few people attending this birth grimace in moral horror as the smiling face of Father Michael glares in the foreground. Christopher Lee's facial expressions alone, his perverse smiles especially, help to mold his performance as something special. His quiet smugness at knowing he has mastered the powers of darkness makes his performance beam with arrogance and self-confidence.

While *The Devil Rides Out*, the first Hammer film based upon Dennis Wheatley literature, was an artistic and commercial success, Hammer went to the

Nastassja Kinski and Richard Widmark in *To the Devil... a Daughter*.

well one more time with Wheatley's *To the Devil... a Daughter*. However, the script was in constant flux and after the ending was filmed (which was deemed too similar to the lightning/fire death of Lee's Dracula in *Scars of Dracula*), giving Christopher Lee's villain an explosive send-off, the climax was recut from already existing film. Now hero Widmark steps into the protective satanic circle, one created with human blood, and throws a rock at Father Michael, striking him square in the forehead, causing him to suddenly vanish from the film. Similar to *Scars of Dracula* or not, give me an ending worthy of disposing of such a villain that Lee has masterfully created, something that ends the movie dramatically by making Father Michael's dismissal worthy of the characterization Christopher Lee created. Also, during this final confrontation between Lee and Widmark, the Father Michael character offers Widmark the physical pleasures of Nastassja Kinski as diversion—she walks seductively toward the camera, sheds her sacrificial robe and displays full-frontal nudity. In today's cinematic arena, Kinski, with her normal God-given breasts, probably would not qualify for onscreen nudity because her natural body would be deemed in need of surgical enhancements.

Disappointing climax or not, *To the Devil... a Daughter* holds up surprisingly well in its uncut, uncensored version. It is sad to see the credits roll by and not recognize any of the personalities typically associated with Hammer in the glory days, but to be fair, *To the Devil... a Daughter* is a most fitting swan song for Hammer.

WAR

Hammer Declares War

by Tom Johnson

We hate message film. We make entertainment.
—James Carreras, *Films and Filming*, October 1959

From 1957 to 1959, when Hammer first burst upon the international scene, the company acquired a well-deserved—and sought-after—reputation as the *House of Horror*. Certainly, the horror movies were there, and good ones, too—among the best ever made. However, what is often overlooked is that, at least until the early '60s, Hammer was making a highly diversified group of films with horror only a part of its output. That output included mysteries, comedies, science fiction, musicals, shorts and war films.

If we pulled out a calculator, we would find that during the above period, just about 30 percent of Hammer's pictures could be considered *horror*. Almost half had a military background. Some of these were, admittedly, comedies, but the fact remains that the company was not simply concentrating on grinding out horror movies to the exclusion of all else. War films were as important to Hammer as any other type.

Hammer's first three serious war movies—*The Steel Bayonet* (1957), *The Camp on Blood Island* (1958), and *Yesterday's Enemy* (1959)—were unusual for their time, and more closely resemble those made during and after Vietnam, when disillusionment with the military set in. What ties these three films together is their lack of conventional John Wayne–style heroics. There are few clear-cut *good guys*. Not only does the *right side* not necessarily win, no one really wins. Due to their bleak outlook, the trio could easily be called "war noir."

The protagonist in each movie is not a young, dashing Errol Flynn-sort, but a weary, beaten man, in *way* over his head. Two of the three *heroes* die—by their own choice. Hammer at War is not the stuff of recruiting posters, but then, neither is the real thing.

THE STEEL BAYONET
What are you worrying about rations for? We'll all be dead tomorrow.
—The Sergeant

SYNOPSIS:

C Company is completely exhausted after a running battle with the Nazi Afrika Tank Korps. While they are awaiting replacements, Colonel Derry orders them to take control of a farmhouse, which is to be used as an observation post. Led by Major Gerard, they must keep this occupation a secret so that they can direct artillery fire from the farm. To preserve this secret, Gerard orders the killing of a German patrol that he would ordinarily have ignored. Captain Mead, atop a windmill tower, directs the fire by radio but is spotted by German scouts. Gerard calls for an all-out attack—one that his weary men cannot carry out. The out-manned British are overwhelmed and evacuation orders are given. The tower is hit by a shell and bursts into flames, killing Mead and pinning Gerard beneath. He radios for a barrage on the farmhouse, destroying both the enemy and himself.

The Steel Bayonet was the first feature film to be directed by Michael Carreras, usually more at home as executive producer. The movie is certainly his best, which could be considered faint praise when considering less than brilliant efforts like *Maniac* (1963), *The Curse of the Mummy's Tomb* (1964), and *The Lost Continent*. Those notwithstanding, *The Steel Bayonet* is a terrific first try and it's shame that Carreras' career as a director never came to much.

Carreras wanted *The Steel Bayonet* to be different from the typical British war picture—he wanted to avoid their "tendency for understatement." Carreras admired the American-style war movie for its more realistic approach to violence and wanted his film to reflect this.

Many of those involved in the making of *The Steel Bayonet* were well qualified to know the realities of war. From Carreras to star Leo Genn to the crewmembers, most were veterans of World War II (Genn had received several medals for his wartime heroics). Carreras felt that, since most of the cast had military training, his job was made easier by not having to teach them how to act like soldiers.

Filming began in the summer of 1956 at the Aldershot Tank Proving Grounds. This area stood in admirably for North Africa. Due to a flare-up of hostilities in the Suez Canal, the British military was on alert, and tanks that had been promised to Hammer were withdrawn. The company then obtained from a

scrap dealer four tanks, which were modified to play both British and German vehicles.

The Steel Bayonet ended production on September 20th and was released in London on June 3, 1957. Reviewers were more impressed by Hammer's approach than by its execution. *The London Times* (May 14), following the trade show, called the film "grim but there is something about the whole thing that does not…ring true."

While some of the *realism* does seem a bit contrived, *The Steel Bayonet* is still far from the propaganda movies that emanated from all sides of the conflict in the 1940s. Perhaps the fact that the war had been over for a decade gave *The Steel Bayonet* a perspective that something like, say, *Sahara* (1943) lacked.

One unique touch was to have the German soldiers speak German with English subtitles. While this was probably not the first time this was done, it was nevertheless a bold move for a low-budget film.

The Steel Bayonet is by no means a classic, or even a great war movie. It's the weakest of the three films being covered here, but it's certainly no worse than some of the better known and more highly praised American and British nonsense that preceded it.

With a big star in the lead, *The Steel Bayonet* might have been a success, but Hammer apparently felt that was out of the question. It's a good thing, too, because the film's lack of star names added to its sense of reality.

Hammer's next war movie would be too real for some. It was the company's most controversial film—and one of its greatest financial successes.

Credits: 1957, 85 minutes, black and white, Director/Producer: Michael Carreras, Screenplay: Howard Clewes, DP: Jack Asher

Starring: Leo Genn, Kieron Moore, Michael Medwin, Robert Brown, Michael Ripper

THE CAMP ON BLOOD ISLAND
This brutal film should not be shown.—*Reynolds News*, April 20, 1958

SYNOPSIS:
    The Allies have defeated Japan, but the brutal overseers of the prisoner of war camp on Blood Island are not yet aware the war is over due to a broken radio. British Colonel Lambert is concerned that Colonel Yamamitsu will kill all of the prisoners when he discovers the truth. Lt. Bellamy, an American airman, parachutes near the camp and is captured, but sizes up the situation and keeps silent. Dr. Keiller has escaped to see his wife in the nearby women's camp, but at the fence is machine-gunned down before her eyes. When the killing starts, Bellamy and Van Elst escape in an attempt to free Mrs. Keiller, who knows a route to safety. Van Elst is shot, but Bellamy manages to elude the guards. When Lambert explains the situation to the men, Beattie goes mad. Under the pretense of giving information, he enters Yamamitsu's office—with a hand grenade. When the grenade explodes, so does the camp, as guards begin firing from watchtowers. Shields climbs a tower to kill a sniper but Lambert, who was distracted, lofts a grenade, killing his friend.
    The prisoners eventually take control of the camp—those few still left alive.

    Hammer had great plans for *The Camp on Blood Island*, which was highly publicized as the company's 50th production. The company hoped that the film would put their name before the public. That certainly happened, but in a way Hammer had never expected.

Jon Manchip White, who in the '50s managed the Lyric Theatre, had been a P.O.W. "He had kept notes scribbled on lavatory paper," Val Guest said. "He eventually gave Hammer the notes. I was called in, we looked them over and I said, 'yes, it's going to be a hell of a movie'!"

It *was* a hell of a movie, but it was a story that many felt was better not being told. While Hammer almost certainly played down the actual violence and brutality of the situation, the studio was assaulted by critics for showing as much as they did. The prevailing attitude seemed to be, "Yes, things like this happened, but let's pretend that they didn't, because it won't do any good to stir things up."

Although *The Camp on Blood Island* was a huge financial success, it was instrumental in creating Hammer's bad reputation—even more so than the similarly vilified *The Curse of Frankenstein* and *Dracula*.

Filming began on July 29, 1957, at Bray Studios and Black Park—both looking remarkably like Southeast Asia. The production ended on September 11, and *The Camp on Blood Island* premiered at the London Pavilion on April 18, 1958. After an extraordinary seven-week run, the film went into general release where it broke records previously set by *The Curse of Frankenstein* (and which would later be smashed by *Dracula*).

Although audiences were lapping it up, most British critics were horrified by the film's brutality. The opening scene set the tone of the horrors to follow: While his friends look on from behind a barbed-wire fence, a P.O.W. digs a grave—his own. When he finishes, he is machine-gunned at point-blank range and topples into the open pit.

The London Times (April 21, 1958) stood alone in its praise: "Whatever the rights and wrongs of the matter, the central situation is an intensely dramatic one. The acting is workmanlike and sincere." Other papers took a less enlightened approach. *The Reynolds News* (April 21): "the most shameful and destructive picture of the year." *The Star* (April 17): "an orgy of atrocities." *The Sunday Times* (April 20): "appalling." *The Observer* (April 20): "an abomination."

Normally, Hammer might have been pleased by the vitriolic attacks, since they usually translated into audience curiosity and box-office success. But this was different. Plans were being made to ban the film in the Far East, which might have been expected. What was not expected were noises to prohibit the showing of *The Camp on Blood Island* in the United States. Most of these noises were being made by Shiro Kido, the chairman of the Motion Picture Association of Japan. He felt that the film should definitely not be shown in Los Angeles, due to the city's large Asian population.

Fortunately, the reaction in the U.S. was far less extreme than in Britain—perhaps due to the lingering memory of Pearl Harbor. Following *The Camp on*

Blood Island's American release, *The New York Herald Tribune* (September 9, 1958) called it "a straightforward and expert melodrama." *The New York Times* (September 18) felt it was "directed and acted quietly to lend an air of credulity." *Variety* (April 23) caught the film in London, and laid it on the line: "It will jerk out of complacency any person who now tends to regard the Japanese as not being as bad as thought."

When comparing the British and American reviews, one wonders how they can be discussing the same movie. The *controversy* was over by the end of 1958 when *Variety* (December 31) reported that Eric Johnston, chairman of the British Motion Picture Association, said he didn't think it was proper to "make films that bring back memories of detestable experiences of World War II," and that he hoped "they would not be produced again." Why not? Shouldn't we be reminded of these things so they *won't* be tolerated?

Eric Johnston's slap on Hammer's wrist had, naturally, little effect. Hammer's next war film would be an even more searing indictment of wartime atrocities—this time committed by *both* sides.

The Camp on Blood Island's basic situation was carried on to a subtler—but more horrific—end in *King Rat* (1965), a brilliant filming of James Clavell's 1962 novel. No one felt that this film was improper—it got excellent reviews and launched George Segal's career. Perhaps Hammer deserves credit for stretching the limits of what had previously been accepted on the screen. This works both ways, of course, resulting in as much garbage as art, but—just perhaps—a movie like *Schindler's List* (1993) might not have been produced had Hammer

and other companies making similar movies not opened the door in the '50s.

Audiences, naturally, couldn't have cared less about the negative reviews and lined up for blocks. *The Camp on Blood Island* joined Hammer's *Dracula* and *Up the Creek* in London's prestigious West End, giving the company an incredible triple success during the summer of 1958.

The film, as did *The Curse of Frankenstein* and *Dracula*, grossed over $4 million worldwide—big money for the late '50s. *Variety* (October 28, 1958) called Hammer "one of the world's foremost suppliers of successful, modest-budget entries." Columbia was so delighted by the performance of *The Camp on Blood Island* that an agreement was reached for Hammer to release 25 films through the distributor over the next five years. Columbia also become a 49-percent owner of Bray Studios—the first such arrangement between British and American film companies.

Watching *The Camp on Blood Island* over 70 years after the war's end and 53 years after its release, it's possible to judge it as a *movie* and forget the baggage it initially carried. What one finds is that it's pretty good. Andre Morell is, as always, excellent and fronts a cast of Hammer "regulars" including Barbara Shelley, Michael Gwynn, Richard Wordsworth and Michael Ripper. Bray Studios and Black Park ably—and incredibly—suggested the Far East, and just *looking* at Jack Asher's gloomy photography makes one sweat. The film is nasty and brutal—even today—and is even more so due to the realism of its subject. Prisoner of war camps, one suspects, were not like *Hogan's Heroes*.

Val Guest's unobtrusive, matter-of-fact direction gives the picture an almost documentary-like feel—a talent that made even fantastic subjects like *The Quatermass Experiment* seem real.

The Camp on Blood Island is not in the same league as, say, *King Rat* or *The Bridge on the River Kwai* (1957)—two of the great P.O.W. films—but, for its budget and exploitative subject matter, it's a minor classic. *The Camp on Blood Island* was a huge financial success, but perhaps Hammer paid too high a price. From this point on, Hammer would be associated with the seamier side of filmmaking—an underserved reputation that would haunt the company forever.

When Hammer's next war film debuted to excellent reviews, the company's name was missing from most of them.

Credits: 1958, 82 minutes, black and white, Director: Val Guest, Producer: Anthony Hinds; Screenplay: Val Guest, DP: Jack Asher

Cast: Carl Mohner, Andre Morell, Edward Underdown, Walter Fitzgerald, Barbara Shelley

YESTERDAY'S ENEMY

Now that you are not fighting spears with guns, you want a code of conduct. This is total war—no quarter given.—Yamazaki

SYNOPSIS:

A group of weary British soldiers make their way through the Burmese jungle, separated from their company. Captain Langford is in reluctant command, due to the Brigadier's injuries. The Padre and war correspondent Max are in disagreement with Langford's style of leadership. They take a village previously held by the Japanese and kill a high-ranking officer in possession of a mysterious map. A captured Burmese—a probable collaborator—refuses to divulge the map's secret, so Langford makes an unpopular decision. He orders two innocent villagers to be shot to frighten the Burmese into talking. It works—he tells Langford that the map outlines a major invasion. Then, following the Captain's orders, Sgt. McKenzie kills him. Langford decides to move out—leaving the wounded behind—to get the information to headquarters, but Japanese troops soon arrive and capture the British. Yamazaki questions Langford about the missing map—and the officer. When Langford refuses to talk, Yamazaki orders Lt. Hastings to be shot. Langford, now out of options, makes a clumsy attempt to use the radio, purposely drawing his guards' fire. Yamazaki wearily orders the remainder of Langford's men to be executed.

Although James Carreras was, at least in print, opposed to "message pictures," *Yesterday's Enemy* was a very painful one to give. With the critical assassination of *The Camp on Blood Island* still fresh in the memory, one wonders why Hammer chose to tread on even more sensitive ground—wartime atrocities committed by the British.

Like so many earlier Hammer films, *Yesterday's Enemy* was based on a BBC

Japanese poster for *Yesterday's Enemy*

Yesterday's Enemy was based on a BBC play and starred Stanley Baker, Guy Rolfe and Leo McKern.

play. Peter Newman's controversial story moved audiences to both assent and anger. One of its many viewers was Michael Carreras, who was so impressed that he immediately put Val Guest on the project of turning it into a movie. "*Yesterday's Enemy*," said Guest, "is one of my four favorite films out of over 90 I've written and directed. This was a labor of love."

It's no wonder that Guest feels so strongly about the picture—it's excellent on all counts. Unfortunately, the film's lack of a superstar in the lead and its unpalatable subject matter will always prevent it from being embraced by a mass audience.

Yesterday's Enemy began production at Shepperton Studios on January 12, 1959, and moved to Bray on February 19. Since Bray lacked the space, the village set was built on a Shepperton soundstage, and Hammer's usual base was used for the swamp set.

A language barrier created an additional problem, since most of the actors playing Japanese soldiers were, in fact, Japanese. Most of them had been recruited from London's Oriental restaurants, and actor Philip Ahn had to interpret Val Guest's direction.

Yesterday's Enemy was trade-shown on June 5, 1959 to an enthusiastic press corps, and premiered at the Leicester Square Empire on September 17. Many military men who had served in Burma were present, and were impressed by

Yesterday's Enemy **does not back away from making a strong statement.**

the movie's accuracy and honesty. Val Guest sat next to the highly decorated Lord Mountbatten, who "recognized" areas of the swampland...not realizing that those scenes were shot at Bray. Adding to the film's realism was the total lack of a musical score. Only jungle sounds were heard—a stipulation insisted upon by Guest.

Following its exceptional engagement at the Empire, *Yesterday's Enemy* went into general release on October 19, 1959. Reviewers were impressed. *The London Times* (September 21): "a well written film that stimulates argument." *The British Film Institute's Monthly Bulletin* (September): "Something of a surprise for those who associate Hammer Film with horror." *The Saturday Review* (October 3): "Serious if not downright philosophical." *The New York Times* (March 4, 1960): "It is the first entry from Hammer Films...that manages to be haunting in the right way."

Stanley Baker, not yet a big star, was well cast as Captain Langford. With command thrust upon him, the character was forced to make choices that are easily criticized, but someone had to make them. Certainly a "real hero" like John Wayne would have followed a stricter code of behavior but, as Yamazaki pointed out, in war there is no code.

While having the British suffer the same fate that they inflicted earlier upon the enemy is a bit contrived, it works onscreen far better than it reads, due to the skillful acting and direction. In a standout group of supporting actors, Richard Pasco shines as Lt. Hastings, tied to a stake, waiting to be executed. If that scene doesn't shake you up, nothing will.

The film makes its point quietly, but does not back away from making it, and it would be difficult to find another movie of this vintage that is so critical of its own armed forces. This type of introspection would be more common a decade later, but for 1959, *Yesterday's Enemy* was on the leading edge.

Credits: 1959, 95 minutes, black and white, Director: Val Guest, Screenplay: Peter Newman, DP: Arthur Grant

Cast: Stanley Baker, Guy Rolfe, Leo McKern, Gordon Jackson, David Oxley

Unfortunately, *Yesterday's Enemy* was one of the last "serious" films Hammer would make in any genre. After *Never Take Candy from a Stranger* (1960—talk about controversy!), *Hell is a City* (1960), and *Cash on Demand* (1962), Hammer settled into an array of horror, science fiction and exotic adventures. Certainly, many of them were good movies, and a few, like *Frankenstein Must Be Destroyed*, were excellent. Nevertheless, it's too bad that the company strayed so far from the diversified films it was making in 1959.

With the release of *Yesterday's Enemy*, Hammer may have reached its peak. *The Curse of Frankenstein, Dracula* and *The Camp on Blood Island* had been huge worldwide money winners, with *Up the Creek* (1958) and *Further Up the Creek* (1959) more than holding their own. *The Hound of the Baskervilles* had just left the London Pavilion after a tremendous four-week premiere engagement. *The Man Who Could Cheat Death* was doing well on the ABC theater circuit and *The Mummy*, then in post-production, would soon be shattering records.

Never again would Hammer have so many financial and/or critical successes on their hands and it's just possible that, with a few more movies like *Yesterday's Enemy*, Hammer's stock might have risen appreciably with the critics.

Taken as a group, this trio of war films shows Hammer in a way that many fans would find surprising. Lacking Technicolor, Victorian sets, Peter Cushing, and low-cut gowns, they are light years away from the typical Hammer production. All three films are available on DVD in the U.K. in Pal format and well worth the search.

Information for this article came from, in addition to the credited sources, Dick Klemensen's *Little Shoppe of Horrors*, Val Guest, Randy Vest and Tom Weaver

Night Creatures

by Gary J. Svehla

Night Creatures, an odd duck Hammer production, pretending to be a pirate movie (in the same vein as *Pirates of Blood River*) but without showing any pirate ships or actual pirates, tends to go for horror overtones by featuring a few scenes with Marsh Phantoms (actually human beings wearing luminescent glow-in-the-dark skeleton outfits). The film, directed by Peter Graham Scott, does not even play like the typical Hammer production, although the presence of Peter Cushing, Oliver Reed, Yvonne Romain and Michael Ripper makes it look like one. Peter Cushing's conversion from bloodthirsty pirate to reformed minister is one of Cushing's splashier performances, his dual lifestyles continuously clashing. He is the leader of a band of smugglers who fight British oppression and unfair taxation, yet his hell and brimstone preaching makes him the moral universe of the small cove-side town. At the same time he attempts to protect his daughter Imogene (Romain) from learning his identity, and tries to help her escape the curse of Captain Clegg and prevent the sins of the father from fall-

Peter Cushing stars in *Night Creatures*

ing upon the young girl. Cushing's performance is another high energy one with complex moral ambiguities, making his lead character heroic but terribly flawed. Oliver Reed's romantic lead is perfect and his physical suffering for his love makes the youthful Reed dashing as he's never been before. Michael Ripper, for once, gets an actual character to develop, and his friendship with Clegg is richly etched, especially in the film's final seconds when he carries the corpse of his friend to his grave, tears welling up in his eyes.

The film's typical Hammer touch and also its flaw is the presence of Tor Johnson Brit clone Milton Reid as the Mulatto, the man who dared attack Clegg's wife and received the punishment of having his tongue cut out and being left for dead. Now, years later, he only lives for reveng,e and his weapon of choice is a steel spear that he wields with expert skill. Somehow his presence seems to be monstrous in a film that focuses on human beings, and his character appears in the film for only two reasons—to provide the horror aspect and to create a way to kill off the sympathetic and now reformed Clegg in a dramatic conclusion.

The sequences of the Marsh Phantoms are wonderfully photographed, garish and blinding as their ectoplasmic forms radiate, frightening all those who face these specters on horseback. Of course the audience understands immediately that these are smugglers wearing glowing costumes, but the manner in which they are photographed is always spooky and demands our attention. Unfortunately, the film opens with one of these sequences and it would seem, in such a talky production, that perhaps it might have been better to hold off, for pacing's sake, on such splashy sequences for insertion later on.

Night Creatures could have used a few more action sequences.

Night Creatures has been built up to be a better film than it actually is because of its scarcity on home video; however, the wonderful Eastmancolor print is deeply saturated and generally blemish free. However, the film is never better than a good programmer with a few excellent performances and tends to be talky in parts. It also lacks a few needed action sequences that would have created the swashbuckling thrill sorely missing from the production.

Hammer Memories

by Sue and Colin Cowie

The first pleasure I thought of when reminiscing about Hammer is my husband, whom I met 22 years ago at the first British convention of the Christopher Lee International Fan club; our 20th wedding anniversary was this Christmas past and our love for Hammer has continued over the years, through two fanzines (*The Horror Elite* and *The Hammer International Fan Club Journal*), and through innumerable friends gained via our love of Hammer. Between us we have been privileged to meet some of Hammer's greatest treasures, and we thought we'd share some of their words with you.

We met Terence Fisher in 1975 and were privileged to be friends until his death. I remember sitting with him, watching Jess Franco's *Count Dracula* and asking him what he thought of it. "Well my dear, for the first 10 minutes I thought, my God...no it's not!" I remember his kindness in watching a fan's amateur film with patience and then spending two hours talking to him about it, his delight at seeing Melissa Stribling again after 20 years, and his unfailing humor when surrounded by fans. The world is poorer for his not being here... so let's share some of his words.

Fisher on Directing:

> I wanted to go into film, to edit films, which is the start of directing because no one can direct a film without knowing how to edit. I was a slow starter, a very slow starter! I didn't really start until I was 28 years old. The films we made at Hammer had pretty small budgets and you had to use glass shots and all the tricks of the game, but that's not the important thing. The important thing is what comes out at the end: whether it catches the audiences' imaginations or not and that is the *only* thing that matters.
>
> You go to see films to be emotionally moved in one form or another...to be entertained is a loose word, but to be emotionally moved, I think, is the most important word about a film that is presented to you. Being an editor first was tremendous because it gave one a chance of analyzing, day by day, everything which the director had done, and as an editor you always attempted to edit, within the material you were given, the greatest expression of what the director was trying to say. You know? Action, reaction, where to cut to, not the person who was expounding on what they felt but upon

Terence Fisher

the reaction of the other person. It also gave you a chance of saying, in a subconscious way, if I'd been the director of this film, I'd have done this scene differently. Of course, it was the most wonderful opportunity of analyzing a director's work and trying to take everything he'd shot and make it into the best possible form. That's the fun of the game isn't it, and it helped develop one's intuition. You see, I don't work analytically, I work intuitively and emotionally.

As a director, I cut in the camera most of the time. Except in certain emotional moments when I get a chance of a crosscut of reaction as opposed to what's being said to them. Yes, I'm an economical shooter, but I will give the editor the emotionalism of presenting the final thing. I don't worry about handing it over to an editor because we discuss it all. Well, we all knew each other in those days. It was a good association, you didn't have to talk a lot. We knew each other so clearly that you only had to say a few words and the others would know what you were talking about. It was a mental thing, between person and person, and that was wonderful.

Peter Cushing in *The Curse of Frankenstein*

Fisher on *Dracula* and *Frankenstein*:

> Dracula is the personification of evil. Frankenstein is a man of idealism who has been tempted by the Devil and eventually decided that he is God himself and can do better than God. Dracula is a sad character, who is not the beginning of evil at all, but a victim of someone else and has evolved into this thing. Frankenstein, of course, the creator, started with the greatest idealisms in the world, of curing a certain amount of physical ills. In the end he came to the mountain, tempted by the Devil and decided, as he said in one film, "I am the creator of man," so he is the greatest evil of all. Dracula is to be pitied. The only one you cry for in a *Frankenstein* film was the victim of what he tried to create and can't. "I am the creator of man," and he never bloody does! He creates something that is going to fail and will always fail because he's creating as a God-like figure. My dear old friend Peter Cushing won't agree with that, and he's quite wrong of course [laughing]...I told him

on the last one I directed, I said, "Peter, really, in this one you're the most ruthless and self-seeking...you're a God..." Peter looked at me out of that blue eye of his and said, "I think you must be right."

Fisher on Period Pieces:

> I'm not interested in working in anything that is contemporary in experience: there are enough people making pictures about contemporary emotions and violence. I like a borderline fantasy. I'd like to do a modern-day vampire story...but not Dracula walking along the King's Road...You can make a contemporary vampire film which is allied to the cultivation and following of Black Magic, and anything else—they're all mixed up together. You can take the cult of vampirism and put it into modern day. After all, where did the superstition of vampirism come from? I was told Transylvania: that's rubbish. You can go back to the first chapter of Genesis where the first vampire is the serpent in the Garden of Eden. When I say vampire, I mean the first personification of evil as such. The serpent had long teeth. You see, vampirism is nothing new, it goes back to Genesis. It's a fable about evil and the Bible is only a fable anyway, and the fable goes back a long time, passed by word of mouth, person to person.
>
> *Horror of Dracula* is a satisfying film; it has survived. I love it because everything was right about it. Very nearly a love story but not quite.

We miss Terry *so* much.

On another occasion, my husband Colin, Keith, and some other friends visited Ms. Ingrid Pitt. She was immensely kind and charming to them, and when he came home my normally monosyllabic spouse was raving. So when we both had a chance to have tea at her home, I was intrigued to meet her. Of that meeting I wrote:

> It may sound fulsome to say it, but she is five times lovelier than any films or photos show her. She is also kind, friendly, funny, a fantastic cook, helpful to interviewers, who dry up whilst gazing at her, acidly witty, fiercely loyal to her friends, and altogether stunning. You sit, fascinated, listening to that delicious voice, amazed at the variety of languages that drop into conversation if they happen to express exactly what

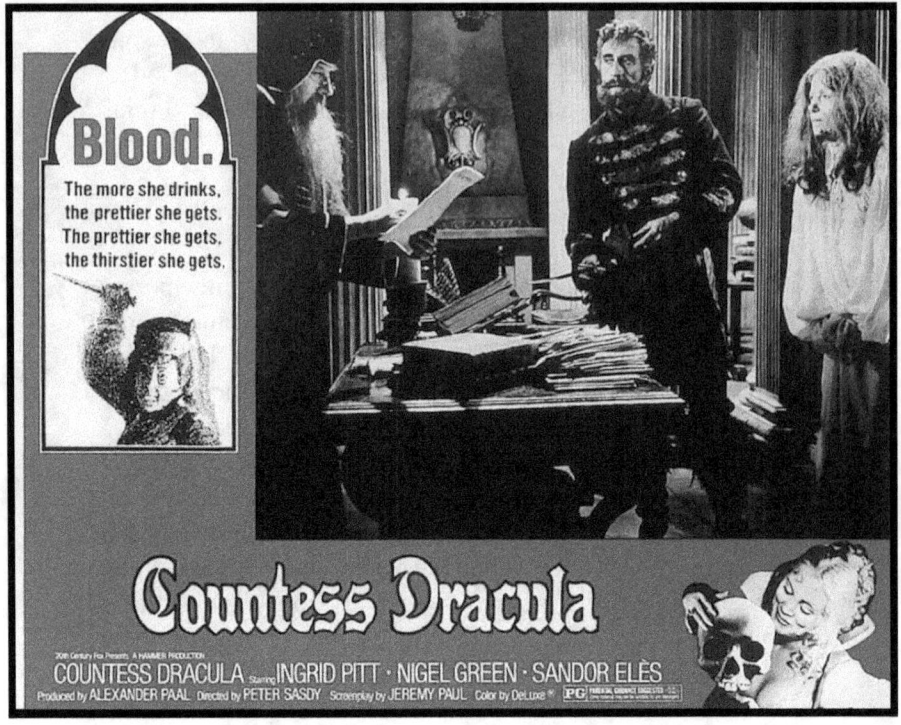

she wants to say, totally unconscious of time passing as she weaves her spell, like an enchantress of legend.

I have never had reason to change my mind. Let me share with you Ingrid in a playful mood...

Ingrid on the Best and Worst of Filming *The Vampire Lovers*:

> The most enjoyable was coming home in a Rolls Royce and the worst was going back at dawn in a vile mood.

On Having a Mask Made and Being Shut in a Coffin:

> The great thing about claustrophobia is that it can be exorcised by a few noughts at the end of your payslip. I just lay there and thought of a trip to France I had planned as soon as shooting was over, and it all seemed worthwhile. I had straws up my nose to breathe and I got...well, you know...stuck in one. I didn't know whether to sniff or blow to get rid of it! Mind you—sometimes it can be a bit heavy. When I was doing *The House That Dripped Blood,* some jokers shut my coffin lid and went off to lunch. My insecurity showed in that I wondered if they were trying to tell me something!

On Being Complimented on the Strength of Characters of Carmilla and Countess Dracula:

> Well, that's all down to the writer and the director. I think it was Noel Coward who said, "Just learn the lines and try not to bump into the furniture." I'm so busy learning my lines and not bumping into the furniture that if anything else comes across up on the screen, I blow a kiss in the direction of the director and thank God for someone who can write a few decent lines! Those ladies...some people, because of their willpower, trigger off events that happen to other people in their own surroundings. all the time it's the doers and the done; the trick is to "do" before you can be "done."

On the Difficulties of Working with a Virtually All-Female Cast:

> It's more difficult working with a virtuous female cast!

On other occasions she can be serious and perceptive about films, but you've probably read all those interviews.

Oh, I almost forgot a spellbinding afternoon with James Bernard and Phillip Martell. I'd like to copy all the conversation, but here a just a few snippets.

Martell on the Musicians:

> If you came to a session—it's staggering. Raymond Cohen comes in with a Stradivarius. Nesbitt who plays with Ricci has a Strad. When they go out for tea it's terrifying—they leave the instruments propped up against chairs. What I think the public don't know at all is the sheer standard of musicianship that you have for a film score; that you have the cream of the world practically. They're better than any symphony orchestra because no orchestra could afford them or keep them. They are the top of their speciality. The sound is unbelievable—it wafts you to heaven. It's the only thing that makes the sweat worthwhile.

On Music for Film:

> When we start on a film we have a synopsis of the story, we've seen the script, and we've already seen a rough cut of the film. That's when we call Jimmy in. He can see anything

FANEX 8 guests pose for a photo: left to right: Ingrid Pitt, Val Guest, Yolande Donlan, Veronica Carlson (with her arm around FANEX host Gary Svehla), James Bernard and Martine Beswicke. Susan and Richard Svehla are peeking out from the back. Since that show we have lost Ingrid, Val, Yolande, James, and Gary's dad, Richard.

he likes, anytime he likes; preferably as often as he likes. I try to go down and see the film at the end of each week's shooting. We spend lots of money on the phone and we sort of somehow agree where the music's going, and what it's going to do and what sort of orchestra we are going to have. Then he sits back, or goes to the West Indies, and I go to the studios and fight. I go and have a fight with the Director or Producer to see how much money they're going to give me for the orchestra, and while I'm doing all the nonsense and the orchestra's being engaged, we come to the day when the rough cuts are available and we both look at them and talk. By the end we will have pretty much agreed. Then we wait for the fine cut which is usually a matter of two weeks. And then we watch the final cut with the producer and director. Often the marvelous thing with Hammer was that Michael Carreras used to stay behind and so did Tony Hinds; they both had very good taste and were very considerate people with whom we got on and could work with very well.

On the *Dracula* Theme:

> J.B.: It came very easily from the name. That came straight away—it was very simple.
> P.M.: Yes, but that was only the top line notes. It's what you do with it, how you build it, what harmonic structures you give it that makes it sound like Dracula. Think about the music over the credits—it's comparable to the overture to an opera. You're setting the mood and atmosphere for what is to follow. And that's where I think he has a great sense of drama.
> J.B.: Another thing, with horror films you need to synchronize the music and action carefully. You can't be subtle because it doesn't work with Gothic horror. There are times though, aren't there Phil, when you can play music through, like a romantic scene; then you just have a pretty tune going.
> P.M.: I think one of the liveliest things we ever did—you wrote it Jimmy, I just waved the piece of wood in the air—was on the long shot of Ursula Andress in *She* where that 60-piece orchestra came in with such a whisper that you had to strain your ears to hear it and then it grew and grew and it was really fantastic. Raymond Cohen led the orchestra. I remember saying to him when we'd got it down to a whisper. "Raymond look, what I'm getting now is forte, now can we have a pianissimo?" He said, "You can't." But we got it. It was a shimmer of sound. That's the fun, when you feel it worked it's terribly exciting. You feel exhilarated by it.

And we were exhilarated by them; may Philip and James rest in peace, making music with the angels.
Sue and Colin Cowie,
England

If you enjoyed this book,
please visit our website
www.midmar.com
or call or write for a free catalog

Midnight Marquee Press, Inc,.
9721 Britinay Lane
Baltimore, MD
USA
410-665-1198

www.ingramcontent.com/pod-product-compliance
Lightning Source LLC
Chambersburg PA
CBHW071305110526
44591CB00010B/779